Philanthropy and Police

Philanthropy and Police

LONDON CHARITY IN
THE EIGHTEENTH CENTURY

Donna T. Andrew

PRINCETON UNIVERSITY PRESS

PRINCETON, NEW JERSEY

Copyright ©1989 by Princeton University Press
Published by Princeton University Press, 41 William Street,
Princeton, New Jersey 08540
In the United Kingdom: Princeton University Press, Oxford

Library of Congress Cataloging-in-Publication Data

Andrew, D. T. (Donna T.), 1945–
  Philanthropy and police : London charity in the eighteenth century / D. T. Andrew.
    p. cm.
  Includes index.
  ISBN 0-691-05557-2
  1. Charities—England—London—History—18th century. 2. Poor—England—
London—History—18th century. 3. Social service—England—London—History—18th
century. 4. London (England)—Social policy. I. Title.
HV250.L8A65 1989
361.7'09421—dc19   88-25416
                                                                     CIP

Publication of this book has been aided by the Whitney Darrow Fund of Princeton
University Press

This book has been composed in Linotron Sabon

Princeton University Press books are printed on acid-free paper, and meet the guidelines
for permanence and durability of the Committee on Production Guidelines for Book
Longevity of the Council on Library Resources

Printed in the United States of America by Princeton University Press, Princeton,
New Jersey

TO ED

For making it all possible

Contents

Preface

WHEN I FIRST BEGAN the Ph.D. thesis on which this book is based, I wondered how I'd ever find anything "original" to write about the eighteenth century, a period about which so many had written so much. Now, entirely too many years later, I wonder whether we yet know enough to properly make any of the sort of general statements I make throughout this volume. However, perhaps in some small way, this work will help to focus and give form to the reconceptualization of the "long" eighteenth century that is now going on.

It is my very great pleasure to be able to thank those people and institutions that have supported and nurtured this project. I would like to thank the Canada Council for awarding me a doctoral fellowship, and its successor, the Social Science and Humanities Research Council of Canada, for subsequent grants that have enabled me to take research trips to England. I would also like to express my appreciation to the various libraries and archives, librarians and archivists, that have given me access to their collections: the British Library, the Goldsmiths' Company Library at the University of London, the Royal College of Surgeons' Library, the Library of the Maritime Museum at Greenwich, the Greater London Public Record Office, and the County of Surrey Record Office.

Central to my work and to this book has been the kindness and benevolent influence of my Ph.D. supervisor and friend, John Beattie. It was his total and passionate commitment to the history of the eighteenth century that convinced me that the life of the historian was attractive and rigorous, and that the eighteenth century was a veritable "new found land." I also wish to thank my friends and colleagues who, as part of the Toronto group in English history, listened to and criticized the various chapters of this book that I imposed upon them, offering both stimulating comments and fraternal support. Furthermore, I would like to acknowledge my gratitude to the University of Guelph, which gave me a home in their history department, allowing me to cease the life of an itinerant teacher and become, finally, a proper scholar and historian.

Special thanks are also due David Levine and Nicholas Rogers, for helping me when I most needed it, to Joanna Innes and Nicholas Rogers, for sharing their great knowledge of the eighteenth century with me, and especially to the editors and readers of the Princeton University Press, and to my copyeditor, Jeff Beneke, who have been unfailingly useful and indulgent to me in all my dealings with them.

Donna T. Andrew
Guelph
June 1988

Philanthropy and Police

Introduction

Give, looking for nothing again, that is, without consideration
of future advantages: give to children, to old men, to the
unthankful, and the dying, and to those you shall never see
again; for else your Alms or courtesie is not charity, but traffick
and merchandise.

—Jeremy Taylor,
The Rule and Exercise of Holy Living (1650)

Our minds become humbled by receiving charity: we have no
longer that ardour, that spring for exertion in youth or dignity
in old age, which keeps us from the commission of little actions.
When a man is forced to thank, and as it were, to bend the knee
for his daily bread, he feels like a slave, and is too apt to act the
part of one.

—William Sabatier, *Treatise on Poverty* (1797)

THESE TWO VIEWS, coming almost one hundred and fifty years apart, rep-
resent extreme expressions of changes in opinion about the nature and
function of charity that occurred in this period. The first saw all advantage in benevolence as accruing to the donor, and urges him to give to all
without discrimination, and without hope of return. The second considered the effect of charitable donation on the recipient, stressing its pernicious influences on the character and personality of the object aided, urging instead a manly self-reliance and determination to be free of the taint
of charity. Changes in practice were equally striking; in 1650 London had
few if any privately organized and financed charitable institutions, by
1800 it had dozens. Historians of this period have seen the genesis of
these changes in attitude and practice in the appearance of a new spirit of
"humanitarianism," which, they say, became significant in the 1740s and
onward. The first practical expression of this new concern was the establishment of the Foundling Hospital in 1740. In chapter 2 we will consider
both the beginnings of the Foundling and the adequacy of "humanitarianism" as an explanation for the wave of charitable theorizing and experimentation that characterized this period. The Foundling, however,
was not the only major charity established at this time. My own interest
in midcentury charity was first aroused by the unexplained and unex-

pected flurry of maternity hospitals and charities that sprang up in London between 1740 and 1760. It was in the attempt to understand the appearance and growth of these institutions that I encountered several circumstances that led me to enlarge the focus of investigation both backward and forward in time and outward in scope. The nature of the evidence, which I will subsequently examine, also urged this course.

THE QUESTIONS

One of the first sources I came across at the beginning of this enterprise was the "declarations of purpose" that each charity had printed as advertisements and inducements to public subscription. When I came to examine these explanations and justifications for their existence, it became clear that all contemporary charities, in promoting their enterprises, explained themselves and their purposes in similar ways, seeing their work as achieving similar goals and, most interestingly, as central to the pursuance of similar national policy aims. This perhaps is not surprising when one realizes that many of the same individuals gave to several current charities, and often took more direct roles in their management and organization. The structure of explanation that these declarations reveal and the goals into which these appeals fit was not, I soon realized, entirely new to the midcentury, but was in many ways the reiteration, the material expression, of well-worn and popularly accepted ways of understanding that stretched back to the seventeenth century. Thus, in attempting to understand the origin of one cluster of charities, I was compelled outward to include other contemporary benevolent organizations, and pulled backward to discover the genesis of the notions and views that shaped them. Driven at first back in time from the midcentury, I found myself wondering what happened to this "trial of experiments"[1] after the initial enthusiasm had passed. And so I was pushed forward, through the 1770s and beyond, to the point where a new system of thought and practice began to reorganize charitable activity under a reshaped view of what constituted the nation's greatest need. This study, then, is the result of two basic convictions that emerged from and gave direction to my research. First, I became convinced that it is not only difficult but futile to study any single charity separate from either the "world of charitable concern" or from ongoing changes in social theory and practice. Only in the general patterning of charitable alternatives and charitable experimentation could the work of any charity or group of charities make sense. Sec-

---

[1] [Jonas Hanway], *The Genuine Sentiments of an English Country Gentleman, upon the Present Plan of the Foundling Hospital* with *A Candid Historical Account of the Hospital . . . for Exposed and Deserted Children*, 2nd ed. (London: G. Woodfall, 1760), p. 33.

ond, I sought to situate midcentury charity both in its own time and place and also to present it in its relation to its predecessors and its successors.

However, before we go any further, it is necessary to explain the title of this book, and to describe the criteria I have used to decide which organizations will be considered and which deleted. For this study is by no means an exhaustive or complete account of all benevolent institutions or groups in eighteenth-century London. The first major omissions are all groups that cared only for their own poor, such as the many Huguenot or Jewish charities. The second are the societies like the Westminster Hospital or the Thatched House Society that, while they attempted to aid the poor, did not in the main try to improve them. I have suggested in chapter 2 that even these charities of relief rather than reform or rehabilitation had an improving quality; their main function, however, was to dispense alms to the needy. I, however, included such organizations as the Societies for the Reformation of Manners, of the 1690s and the Proclamation Society, of the 1790s, though at first glance these scarcely appear charitable. For the purpose of this book is to cast light upon a specific sort of charity, to differentiate philanthropy as "an Inclination to promote Publick Good" from broader and more diffuse streams of "love, kindness or natural affection," which the notion of charity often entails. Although the words philanthropy and charity are used interchangeably in this book, it is this narrower meaning, which Bacon defined as pertaining to "the affecting of the Weale of Men," that explains the parameters of this work. The charities I will discuss were those that are broadly based and metropolitan, that were nondenominational and associational, that sought not only to relieve, but to directly benefit the nation.[2]

Along with an attempt to see what the course of charitable activity can tell us more generally about eighteenth-century English culture, four other interrelated questions form the locus of this study. The first, dealt with most explicitly in chapter 1 but present throughout, is whether the notion of a charitable tradition can be used to explain the continuance and expansion of giving. If tradition is more than merely the dead hand of the past, we need to understand and account for changes as well as continuities in traditional ways of seeing and doing. For it is the contention of this book that the retention and reformulation of ideas is as important and as worthy of historical investigation as their rejection. Ideas

[2] J.A.H. Murray, *The Oxford English Dictionary* (Oxford: Clarendon Press, 1961). Jacques Donzelot, in *The Policing of Families* (New York: Pantheon, 1979), p. 16, uses a similar definition: "the consolidation . . . of all the forms of direction of the life of the poor, so as to diminish the social cost of their reproduction and obtain an optimum number of workers at minimum public expense; in sort, what is customarily termed philanthropy." Much of Donzelot's analysis about the differences between charity and philanthropy are very apposite to the English case (see pp. 60–69).

and practices change and traditions are refurbished when a combination of new situations and new notions necessitates such a reappraisal. Nothing is ever mechanical nor entirely new.

The second question that this study addresses—what were the social functions of charity in the eighteenth century—contains and perhaps obscures a central assumption, that is, that charity had recognized social roles to fulfill. Chapters 1 and 4, which deal most directly with theories of what the functions of charity should be, as well as chapters 2, 3, 4, and 6, which are concerned with its practice, are both justifications and illustrations of this contention. I have argued throughout that it is impossible to understand eighteenth-century charity without coming to grips with its perceived social utility, which changed as circumstances mandated. It was therefore necessary to reconstruct those larger worlds of hopes and purposes implicit in, and giving shape to, various charitable proposals and schemes. It was also necessary to locate their often self-contradictory ideas and practices within a universe of discussion, a universe filled with unresolved problems and unclearly articulated points of view. In studying this universe, we come to see how theorizing and practice are intimately conjoined; for this universe of discussion is both an intellectual construction and a normative description or prescription of the world as many people wished it to be.

Eighteenth-century polemicists and philanthropists summed up this social function of charity under the term "police." To our ears "police" consists of a group whose job it is to keep the peace, to arrest malefactors, and to protect innocent citizens from harm. The work they do we call "policing." However, the word "police" had a much wider usage in eighteenth-century London. Related to the word "polished," it referred to the maintenance of a civil order, a civilized society, and a refining process.[3] Police was the practical, consensual expression of a society's social arrangements, mores, and beliefs. The notion of police, however, which was originally used in a domestic sense, came to have larger significance as the century progressed, and came to include all those items of importance to the national welfare not completely or adequately handled by public officials. The needs of police, or its defects, encompassed that series of political hopes and aspirations that many publicly minded and prolific social commentators, as well as the hosts of ordinary citizens who in a sense they represented, thought central to the maintenance and expansion of England's role in the world, and her peace at home. A central argument of this work is that, at any given time, there was something like consensus

[3] See, for example, William Blackstone, *Commentaries on the Laws of England*, a facsimile of the first edition of 1765–1769, 4 vols. (Chicago: University of Chicago Press, 1979), 4:162. Also note the title (and message) of Jonas Hanway's *The Defects of Police, the Cause of Immorality* . . . (London: J. Dodsley, 1775).

among those involved in charitable activities about what sort of society they wished for Britain. Although they may have differed widely on the best methods to achieve these national ends, they agreed substantially on what the goals were. Charitable societies maintained that their efforts would promote these national policies, for a good national "police" was not to be achieved solely by politicians or by a professional corp of "police," but by publicly concerned, philanthropically minded citizens.

Following from this notion of police, the third question that this study considers is why English men and women turned to voluntary agencies to ameliorate poverty. What did they hope to accomplish through these means that they thought was not within the scope of the Poor Law? Why did they feel that charitable societies were more sensitive instruments of national policy? How did they think that the very processes of donation and distribution aided the national and international strength and wealth of Britain?

Finally, how were different systems of value melded into workable, if not entirely coherent systems of action? How did religious precepts, mercantile purposes, and the general drive for social improvement come together to provide both the rationale for the establishment of, and the strength and determination to manage, the many time-consuming and expensive charities of the day?

THE SOURCES

Before we can turn to the answers to these questions, we must pause briefly to examine sources. For, in some part, this study has been shaped by the nature of the sources available. Since many of the charities discussed have disappeared, the manuscript sources for the operations of these charitable institutions are scant.[4] Even if they had been more plentiful, however, another type of source would have to have been consulted. For while detailed records allow us to observe the day-to-day practice of the charities under consideration, they seldom and only indirectly give us clues to the nature of that larger world of goals and purposes that this work addresses. Thus, this study has been shaped by two sorts of evidence: a general body of materials dealing with charity, poverty, economic health, and police; and a more specific set of documents that discuss the charities in their particularity—their donors, finances, problems, and successes.

Much of the argument of this book rests on an investigation of the writings of late-seventeenth- and eighteenth-century clerics. Not only did

---

[4] Only the papers of the the Foundling Hospital, the General Lying-in Hospital, the Marine Society, the Lock Hospital, and the Philanthropic Society are available and have been used in this study.

clergymen themselves directly contribute to a public awareness of the importance of benevolence, they also provided historically important rebuttals to writers, like Mandeville, who questioned its efficacy. In addition to the works of the most obvious and notable religious thinkers and writers, men like Butler and Law, Paley and Tucker, charity sermons and miscellaneous clerical essays on poverty, charity, and the economy were also consulted. Charity sermons are especially interesting and understudied. Those preached for the new, privately funded and managed charities of the midcentury were, like their medieval predecessors, an attempt to win fiscal support for their organizations. However, since mid-eighteenth-century charities were largely funded by private individuals, their success depended not only upon convincing the public to subscribe once, but also to subscribe year after year, again and again. The sermons were attempts to explain to potential and present donors not only the efficacy of their particular charity, but also the larger social or police value of the entire branch of charity in which they were engaged. Charities that did best financially used what might be described as the multimotive or shotgun approach toward convincing citizens to subscribe. Donation to their charity, each proclaimed, would not only be pleasant to the donor, but would also be profitable to him in his capacity as an economic agent, a citizen and a soul, both here and hereafter. The most successful preachers were able to tailor their sermons to appeal to this hodgepodge of motives; those charities that fared least well in terms of amounts raised, like the Lock Hospital, most often featured sermons that appealed only to sympathy and benevolence. Charities that did moderately well, like the lying-in hospitals, appealed both to sentiment and to sound money sense. The charity that did best of all, the Marine Society, also promised its subscribers the largest worldly returns.[5] Thus, the charity sermons speak to us in voices louder than their own, for, when successful, they articulated the hopes and motives of their audiences, whose opinions otherwise are almost entirely unknown and unrecorded.

Though clerics were important in setting the tone and practice of eighteenth-century charity, writers on economic policy and affairs were also significant. I have deliberately chosen to look only at works that were read and discussed in the coffeehouses and the stock exchange and that therefore influenced the opinions of policymakers, executors, and philanthropists alike. Two groupings of such thinkers are considered in this study; the first, which I have called the "political arithmeticians," and the

---

[5] The Marine was able to attract £4,721 in its first year. The Magdalen House subscribers contributed more than £5,600 from 1758 to April 1759. On the other hand, the Lock's average annual income for its first five years of operation was less than £700.

second, the "political economists."[6] Their writings were read by and formed the backdrop to discussions of national policy for those most actively concerned about the care of the poor, men like Thomas Coram and Jonas Hanway (discussed in chapters 2, 3, and 4) or Thomas Bernard and Robert Young (discussed in chapter 6). Such informed polemicists for and practitioners of benevolence saw charitable activity as one major way in which an active and involved citizenry could affect and promote national goals.

Having studied the milieu in which charitable ideas were formed and philanthropic experiments advocated, we come to the work, and sources for the study, of the charities themselves. First, of course, all surviving manuscript sources have been consulted. Of equal importance, however, is the wide variety of printed sources that remain. We have already mentioned the "declarations of purpose" that many institutions printed. In addition to these, many charities also published a range of materials to advertise their work. Often an especially popular and successful charity sermon was published with the charity's financial statement. Sometimes a subscription list and a "potted" history of the charity's "objects" (as the recipients of charity were called) was also included. The completeness of these last two sorts of information varies enormously from charity to charity and year to year. Some lists are full, with names, addresses, and amounts subscribed. Others merely record the names of donors with no more information attached. Most records give some sense of the admission and dismissal rate of the institution. This allows us roughly to gauge changes in this vital phase of a charity's operations. The financial records, even when incomplete, are other useful and illuminating sources of information. For the financial statements of these charities can be seen as barometers of their ongoing success or failure. When a charity's funds continued to grow year after year, one feels confident that its aims and management pleased its members. On the other hand, when charities failed to attract donors, when their finances and their subscribers dwindled, it is equally clear that they had lost the confidence of the public, or that a competitor had been more successful in squeezing them out of the struggle for charitable funds. In addition to giving us clues about changes in levels of public support, the financial records also allow us to see the techniques used by charities in their fundraising. We can see the extent to which they depended on ongoing subscription and monies collected be-

---

[6] I have chosen to call these two groups of theorists the "political arithmeticians" and the "political economists" for two reasons. The first is that that is what contemporaries called them. But even more important is the unnecessary bother and unfruitful argument that would be created if they were described as "mercantilists" and "classical economists," or some other such nomenclature, since a vast and irrelevant (for the purposes of this book) literature centers around these terms.

fore and after sermons, dinners, and special events, like benefit plays and operas. We can also tell how successful each charity was in one of its fondest ambitions, making the work of its inmates pay. Perhaps potentially even more valuable than these accounts of receipts and expenditures are the lists of the charity's subscribers. An analysis of them helps reveal who these unknown donors were, what sorts of people different charities appealed to, and whether or not any common patterns can be found among them. The results of this examination are scattered throughout the study; a more detailed discussion of what I have called the "charitable community" of donors will be found in chapters 3 and 6. Also included is an examination of the wills of a sample of subscribers, which both tells us more about their motives and backgrounds and provides information about the nature and scope of their charitable bequests.

Having considered both the structure and the sources for this study, we return to our beginnings. How can the change in theory and practice exemplified in the opening quotes be explained?

CHAPTER ONE

"All Mankind's Concern": Religion, Commerce, and Charity, 1680–1740

> Thus God and nature linked the gen'ral frame
> And bade self-love and social be the same
> —Alexander Pope, *Essay on Man* (1733)

ENGLISH MEN AND WOMEN of the eighteenth century judged it to be a great age of benevolence. They were convinced that a new phase in England's care of the poor had been initiated, vindicating for all time the superiority of the Protestant faith, which, while not making good works the method of salvation, showed its true Christianity by its overflowing beneficence.[1] It was said that as soon as a need was found, a charity was established to care for it. This is an interesting though not entirely accurate assessment.

Until quite recently we have known very little about the shape of eighteenth-century giving. Perhaps too easily convinced by Tawney and his followers that the mercantile spirit was a mercenary one, we have not, on the whole, despite appeals from Charles Wilson and others, really understood either the spirit or the course of charitable operations in this century. In this chapter we will attempt to trace the intellectual roots of that benevolence and understand its nature.

David Owen, the most prominent historian of the charities of modern England, has warned us of the dangers of speculating about motives. He wrote that "it would be hardly rewarding to speculate at length on the motives which inspired [Londoners] to donate or bequeath sizeable sums for public purposes." Yet, when Archbishop Secker addressed those very Londoners who formed the many committees that made charities function, he warned them that motive was all: "To the Poor indeed it is all one from what Principle we give, but to us the Difference is Infinite. In

---

[1] See M. G. Jones, *Hannah More* (Cambridge: Cambridge University Press, 1952), and James P. Malcolm, *Anecdotes of the Manners and Customs of London during the Eighteenth Century* [1800], 2nd ed., 2 vols. (London: Longman, 1810), 1:16. A correspondent to the *Gentleman's Magazine* (April 1747), p. 163, held that "since the Reformation has banished ignorance and restored Christianity, we have nobly distinguished ourselves by donations of another kind [from those of the Catholics], such as are truly stiled *charities*."

the Heart lies all the Value."[2] Thus, despite Owen's apt and sensible warning, we are impelled to search the treacherous and murky waters of motivation, to discern and disentangle, so far as we are able, the complex currents of the heart.

Many historians, in seeking to explain the midcentury outpouring of charitable assistance, have fallen back on the notion of tradition, in this case a "tradition of benevolence." That people gave to charities because their forebears had, and because it was expected that they too would, while undoubtedly true, does not explain why they gave in the manner they did or why such giving, over the course of the century, sought different objectives for its goals. Nor, in fact, does it help us to understand more clearly the psychology of motivation. The idea of a tradition of benevolence as an inexorable weight pressing relentlessly and constantly upon its hapless victims (or, in this case, donors), coercing them, willy-nilly, into reaching into their pocketbooks and giving to whatever comes along, explains little.

In fact, tradition is a more delicate and complex organism, responding creatively to new stimuli within a wide framework of past choices. Tradition is that living past, reinterpreted and modified by the views and needs of the present. If we think of tradition in this fluid and nondeterministic way, we can discuss the complex of traditions that fueled the charitable sentiments of this period. What I wish to do then, is to look at a series of "traditions" in order to locate and describe the concurrence of convictions that set the stage for the emergence of the charities of the midcentury.

CHRISTIANITY AND CHARITY

The first of the traditions that I would like to examine is the religious one, that is, the general role and specific views of English clerics toward poverty and charity. The question of the nature and ultimate reason for the existence of poverty has always been a central theological question. However, with few notable exceptions, historians of the eighteenth century are still laboring under the view, proposed by R. H. Tawney many years ago, that such thought either does not exist, or is not worth studying. Tawney claimed that after the Civil War "religious opinion laid less emphasis on

---

[2] David Owen, *English Philanthropy* (Cambridge, Mass.: Belknap Press, 1964), p. 69; Thomas Secker, *Sermons on Several Subjects*, 5 vols. (London: J. & F. Rivington, 1790), "On the Duties of the Rich," 3:215. Secker (1693–1768), archbishop of Canterbury, was at school with Joseph Butler, was recommended for his first ecclesiastical appointment by William Talbot, and was a close friend and brother-in-law of Martin Benson. The *Dictionary of National Biography* (*DNB*) calls him a typical "orthodox eighteenth century prelate," known for his "plain good sense" (2:258).

the obligation of charity than upon the duty of work, and that the admonitions which had formerly been turned upon uncharitable covetousness were now directed against improvidence and idleness."[3] The Puritan ideal, Tawney held, undermined the old criticisms of uncharitableness to the poor by instead stressing the need for the poor to support themselves, that alms were of less importance in salvation than that faith which manifests itself in acquisition and material attainment.

Tawney maintained that "the growing individualism of the [post–Civil War] age . . . saw in misfortune, not the chastisement of love, but the punishment of sin."[4] An examination of the religious writings of this period reveals a much more ambiguous attitude toward poverty than Tawney had led us to expect. From the eminent dissenter, Thomas Gouge, writing in the 1670s, through the bishop of Gloucester, Martin Benson, writing more than fifty years later, clerics strongly asserted (as had their medieval and early modern predecessors) that poverty was the result not of sin, but of God's providential plan for the world; that poverty was God's gracious method of allowing men to win salvation in the exercise of their mutual ties of obligation and gratitude. Thus, in a sermon entitled "The Value of Charity," the Anglican theologian Daniel Waterland, noting that "God could have provided for [the poor] in a thousand other ways," stressed the beneficial effects of almsgiving to the donor.[5]

Charity was accorded a central role in religious life. Isaac Barrow; the bishop of Durham, William Talbot; the Jacobite bishop Francis Atterbury; the theologian Daniel Waterland; and Knightly Chetwood, dean of Gloucester, all held that charity was the main element in true Christian observance. Talbot, for example, wrote that "the excellency of this Grace [charity] is that 'tis preferable to Faith and Hope, the very bond of perfectness, the fulfilling of the Law, and that it shall cover a multitude of sins." And although Atterbury and Benjamin Hoadly disagreed about most things, Atterbury, like Hoadly, thought that "to practice 'virtue and charity under the belief in a Supreme Governor' was to be religious."[6]

---

[3] R. H. Tawney, *Religion and the Rise of Capitalism* (London: John Murray, 1943), p. 264. An interesting current variation on the Tawney thesis is the claim, made by a recent historian, that unlike Catholic France, whose religion stressed "the value of good deeds to the doer as a means toward earning his own salvation," in England such motives were undermined by a "Calvinist influence on religious thought." See Ruth McClure, *Coram's Children* (New Haven: Yale University Press, 1981), p. 14.

[4] Tawney, *Religion*, p. 14.

[5] Daniel Waterland, *The Works of Daniel Waterland*, vol. 5 (Oxford: Oxford University Press, 1843), "The True Nature of Charity," p. 563. Waterland (1683–1740), vice-chancellor of Oxford University and archdeacon of Middlesex, is credited by the *Dictionary of National Biography* with having done "more than any other divine of his generation to check the advance of Latitudinarian ideas within the Church of England" (20:904).

[6] William Talbot, *Sermon before the . . . Governors of the Several Hospitals of the City*

If poverty is providential, then Christians, if they wish salvation, clearly stand obliged to care for and succor the poor. However, it is at this point that difficulties and distinctions arise. What is to be the nature of this charity? What is the strength of the obligation to give to the poor? What can or should one expect from one's alms? It is to these questions that we must turn.

That charity is the heart of Christianity is merely platitudinous unless given some more substance. This, some eighteenth-century divines were prepared to do. Following medieval precedents, Chetwood argued that charity was not merely voluntary benevolence, but mandatory justice entailed on the enjoyment of any form of property. "We are apt," he noted, "to take it for granted that our Estates . . . are entirely at our own Disposal, legal Debts being discharg'd; but this is a great Mistake, Charity is a principal Branch of Justice, . . . we are but Stewards, not Proprietors, even when Estates are gotten by the most justifiable Means." As late as 1734, Joseph Roper could argue "that if we have not disposed of those good Things, which he hath deposited in our Hands, according to the Will and Intention of the Sovereign *Proprietor*, that we are guilty of gross Mis-application."[7] This view had not yet disappeared in the 1740s, when Henry Layng characterized all wealth as "the gracious Gift of God only,"[8] or when the future bishop of Rochester, Zachariah Pearce, refuting the Lockean notion that the right to property derives from human labor, asked whether even this was not God's bounty, "for who gave the prosperous Voyage to the Vessels, which came home freighted with thy Riches? Was it not God?"[9]

---

of London . . . (London: Thomas Bennett, 1700), p. 26. Talbot (1659–1730) was the patron and friend of Joseph Butler and Thomas Secker. Benjamin Hoadly, quoted in Lewis Perry Curtis, *Anglican Moods of the Eighteenth Century* (Hamden, Conn.: Archon Books, 1966), p. 8. Hoadly (1676–1761), bishop of Bangor and father of the "Bangorian Controversy," spent most of his career fighting with his ecclesiastical colleagues. See also Waterland, *Works*, "The Duty of Doing Good," p. 303.

[7] Knightly Chetwood, *A Sermon Addressed to the Lord Mayor, Aldermen, Sheriffs and Governors of Several Hospitals of the City of London* (London: Jonah Bowyer, 1708), p. 29. Chetwood lived from 1650 to 1720; Joseph Roper, *Sermon Preached . . . before . . . the Governors of the Several Hospitals of the City of London* . . . (London: W. Innys and R. Manby, 1734), "The Character of a Liberal Man," p. 10. See also William Lupton, *Spital Sermon* (London: D. L. for J. Cleave, 1713), "The Necessity and Measures, the Excellency and Efficacy of Works of Charity Represented," pp. 8–9. I have not been able to uncover any information about Roper; Lupton (1676–1726), prebendary of Durham, had a reputation as a good preacher.

[8] Henry Layng, *A Sermon Preached . . . before the President and Governors of the County Infirmary for Sick and Lame Poor* (Northampton: W. Dicey, 1746), p. 10. Layng was rector of Paulersbury.

[9] Zachariah Pearce, *A Spital Sermon before . . . the Governors of Several Hospitals* . . .

Charity was thus a natural and inevitable activity for all good Christians. Through the first five decades of the eighteenth century, contrary to Tawney's view, clerics continued to insist that almsgiving, directed by the spirit of sacrifice, was essentially a self-regarding religious act. "True Charity" said Jabez Earle in a sermon of 1728, mirroring the same sentiment expressed earlier by Waterland, "is for God's sake." Charity then was an act of devotion involving the giver and God; it was a demonstration of the sincere believer's faith in Providence. The man who gives his substance to the poor "does therefore plainly own it to be in God's power to afford him a fresh supply of all things that are necessary for him."[10] This cheerful resignation of the goods of the world has the happy effect, not only of "covering sins" at the day of judgment, but also of insuring God's blessings on our enterprises in this life. "Liberality," said Isaac Barrow in his most famous sermon, "The Duty and Reward of Bounty to the Poor," "is the most beneficial trade that can be. . . . We thereby lend our money to God, who repays with vast usury; an hundred to one is the rate he allows at present, and about a hundred million to one he will render hereafter."[11]

In addition to this central religious motive to acts of kindness, beneficence also had important social consequences. Though Tawney remarked that railings against covetousness ceased along with the demand to be charitable, we can see the old tradition continuing unbroken from Barrow to Thomas Secker, who saw in charity the best medicine for the sin of covetousness, preventing "the Love of Money from fixing and growing upon us." Not only was charitable donation a remedy for miserliness, but charity was also seen as springing from a sense of common humanity. For, "as we are all Children of the same Father" we cannot help being "affected with the Wants and Miseries of our Fellow-Creatures."[12]

(London: John Watts, 1743), p. 11. Pearce (1690–1774) left £20,000 to charity. See also Secker, *Sermons*, "As We Have Opportunity, Let Us Do Good to All Men," 4:181.

[10] Jabez Earle, *Dispensing and Giving to the Poor Considered* (London: J. Grey, 1729), p. 4. Earle (1676–1768), a Presbyterian minister and chaplain to the duke of Douglas, was one of the original members of the Society for the Reformation of Manners. Thomas Lynford, *A Spital Sermon* (London: Joseph Downing, 1712), "The Charitable Man Bears Much Fruit," p. 13. Lynford (1650–1724) was chaplain-in-ordinary to William and Mary and canon of Westminster.

[11] Isaac Barrow, *The Theological Works of Isaac Barrow*, Alexander Napier, ed., 6 vols. (Cambridge: Cambridge University Press, 1890), "The Duty and Reward of Bounty to the Poor," 1:81. Barrow (1630–1677), a friend of Tillotson's and master of Trinity College, Cambridge, was regarded by John Locke as author of sermons that were "masterpieces of their kind."

[12] Secker, *Sermons*, "As We Have Opportunity," 4:54–56. See also Barrow, *Works*, "Motives and Arguments for Charity," 2:382. Edmund Gibson, *A Sermon Preached . . . at St. Sepulchre* (London: Joseph Downing, 1716), "The Peculiar Excellency and Reward of Supporting Schools of Charity," p. 20. Gibson (1669–1748) was bishop of London and an

But to whom should the good Christian be charitable? Should he be kind only to good Christians, or to those clearly deserving? What should be hoped for as a consequence of such charity? The single most frequent, and somewhat misleading, response to the first question is that we should be charitable to all, that we should give even to those who may be wicked, or to those from whom we can expect no advantage.[13] Furthermore, the preachers warned the charitable not to slacken their efforts under the misapprehension that misery was the just reward of vice, and thus not to be ameliorated by alms or care; Waterland called this "the drawing rash and uncharitable conclusions from greater suffering to greater sins." As to the ends of charity, clerics like Atterbury, William Lupton, and Secker urged their hearers to exercise "a calm settled Benevolence on all fit Occasions, because we ought; without hoping to succeed very often, or to produce on the whole a remarkable Change for the better."[14]

Despite this seeming urging to indiscriminate almsgiving, directions and limitations on charity were recognized and recommended. Secker, for one, set out a list of priorities for benevolence that would not have been out of place in a medieval text, beginning with kindnesses to kindred and ending with those due the poor. But, in fact, priorities and expansive generosity were not mutually exclusive. "Our part," said Atterbury, "is to chuse out the most deserving Objects, and the most likely to answer the Ends of our Charity, and when that is done, all is done, that lies in our Power: the rest must be left to Providence. . . . What we bestow on these Occasions is given by us, not as unto Men, but as unto God. . . . And, with him, the Value of our Gift depends not on the Success of it."[15]

---

eminent Anglo-Saxon scholar. He strongly opposed the moral laxity of his day. Richard Grey, *A Sermon before the Governors of the Northampton County Infirmary for the Sick and Lame* (London: William Dicey, 1744), "The Encouragement to Works of Charity and Mercy," p. 7. Grey (1694–1771) was a prebendary of St. Paul's.

[13] John Norris, *The Theory and Regulation of Love* (Oxford: printed for Henry Clements, 1688), pp. 58–59. Norris (1657–1711) was one of the last to be influenced by the Cambridge Platonists. See also Waterland, *Works*, "The Duty of Loving Our Neighbours as Ourselves," pp. 440–41; Lynford, *Spital Sermon*, p. 6.

[14] Waterland, *Works*, "The Case of Passing Judgment Concerning Calamities Examined," p. 502. Archbishop Secker in fact commended charity to the wicked by rhetorically asking, "How do we know, that Mercy exercised prudently, will not reclaim them; or that refusing it will prove a Warning to Them, or to others?" *Fourteen Sermons*, vol. 2 (London: J. & F. Rivington, 1771), "Preached before the Governors of the London Hospital, 1754," p. 251. Secker, *Sermons*, "And the Second is Like Unto It, Thou Shall Love Thy Neighbour as Thyself," 2:99.

[15] Francis Atterbury, *Sermons and Discourses on Several Subjects and Occasions*, 2 vols. (London: J. Bettenham for C. Bowyer, 1730), "Spital Sermon 1709," 2:231–33. Atterbury (1662–1732) was characterized as "the best preacher of his day" by the *Dictionary of National Biography*, 1:705–10. See also Lupton, *Spital Sermon*, pp. 12–13; Secker, *Sermons*, "On the Duties of the Poor," 4:223–24.

In looking at the social and charitable attitudes of clerics for the decades preceding 1740, we have so far stressed the continuity of thought and admonition between these eighteenth-century churchmen and their predecessors. However, since tradition is a living thing, these opinions did not and could not remain unchanged, and were, in fact, sometimes subtly, sometimes massively, reinterpreted and renovated. Often the same cleric held two different, and contradictory views simultaneously. These contradictions illustrate the difficulties of revivifying a received tradition.

We have already noted that clerics continued to believe that poverty was a providentially arranged condition, ordained by God so that men could earn salvation through the reciprocal processes of kindness and gratitude. At the same time, clerics also began to give other explanations for this vexatious condition. Secker, for example, thought poverty an inevitable result of the combination of natural inequality and the transmission of property.[16] This new insight into the nature of poverty rested on a new understanding of the limits and obligations of property. Those who viewed poverty entirely as providential had seen charity as the rent annexed to the use of property, and thus judged almsgiving to be merely the workings of justice. In the new proprietary view, however, justice had become detached from the duty to charity, and attached to the promulgation of private property. "Hence it appears," noted Bishop Thomas Sherlock, "that Property is established . . . by the positive Law of God; which is to us the highest Reason and Authority. . . . And to this Right of his own establishing even God himself submits." How then were the poor to be cared for? "The Poor are his [God's] peculiar Charge; his Providence stands engaged for their Support: But neither does God force us to part with our Estates to the Poor, or give the Poor *any Right* to serve themselves out of the Abundance and Superfluity of others." They are to be maintained "by the *free and voluntary* Gift of such as can spare from their own subsistence some Part of what they enjoy."[17]

With charity removed from the realm of obligation to that of voluntary action, from justice to mercy, clerics also began to reassess the amount or portion of one's property that one was bound to give away. Bishop Gilbert Burnet, interpreting Christ's command to "sell all that thou hast, and give to the poor," noted that this injunction was meant to apply only in times of "famine or persecution," but that "in ordinary cases to do it, might be rather a tempting of Providence than a trusting to it, for then a

---

[16] Ibid., 3:223–24.

[17] Thomas Sherlock, *Several Discourses Preached at the Temple Church*, 4 vols. (London: printed for J. Whiston and B. White, 1754–1758), 3:108–9; emphasis added. Sherlock (1678–1761), bishop of London, attained extraordinary popularity as master of the Temple. In addition to being an important political ally of Walpole's, he maintained kindly relations throughout his life with Dissenters.

man should part with the means of his subsistence, which God has provided for him, without a necessary and pressing occasion." Burnet concluded by urging moderation even in the virtue of charity. "We should be," in the words of the prebendary of St. Paul's, Richard Grey, "merciful *after our Power*."[18] Though God expects charity from all, noted Archbishop Secker, the amount required is left to individual discretion. Even clerics like Lupton, who maintained that "God is the sole Lord, who hath intrusted us with Treasures, to be disposed of not as our own humours direct, but according to his express direction and commandment in supporting and comforting the Needy and Afflicted,"[19] felt it would be unreasonable, not to say dangerous, for the rich overzealously to dispossess themselves of their property, or even of their superfluities. It was only in the enjoyment of such property that rank and hierarchy, as well as the true church, could be maintained. Indeed, all that was required was that people of wealth "retrench unnecessary expenses at least, abridge their pleasures, shorten their diversions, cut off as much as possible from the pomp and pride of life, to spend upon the poor." And while covetousness was still decried as a sin, frugality, its near kin, was seen as a necessary virtue.[20] The getting and enjoying of wealth, rather than making it more difficult to attain salvation, was now described as a beneficial and moral state. The good Christian, according to Thomas Lynford, "is neither any Way dishonest, nor oversolicitous in the Management of his Affairs, but yet is very careful and industrious, that so, if it be possible, he may procure to himself a comfortable subsistence in the World." In fact, clerics began to warn of the possibility of overcharitableness. "Some have carried their public spiritedness too far and piqued themselves on manifesting Good-Will to their Fellow-Creatures, by Undertakings out of their Province, and even beyond their Abilities."[21]

With this softened emphasis on the importance and justice of charity to the Christian life came a reconsideration of the notion that the poor have a right to the assistance of the rich. This rethinking led to different responses. Some, like Nicholas Clagett, denied that the poor had any temporal rights to the property of the rich since "the crime of uncharitableness is what appertains to another and a higher jurisdiction, and is one of

[18] Gilbert Burnet, *An Exposition of the Thirty-Nine Articles of the Church of England* (Oxford: Oxford University Press, 1831), p. 183. Burnet (1643–1715), bishop of Salisbury, a "singularly effective preacher," was said to be as "unsparing in labour as in charity." Grey, *Sermon*, p. 8; emphasis added.

[19] Secker, *Fourteen Sermons*, "Sermon before the Lord Mayor, 1738," p. 70; Lupton, *Spital Sermon*, pp. 8–9.

[20] Ibid., p. 6; Waterland, *Works*, "The True Nature of Charity," p. 565.

[21] Lynford, *Spital Sermon*, p. 3; Secker, *Sermons*, "Thou Shall Love Thy Neighbour," 2:80.

those reserved cases, that God, the supreme judge of mankind, must be supposed to keep in his own hands."[22] Others, like Sherlock, thought that "Charity is the Inheritance of the Poor; it is, as I may say, their Property," and thus allowed of the propriety of certain poor people being allowed to beg alms: "those who have a Right to this kind of Maintenance, have a Right to ask for it, that is, to beg the Charity of all well-disposed Christians." Still others, like the chaplain of the earl of Hume, thought the poor had a real right to "a Part of our Substance, provided we are sensible that our Alms will do him a *real Good* and ourselves no great prejudice."[23] This notion, that charity must be so directed that it would not only be of short-term benefit to the poor, but also would be to their long-term welfare, seems a growing sentiment. "Hence it follows," said John Norris in a provocative piece called "The Theory and Regulation of Love," "that we ought to tender the Interest of his Soul more than the good of his Body; . . . that we stick not to prick and lance him in order to his Cure, and (when both can't be done) that we chuse rather to profit him than to please him. For this is true Charity, tho' a severer sort of it." The sensible donor would not be indiscriminate; he would deny the requests of the poor or meet them only in such a way as to promote their real interests.[24]

Discrimination, though it had always been present in discussions of charity, was now reemphasized in the philanthropic relations between the rich and the poor. Both in terms of whom to aid and how to give, differential treatment was urged. The charitable Christian was increasingly being advised to disburse his charity during his lifetime, in order to have greater control over its direction. "He is fearful lest his Legacie should be lost, or not dispos'd of according to his Mind and Intention. And therefore takes Care to distribute a good Part of his Charity with his own Hands." Furthermore, in the choice of objects of charity, the clerics were of one mind. From Gouge to Secker, all quoted St. Paul's dictum "that if any would not work, neither should he eat."[25] By this they meant simply that "they indeed who prefer an Idle and vagabond Life of Beggary before honest labour, ought not to be encouraged in it by Relief, but abandoned

[22] Nicholas Clagett, *Sermon Preach'd before the Lord Mayor of London* . . . (London: John Pemberton, 1733), p. 3. Clagett, bishop of Exeter, died in 1746.

[23] Sherlock, *Several Discourses*, 3:110; Thomas Holme, *Sermon for the Northampton Infirmary* (Northampton, 1745), "The Duty of Almsgiving Stated and Recommended," p. 10. Holme was rector of Wilden. Emphasis added.

[24] Norris, *Theory and Regulation of Love*, p. 123; Lynford, *Spital Sermon*, p. 7.

[25] Ibid., p. 9; Thomas Gouge, *The Surest and Safest Way of Thriving* (London: S. and B. G. for N. Simmons, 1676), pp. 59–60. Thomas Gouge (1601–1681), a nonconformist divine, gave two-thirds of his annual income to the poor, usually in the form of provision of flax and hemp for the employment of able-bodied workers looking for labor. A friend of Thomas Firmin, it has been suggested that it was his example that encouraged Firmin in charitable employment. See also Secker, *Sermons*, "On the Duties of the Poor," 3:247–48.

to the Wretchedness which they chuse." But, as Secker added, this does not apply to "Persons, whom Providence hath rendered incapable of supplying their own Necessities. They have nothing to be ashamed of, but ought to be assisted with Tenderness and Respect." Thus, though clerics saw charity's real goals to be in the maintenance of the impotent and the refusal to encourage the idle through relief, they also increasingly stressed as charity's main goal the gainful employment of the poor. "For the best Method of relieving the able Poor is employing them."[26] We will soon see how this charitable employment coincided with contemporary economic thought and policy.

Two more themes must be noted. The first, a rather minor one, seems to accord with the increasingly practical appeals that clerics made to their audiences for charitable donations. Charity was increasingly recommended as having specific benefits to the nation or to the national church. Thus, Atterbury remarked that the public charities of Anglican England were a noble rebuke to the Catholic claim to a monopoly on benevolence. Talbot assured his listeners that their charity, like that of the earliest Christians, "will ever be a most certain method to secure and propagate our Religion." John Nixon even maintained that it was only the charity of the English that "engag'd [God] to restrain the Enemy [in this case, the Scots] from ravaging our Territories." The effects of such cooperative ventures of benevolence would be widely felt. Christians gathered together in charitable service would also be better citizens, for almsgiving knits together the donors in one bond of concern and activity. "Ever sacred charity" was credited with the power "to still even the noise of party rage and the madness of the people."[27]

Gradually then, though the older ideas did not disappear and the importance of charity as a prime religious obligation continued to be stressed, clerics also mentioned other, more mundane reasons for encouraging benevolence. These new themes did not displace the older ones, but rather reinforced and reinterpreted them. They did not deny the religious value of almsgiving, but added the social and practical value, the private- and public-interest aspects. We see this multiplicity of motives in a 1712 sermon of Thomas Lynford, "The Charitable Man Bears Much Fruit." In a call to Londoners to solve the problems of beggars, Lynford reminded

[26] Secker, *Sermons*, "As we have opportunity," 4:67, 53; "On the Duties of the Poor," 3:247.

[27] Atterbury, *Sermons*, "Spital Sermon 1707," 2:174; Talbot, *Sermon*, p. 30; John Nixon, *Sermon Before the Governors of the County Infirmary* (Northampton: William Dicey, 1749), p. 24; Martin Benson, *A Spital Sermon Preached . . . before the Lord Mayor of London* (London: J. J. Pemberton, 1736), p. 15. Benson (1689–1752), bishop of Gloucester, was Secker's friend and brother-in-law and a friend of Joseph Butler. See also Holme, "The Duty of Almsgiving," p. 39.

his listeners that "the Care of Religion, a due Regard for Trade, the Honour of this famous City, the Spiritual as well as Temporal Welfare of your Neighbours" all demanded immediate action. Getting the poor out of sight was openly acknowledged as a desired end for charitable action, and preachers like Nicholas Clagett felt no embarrassment in using the uneasiness that misery engendered to persuade Londoners to support their city hospitals, warning them if they had not, "Would it not have abated much of the pleasure we now justly take in beholding the beauty, the riches, and magnificence of this flourishing city, if but a small part of the great number I have mentioned had been . . . permitted to lye languishing, and even expiring in our view."[28]

As the absence of charity could cause pain, benevolent actions were inherently pleasurable, especially to the philanthropist. "The Pleasure of doing a Kindness is pure and unmixed"; whereas the recipient of charity is burdened with shame and gratitude. Secker, like Waterland, spoke eloquently of the joys of philanthropy, claiming that both success and failure brought pleasure. "If we succeed, we have exquisite Joy: if we fail, it is no inconsiderable comfort that we meant well." In addition to pleasure, however, charity brought in its wake "great worldly Advantages."[29] What was the nature of these advantages? For one thing, the "willingness to do good is always rewarded by the Esteem of Mankind." Roper, in his sermon "The Charity of a Liberal Man" went even further and asserted that great business advantages resulted from liberality; "the Reputation of one handsome Action," Roper claimed, "has been known to do a Person more real Service in promoting his Interest in the World than the Acquisitions or Hoards of Years."[30]

Last, but not least, charity was recommended in so far as it promoted and justified existing social and property relationships. Chetwood, for example, cautioned the owners of estates that "it seems advisable for the more *quiet* Possession, to take in the Title of the Poor." Richard Grey was even more explicit. "Charitable foundations," he felt

give the *Poor in general* grateful and honourable sentiments of and inspire them with a proper Love and Reverence toward their Superiors, to see them thus Active and Solicitous for *Their* Good; and by consequence promote the *Harmony* and *Subordination*, in which the Peace and Happiness of Society consists.[31]

[28] Lynford, *Spital Sermon*, pp. 22–23; Clagett, *Sermon*, p. 23.

[29] Lynford, *Spital Sermon*, pp. 9–10; Secker, *Sermons*, "Thou Shall Love Thy Neighbour," 2:96–97.

[30] Secker, *Fourteen Sermons*, "Sermon before the Lord Mayor, 1738," p. 65; Roper, "Character of a Liberal Man," p. 17.

[31] Chetwood, *Sermon*, p. 29; Grey, *Sermon*, pp. 20–21.

Thus, in the years between 1670 and 1740, charity remained an important topic for preachers, ministers, and theologians. Charity sermons often evoked the best efforts of England's finest divines. Much of the substance of these sermons was old; worn but not threadbare, for the thinning spots were filled in and darned as the occasion demanded. Poverty, though seen as a part, not a flaw, in the Divine design, was also seen as the natural consequence of the fruits of unequal acquisition. The rights of the poor to the superfluities of the rich became reinterpreted into the right of the impotent to beg alms from the merciful. Discussions of the nature of the benefit that almsgiving bestowed on the donor shifted from primarily religious and moral goods to material and social ones. Though the value of charity to the donor continued to be emphasized, its value to the recipient became increasingly more important. Discrimination in the methods of philanthropy thus became more central. Different classes of the poor were to be aided and treated differently if substantial improvements were to be effected in their condition. The advice of religious leaders was increasingly pragmatic in nature, and though still concerned about benefits in the hereafter, was more worldly and present-minded in its demands for an active, discerning, and effective charitable community. Still, the vision of a Christian community, tied together by gratitude and acts of kindness, by brotherly feelings in Christ's name, continued to occupy an important place in social thought.

COMMERCE AND CHARITY

Clerics were not the only group who were concerned with understanding and overcoming poverty. A group of writers and thinkers who, for convenience's sake, we will call the political arithmeticians, also made this problem one of their central concerns. What was the nature of their economic analysis? Like most schools of thought, the arithmeticians disagreed almost as much among themselves as they did with other schools. Therefore, I have chosen to describe what might be called "minimal" political arithmetic, that is, to provide a definition that will take in the greatest number of thinkers without being totally vacuous and devoid of content. Seen in this way, political arithmetic was the system of social thought that believed that the nation's economy should be a commercial one, but should be managed either by a prince or some other sovereign power for national goals. It is important to stress the social aspects of this type of thinking. The arithmeticians viewed commercial society as a delicate mechanism constantly in need of fine-tuning. Though economic activity was its mainspring, the distribution of its motor forces had to be properly regulated so that all of society's cogs and wheels performed their assigned tasks without jarring or intruding on each other. Thus, the promotion of the nation's wealth, power, and virtue, and not the accumulation of riches or the improvement of living standards, was the great end of economic, and all other, activity. In attaining these national purposes, however, a great many more limited sectional or individual interests would also be enhanced. Thus, this economic worldview offered a vision of a national purpose that transcended particular purposes or interests, without in any way denying the value of those interests or attempting to eradicate them.

Yet, while the arithmeticians augured in a new world, they were not entirely of it. Like their clerical contemporaries, they were trying to grapple with new realities, endowed with a Christian vocabulary that sometimes sounds jarring and incongruous following a discussion of bullion flow, or the cash value of human labor. Thus, when Sir George Mackenzie, in a work called *The Moral History of Frugality*, lashed out at the avaricious, because their overwhelming passion for gain made them "starve the Poor, bribe, cheat and oppress," we might be tempted to call this cant. Or when Sir Josiah Child, "tyrant" of the East India Company, declared "that it is our Duty to God and Nature" to care for the poor, and described the neglect of this duty as "one of the great Sins," this might be considered mere humbug. It is more difficult, however, to dismiss the writings of John Bellers, political arithmetician and Quaker philanthropist. Bellers, unconscious of incongruity, used the biblical language of stewardship to describe the proper relations between rich and poor. The vocation of the former, "the greater Stewards by their Leisure, Opportunity and Interests," was "to direct the Poor in their Labour, and to Influence and Instruct them in Virtue."[32]

Despite the language of religion, the arithmeticians' vision was entirely practical. Wishing a strong, wealthy state of many employed and virtuous citizens, they recognized that the source of such national wealth and power lay in labor and the laborer. The productivity of the laboring poor was the great motive force that kept the state healthy and growing. People, and especially laboring people, were seen as having a concrete value, quite distinct from their spiritual or intellectual worth. Laborers were often discussed as units of production, as "hands," and their value measured in monetary terms. Lawrence Braddon, solicitor to the wine excise board, calculated that every "poor young child . . . as soon as born, and likely to live, upon a political account, may be valued at £15." Braddon

---

[32] Sir George Mackenzie, *The Moral History of Frugality with its Opposite Vices* (Edinburgh: Andrew Orelman & Joe Vallence, 1691), p. 30; Sir Josiah Child, *New Discourse of Trade* [1693] in *Selected Works, 1688–97: A Collection of Seven Rare Works by, or Attributed to Sir Josiah Child* (Farnborough: Gregg, 1968), pp. 56–57; John Bellers, *Essays about the Poor, Manufactures, Trade, Plantations and Immorality* [1699] (London: E. P. Publishing, 1972), p. 15.

added that these children, "when well bred up, may be made the greatest wealth and strength of the nation."[33] The actual wealth and strength of the state depended upon having a large and growing population that was, to use Braddon's phrase, "well bred," that is, trained and working. A central concern of national policy, therefore, was to deploy all labor efficiently. There were three aspects to such a maximal utilization of labor: population growth, the provision of employment, and the maintenance of national virtue or morale. If all these conditions were satisfied, men and women not only could labor, but would labor, and labor willingly. Furthermore, these three goals were related and reciprocally reinforcing, so that any advance in one area would result in improvements in all.

Population growth was seen as a cause of both national strength and national prosperity. The more people a nation had, the more formidable would it be both in war and peace. A large population was necessary to maintain international power, to man the fleet and armed forces, and to act as a bulwark against foreign depredations.[34] So evident was the connection between numbers and power to political arithmeticians, that how, and not why, population should increase became the problem tackled in pamphlets with titles like *An Essay or a Modest Proposal of a Way to Encrease the Number of People and Consequently the Strength of the Kingdom* (1693).

We have already noted Braddon's assessment of the value of every well-trained child to the nation as £15 per annum. Clearly, the more units there were that could be multiplied by fifteen, the larger would be the national product. In addition to the direct value of the labor of a growing population, there would be beneficial side effects. A large population would, through a more intensive cultivation of land, produce more food as well as more trade. The crowding together and the increased pressures of necessity would induce people not only to expand trade, but also to live more frugally. The price of wages would fall and industriousness increase, as, spurred by smaller wages, people, "to compensate for the diminution of their immediate profit, must study every method to render trade more certain and extensive than before."[35]

The encouragement of virtue and the discouragement and eradication

---

[33] Lawrence Braddon, *The Form of a Petition for Relieving, Reforming and Employing the Poor* (London: Printed for T. Warner, 1722), p. 19.

[34] Lawrence Braddon, *Particular Answers to the Most Material Objections Made to the Proposal Humbly Presented to His Majesty, for Relieving, Reforming and Employing All the Poor of Great Britain* (London: n.p., 1722), pp. 10–12.

[35] William Bell, *A Dissertation on the Following Subject, What Causes Principally Contribute to Render a Nation Populous? And What Effect has the Populousness of a Nation on Its Trade?* (Cambridge: J. Bentham, 1756), pp. 35, 33. See also *Britannia Languens, or a Discourse on Trade* [1680], in J. R. McCulloch, ed., *Early English Tracts on Commerce* (Cambridge: Cambridge University Press, 1954), pp. 345–50.

of vice was the third plank of national policy. For a virtuous population would not only advance the nation's interest through rapid and numerous propagation, but would also directly contribute to the national welfare. Since the state's spiritual integrity was accorded a palpable role in its destiny, the care and preservation of a healthy national temper became one of the prime areas of social concern. The reinvigoration of the social spirit would swell the total numbers of laboring people, both by filling the drones of society—the shirkers and loafers, the prostitutes and vagrants—with the desire to live honestly by work, as well as by increasing England's population through encouragement to lawful and plentiful procreation. As well as increasing the quantity of labor, a further aim of national police was the promotion of virtue, and especially of sexual virtue, in order to increase the quality of labor. A more virtuous population would not only work longer and harder, but would find little time for crime, sexual license, or other counterproductive activities.

Thus, the concept of growth played a central role in the thought of the political arithmeticians. Their writings were filled with it; expansion, the creation and expenditure of energy, provide its leitmotiv. Potentialities for development seemed both infinite and imminent. Arithmeticians had ambitions to "ingross the trade of the Universe," to improve England "to the utmost Perfection."[36] A lively and well-regulated trade was to be both the expression and vehicle for this endless progress. Described as "the best Jewels in the crown of their princes and the richest flower in their Diadem,"[37] trade and commerce roused people to activity, made the nation prosperous and populous, and civilized simultaneously.

What stood in the way of the accomplishment of this dream? Why were many English men and women poor or in need of assistance? What explanations did the arithmeticians give for the presence of poverty? To some extent they, like the divines, felt poverty to be providential. All would have agreed with Bishop Sherlock that "labour is the Business and Employment of the Poor: it is the Work which God has given him to do."[38] Poverty in this sense, the condition that necessitates constant labor in order to supply the requisites of subsistence, was clearly divinely ordained. But when men did not labor, the state of beneficial providential poverty leading to productive activity gave way to a destructive poverty leading only to nonproductive consumption. Labor was the key element in keeping the great mass of the nation in the first, desirable kind of pov-

[36] *England's Greatest Happiness* [1677], in *Early English Tracts*, p. 261. See also *Considerations on the East India Trade* [1701], ibid., p. 582.

[37] This early articulation of the gemlike value of trade, found in Lewes Roberts, *The Treasure of Trafficke* [1641], ibid., p. 105, came to be commonplace in the late seventeenth and eighteenth centuries.

[38] Sherlock, *Several Discourses*, p. 40.

erty and out of the second, impoverishing sort. The arithmeticians, how-ever, recognized that some of the poor did not labor because they could not, that is, they were too old, too young, or infirm. For those that could not labor, for the impotent poor, it was universally agreed that they had a right to expect relief. Even Daniel Defoe, in his *Giving Alms No Char-ity*, urged "the Sons and Daughters of Charity" to seek out and succor those "poor Families, where the children are numerous and where Death or Sickness has Deprived them of the Labour of the Father." According to Bellers, the right of these poor to relief in illness flowed naturally from their duty to labor when well.[39]

How did the arithmeticians explain the vast numbers of unemployed? Many of their responses were addressed to general economic activity and urged the readjustment of the economy as a whole to eliminate or evap-orate the "problem" of the poor.[40] Most argued that little had been done to grapple properly with the problem, and that often the steps taken to relieve the poor had, in fact, only exacerbated the difficulties. The Poor Law, because it provided the poor with the certainty of relief, was blamed for discouraging initiative and thrift among the poor. "Our Laws relating to our Poor are a vast Encouragement to Idleness," said Matthew Decker in 1744. Not only did the regular care afforded by parish relief encourage sloth, but charity itself, given indiscriminately to beggars or through ca-sual solicitation, contributed to the same evil.[41] Aid due to the infirm or impotent should never inadvertently contribute to the idleness of the able. While it is charity to give to the former, Charles Davenant sternly re-minded his contemporaries, "it is a justice we owe to the commonwealth, not to suffer such as have health, and who might maintain themselves, to be drones, and live upon the labour of others." True charity to those able to labor consisted of the provision of employment. "And as Manufacture seems a kind of *debt* to the labourious part of the people, who by nature are entitled to live, so it is the highest of all Charities; as it is the most substantial and universal."[42] And as the provision of employment was the

---

[39] Daniel Defoe, *Giving Alms No Charity* [1704], in *The Works of Daniel Defoe*, John S. Keltie, ed. (Edinburgh: W. P. Nimmo, 1869), p. 51; John Bellers, *An Essay toward the Improvement of Physick* (London: J. Sowle, 1714), pp. 5–6.

[40] See, for example, [John Blanch], *An Abstract of the Grievances of Trade, which Op-press Our Poor* (London: 1694); and John Cary, *An Essay on the State of England in Re-lation to its Trade, its Poor and its Taxes* (Bristol: W. Bonny, 1695).

[41] [Matthew Decker], *An Essay on the Causes of the Decline of the Foreign Trade* [1744], 2nd ed. (Dublin: G. Faulkner, 1749), p. 32; Bellers, *Essay of Physick*, p. 31.

[42] Charles Davenant, quoted in F. M. Eden, *The State of the Poor* [1797], 3 vols. (Lon-don: Frank Cass & Co., 1966) 1:231. See also D. M., *A Present Remedy for the Poor* (London: Jonathan Riding, 1700), p. 5, and *Britannia Languens*, pp. 300–301. A typical reiteration of this viewpoint is from Letter XVIII of *The National Merchant*, reprinted in *Gentleman's Magazine* (January 1736), p. 26: "[Employment] would not only nourish, but

greatest charity, philanthropists, it was often said, would provide such work more equitably than could state or even local officials. Sir Matthew Decker, a director of the East India Company and a Tory M.P., thought that charity voluntarily administered by reasonable citizens would be more effective than relief from the parish poor rates. These citizens, Decker held, would be more efficient because they would be "Persons of Character and Fortune [who] will, for their own Honour, by their Delicate Sense of Publick Good, and for their love of true Charity, take care to distinguish between the real and pretended Objects of Charity." The management of the poor by parish officers who were appointed by unwilling election or applied for the post in order to obtain an easy salary, was unfavorably compared with those who took on such concerns "willingly and with a ready Mind."[43] Private charity, therefore, especially in its associated form, was often seen as being better suited than public relief for the effective discernment of real cases of distress and the appropriate care of the needy.

Not only would philanthropically minded citizens be more efficient than parish officials, but because their motives were benevolent and not narrowly self-interested, they would not attempt to underpay or squeeze the needy laborer. For the philanthropist, unlike the manufacturer, "whether it turns to present profit or not, is not much material." Thomas Firmin, London's "almoner-general" thought the loss of two pence on the shilling worthwhile in the cause of charitable employment. Unlike "the Trading-Master [who] looks for his profit, and if his Stock turns not to him for gain, he gives over, or reduceth the Workman to inconsiderable Wages, that his own gain may be greater," the philanthropist, "as long as [his] Stock makes but good itself, or be managed without considerable loss, it attains its End, and therefore may give competent Wages."[44] Philanthropists from Bellers to Firmin, and merchants like John Cary and Child, proposed a wide range of charitable projects to provide employment. Both Lawrence Braddon and Bellers advocated the establishment of "collegiate cities," or communities of unemployed families. These centers, founded partly by charity and partly by private enterprise, would house and employ "all the capable, which are chargeable Poor, within the

---

increase the Numbers of the People, of which many Thousands perish every Year, by those Diseases contracted under a slothful Poverty; and to promote this would be a greater Charity and more meritorious, than to build Hospitals, which very often are but so many Monuments of ill gotten Riches, attended with late Repentance." This is a loose paraphrase of Davenant's views of more than forty years before.

[43] Decker, *Essay on Foreign Trade*, p. 100; Secker, *Fourteen Sermons*, pp. 255–56.

[44] Child, *New Discourse*, p. 75; Matthew Hale, *Discourse Touching Provision for the Poor* [1683] (London: Peter Davies, 1927), p. 66. See also Bellers, *Essays about the Poor*, p. 6, and *Some Thoughts concerning the Maintenance of the Poor* (London: T. Goodwin, 1700), p. 16.

Bills of Mortality, from three years of age and upwards," and each would consist of about twenty thousand inhabitants. The addition of productive energy would be so great that through the creation of these cities, the poor would "turn all our Wastelands into Fruitful Fields, Orchards and Gardens, and their mean Cottages into Colleges, and fill our Barns with Plenty of Bread and our Store-houses with Manufactures."[45]

Another proposal to increase national productivity while caring for the poor involved a reevaluation of the potential labor of some of the impotent themselves. Women with small children, the aged, and the infirm might and ought to do what they could to care for themselves and become productive citizens. "All should be set to Work that are any ways able." One method of making this possible involved the provision of "stock," of raw materials, for the poor to work on in their own homes. "For suppose a Woman hath a sick Husband or child or some Infirmity upon herself, in all such cases she may do something at home, but cannot leave her own House."[46]

Despite all attempts to find new solutions and employments, most of the proposed schemes turned out to be variations of the workhouse. The idea of a workhouse for the provision of employment for those who could not find jobs may have been suggested by the work carried on in existing houses of correction. These establishments were built to force employment upon vagrants, beggars, and others willfully idle. Unlike the houses of correction, however, the residents of workhouses were provided with employment not to punish them for their want as to aid them to earn a living. Workhouse inmates seem to have left whenever they wished, that is, whenever they had prospects of other employment.[47] The aid given at the workhouse was primarily intended to see the unemployed laborer through a period of trade depression. Thus, one of the earliest workhouses, set up in London by Thomas Firmin, arose out of the difficulties created by one such trade dislocation. In Bristol, Cary established a similar institution, which employed its workers in spinning flax, while Robert Nelson was actively involved in the organization and administration of the Dublin workhouse.

The workhouse also differed significantly from the private manufactory, as we have already noted, in that profit was rejected as a legitimate

---

[45] Braddon, *Particular Answers*, p. 12; Bellers, *Essay of Physick*, p. 42. See also *Consideration on East India Trade*, in *Early English Tracts*, pp. 626–27.

[46] Bernard Mandeville, *The Fable of the Bees* [1723], Philip Harth, ed. (Harmsworth, Middlesex: Penguin, 1970), p. 274. See also Thomas Firmin, *Some Proposals for the Imployment of the Poor and the Prevention of Idleness* (London: Brabazon Aylmer, 1678), pp. 4–5. Firmin (1632–1697) was a good friend of both Tillotson and Gouge.

[47] T. V. Hitchcock notes that the rule against leaving the house "seems rarely to have been translated into practice": "The English Workhouse: A Study in Institutional Poor Relief" (diss., Oxford University, 1985).

goal. Despite historians' condemnations of the advocates of the work-house as self-interested capitalists concerned only with wringing maximum profits from the labor of the poor, the arithmeticians praised the charitably funded, "nonprofit" workhouse because it would offer the poor a desirable alternative to the corrupt practices of the private manufacturer. The goal of the workhouse was the maintenance and industrial education of the unemployed. Firmin thought so much of this work that he sold his coach to support his workhouse, rather than turn out any of its inmates.[48]

In addition to providing employment, the workhouse was intended to be a training school for those without skills, helping them to become productive citizens. John Locke, no friend to the poor, acknowledged that some of the indigent were unemployed "either through want of working provided for them, or their unskillfulness in working." He recommended working schools to teach these to labor profitably. Industrial training was advocated for children in the workhouse, as well as for those in charity schools.[49] Certainly one of the reasons for the rapid growth and massive support that the charity schools received was due to the widespread desire to insure such an education for the children of the poor. Not only did many of these schools provide vocational training (the girls' charity schools were almost entirely concerned with religious and vocational education, stressing those qualities needed in a trusted and able servant) but their general curriculum was constructed for the formation of a more sober and hardworking laboring class. It was hoped that by the imposition of work discipline at an early age, whether in the workhouse or the school, succeeding generations would not only have the needed skills, but also those habits equally necessary to persevere at a job.

Third, it was thought that workhouses would insure a more equitable and efficient distribution of charitable funds. Much of the money given as charity was being wasted, contemporaries felt, by going into the pockets of sharpers and vagrants who could skillfully play on emotions of compassion and pity. If these monies were all given to the workhouse, the worthy poor could be properly taken care of, and idleness and vagrancy suppressed. For, as Matthew Hale had pointed out, the existence of work-houses was the precondition for the final elimination of beggary. "Indeed

[48] See Hale, *Discourse*, pp. 24–25; Child, *New Discourse*, p. 75. For Child, profit was not the aim of workhouses: "whether it turns to present profit or not, is not much material, the great Business of the Nation being first but to keep the Poor from Begging and Starving, and inuring such as are able to Labour and Discipline, that they may hereafter be useful Members to the Kingdom."

[49] John Locke quoted in Eden, *The State of the Poor*, 1:245. See also M. G. Jones, *The Charity School Movement: A Study of Eighteenth-Century Puritanism* (London: F. Cass, 1964); Bellers, *Essays about the Poor*, pp. 2–3.

were there a clear means practiced for the Imploying of Poor Persons, it were an uncharitable action to relieve them in a course of Idleness."[50]

The employment of the poor, Josiah Child noted, was "an act of great Civil Prudence and Political Wisdom: for Poverty in itself is apt to Emasculate the minds of men, or at least it makes men tumultuous and unquiet." The philanthropic employer, while doing good to the poor, would also be "more secure in [his] goods, by how much there will be fewer persons, who have the temptation of extream want to make them steal and to be injurious to others in their possessions."[51] Employment and the pride of self-support would give men a stake in the future of their country; not only would any property they acquired through this employment encourage national tranquility, but equally "he that hath something of his own, and lives Comfortably, will stoutly defend the Nation against Invaders." A fully employed nation would be a nation at peace, tied together in bonds of mutual dependence. In such a state there follows "a sweet Harmony . . . when every one's Hand and Head is employed, and when there comes a reciprocation of advantage to the landholders, and all others, as necessarily there must."[52]

In addition to increasing national strength and security through the charitable provision of employment, such aid would increase the nation's wealth. Through employment, the poor would no longer be a nonproductive drain on the national economy. A novel contribution made in the later seventeenth century was the notion that all might be able to labor, whether fully or only partially capable. The work of all hitherto unemployed would have positive, visible effects in spurring economic growth. For, in the proper employment of the poor, contemporaries saw a great wasted but potentially immense economic resource. Their employment would lead to a self-perpetuating spiral of growth and wealth. We get a glimpse of this vision of unlimited economic progress in John Cary's *Reasons for Passing the Bill for Relieving and Employing the Poor*: "If the Poor be set to work, they will consume more of our Manufactures themselves than now they do, and pay for them out of their own Labours. . . . There will be a greater Consumption of Cloth, . . . and thereby many more People will be employed."[53]

MANDEVILLE AND CHARITY: CHRISTIANITY VERSUS COMMERCE

The religious and the secular approaches to philanthrophy and poverty ran concurrently, melding into each other with little friction for several

---

[50] Hale, *Discourse*, p. 3.

[51] Child, *New Discourse*, p. 3; Firmin, *Some Proposals*, p. 23.

[52] Cary, *Essay*, p. 165; *Britannia Languens*, p. 300.

[53] [John Cary], *Reasons for Passing the Bill Relieving and Employing the Poor of this Kingdom, Humbly Offered* (1700), p. 6.

decades following the Restoration. Both clerics and merchants used the analogy of the individual and family to discuss the condition of the nation; what was good for a single family was good for the state. Both believed prodigality should be curbed, and monies thus saved used either directly or indirectly for the employment of the poor. Both believed that the employment of the poor was the prime object of national policy and private charity. And both had visions of the nation as a moral and/or economic community, tied together by bonds of public concerns and general interests that transcended private goods and ends. The arithmeticians, admitting that it was possible for the state to languish while some merchants grew rich, thought that the general good must come before that of the individual, while a standard clerical argument in favor of Christianity was that "it teaches us to prefer the publick *good* before our *private*, to prefer what is *just* to what we judge *commodious*, to abridge our selves of our own liberties for the good of others."[54]

There was, however, a strand of economic thought that challenged both traditional clerical and arithmetical assumptions. Starting late in the seventeenth century with writers like Dudley North and Nicholas Barbon, this type of analysis questioned contemporary notions about getting and spending, and while opposed to covetousness on economic grounds, sang the praises of self-indulgent prodigality. Rejecting the notion that if frugality was the best economic policy for families, it was also the best for states, these economic individualists held that "he that spends more than he is able to pay for, is either fool or knave, or in great necessity; but I suppose this not to be the Nation's case."[55]

This "liberal mercantilism," as W. Grampp has dubbed it, exalted and gloried in the fructifying effects of emulation on the nation's productivity. It held that men would work to gratify their "exorbitant desire," and since "the wants of the mind are infinite"[56] they would work without ceasing. The dissatisfaction and envy of individuals was thus conducive to the acquisition of national wealth and trade. The social world they described, a world of restless and constant comparison, was essentially urban, where folks lived in close proximity. "Man being Naturally Ambitious, the Living Together, occasions Emulation which is seen in Outvying one Another in Apparel, Equipage and Furniture of the House."

[54] Richard Kidder, *A Demonstration of the Messias* [1684–1700], quoted in Richard Steele, *The Christian Hero*, R. Blanchard, ed. (London: Oxford University Press, 1932), p. xxi.

[55] *England's Greatest Happiness*, in *Early English Tracts*, p. 261.

[56] W. D. Grampp, "The Liberal Elements in English Mercantilism," *Quarterly Journal of Economics*, 66 (1952); *Discourses Upon Trade* [1691], in *Early English Tracts*, pp. 529, 528. See also Nicholas Barbon, *A Discourse of Trade* [1690] (Baltimore: Johns Hopkins University Press, 1903), p. 14; *England's Greatest Happiness*, pp. 61–62.

This life of endless consumption "is another great Advantage to Trade."[57] And in this world, as Mackenzie lamented in the 1690s, appeals to private interest were the only ones likely to gain attention. Private interest, the endeavor to accomplish ones' own desires regardless of their consequences for the public weal, became the central category of all action in the analysis of these writers.

This strand of thought, however, was largely ignored by the contemporary public and was often written off as "crass" or "self-interested," partly because its exponents published anonymously or were merchants and therefore "interested" parties,[58] but also because the economics of individual self-seeking had an unsettling novelty about it. As Joyce Appleby has so ably argued, the adoption of this strange new doctrine would have necessitated radical changes both in social structure and social ideology.[59] Only with the publication of Bernard Mandeville's full *Fable of the Bees* in 1723 did the value of private interest find a disinterested and hence popular advocate.

Little is known of Mandeville's life. A Leyden-trained physician, he published *The Grumbling Hive* (1705), the core of his latter, more famous work, *The Fable of the Bees*, less than a decade after settling in London. Neither *Hive* nor *Fable* (first published in 1714) seems to have made any impact, and it was not until 1723, when the second edition included the infamous "Essay on Charity and Charity Schools," that Mandeville's ideas attracted much attention. It was the charity essay that seemed to rivet contemporaries.[60] The year after the appearance of the second edition, the work, along with Cato's charity essays, was presented to the Middlesex Grand Jury and condemned. Through the 1720s and 1730s the *Fable* continued to be read and widely attacked.

Mandeville began his famous "Essay on Charity and Charity Schools"

[57] Barbon, *Discourse*, p. 34.

[58] The public career of one of the most prominent of the liberal mercantilists, Nicholas Barbon, must have influenced many against this entire school (*Dictionary of National Biography*, 1:1070–71). Trained as a physician at the University of Leyden, he first came to public attention when his efforts as a London land developer led to a riot between his workmen and the lawyers of Gray's Inn. Barbon followed up the building-over of Red Lion fields with the conversion of Essex House into "houses and tenements for tavernes, ale houses, cooks-shoppes, and vaulting schools, and the garden adjoining the river into wharfes for brewers and woodmongers." His first written work was a defense of debasing the currency, and when he died he instructed his executor not to pay any of his outstanding debts.

[59] Joyce O. Appleby, *Economic Thought and Ideology in Seventeenth Century England* (Princeton: Princeton University Press, 1978).

[60] Richard I. Cook, *Bernard Mandeville* (New York: Twayne Publishers, 1974), p. 117, comments that "No English author since Thomas Hobbes had touched so raw a nerve." See also Thomas Horne, *The Social Thought of Bernard Mandeville* (London: Macmillan, 1978), p. 51; M. M. Goldsmith, *Private Vices, Publick Benefits* (Cambridge: Cambridge University Press, 1985).

with what F. B. Kaye has called a "rigorous" or purist definition of charity:

> Charity is that Virtue by which part of that sincere Love we have for our selves is transferr'd pure and unmix'd to others, not tyed to us by the Bonds of Friendship or Consanguinity, and even meer Strangers, whom we have no Obligation to, nor hope or expect any thing from. If we lessen any ways the Rigour of this Definition, part of the Virtue must be lost.

Mandeville added that the practice of giving true charity "consists in giving away (whilst we are alive) what we value our selves." Thus, for Mandeville, for charity to be genuine, it must be both disinterested and self-denying. While Mandeville could find no fault with such rigorous virtue, intimating often that it would be in such a society that he would have chosen to dwell, he presented himself as forced sadly to conclude that the practice of such goodness was not compatible with a prosperous and powerful state. "Bare Vertue can't make Nations live in Splendor," said Mandeville in the Moral of *The Grumbling Hive*, "they, that would revive / A golden Age, must be as free, / for Acorns, as for Honesty." For Mandeville, true virtue and poverty were inextricably tied, and men's "vilest and most hateful Qualities are the most necessary Accomplishments to fit him for the largest, and according to the World, the happiest and most flourishing Societies."[61] Thus, Mandeville intimated that the purists' view of charity was unacceptable because it was unsuitable for the sort of state England was, and desired to be.

Mandeville also attacked the less stringent definition of charity, held by many of England's clerics and arithmeticians, which stressed the identity of charitable virtue and mercantile interests. Writers like Lynford and Lupton held that while charity was indeed a virtue, it neither was, nor needed to be, disinterested or self-denying; the impulse to relieve the poor or distressed arose from a deep wellspring of human sympathy and compassion, and in relieving distress, the philanthropist simultaneously relieved himself. Mandeville dismissed such providential views of the concord of interest and virtue with derision: "Oh rare Doctrine! Oh easy Christianity!"[62] Rather than see London's many benevolent foundations as emanating from true charitable sentiment, he wrote that "Pride and Vanity have built more Hospitals than all other [Christian] Virtues together." The presence of charitable institutions owed more to self-seeking than true charity, he asserted. Some philanthropists, he maintained, wished for praise, for the reputation of worthiness, or merely for "the

---

[61] Mandeville, *Fable*, "An Essay on Charity and Charity Schools," pp. 263, 53.

[62] Bernard Mandeville, *Letter to Dion* [1732], Augustan Reprint Society, no. 41 (Los Angeles: University of California, 1953), p. 24.

Satisfaction there is in Ordering and Directing" their poorer brethren. Others gave to relieve the "great Pain and Anxiety" that viewing or hearing a creature in distress automatically aroused. Still others gave to cover their sins, to posthumously secure themselves a throne in heaven despite a life of indulgence and total self-regard. And others still, mocked Mandeville, gave to charity in hope of solid financial rewards for their liberality.[63] All seeming charity, in Mandeville's view, sprang from selfish motives.

On the basis of this criticism, Mandeville constructed a counterview to that of most of his contemporaries. When he argued that men are creatures of passion, driven by the desire for self-gratification, many clerics might have agreed. However, rather than engaging in futile deprecation of the passions, Mandeville thought the self-interested passions could be a powerful force for public benefit if prudently channeled by astute statesmen. Unlike the political arithmeticians who wanted political intervention to repress self-serving inclinations and subordinate them to the public good, Mandeville asserted that it was useless, nay harmful, to attempt to eliminate such vicious passions if a wealthy and powerful trading nation was desired. For virtue leads to stultification and stupidity, not to the active, intense life of the merchant-adventurer.[64] The message of the *Fable*, loud, clear, and unambiguous, is that "Lust and Vanity" employ millions and contribute more to the progress of a strong, stable nation than the entire catalog of Christian virtues.[65]

Not only was Christian virtue unimportant to the creation of a wealthy and powerful nation, but charity might well be dangerous; "charity where it is too extensive, seldom fails of promoting Sloth and Idleness, and is good for little in the Commonwealth but to breed Drones and destroy Industry." Charity was responsible for "crowding too much Treasure into the Dead Stock of the Nation." Even charity in small doses could be most disruptive. By "over educating" the poor (and Mandeville considered any education as overeducation), by bringing them into closer physical or intellectual proximity to their betters, the nation would lose

[63] Mandeville, *Fable*, "Essay on Charity," pp. 269, 287, 264. Referring to mercantile sponsorships of charity schools, he wrote: "They have no Thought of Interest even those who deal in and provide those Children with what they want, have not the least design of getting by what they sell for their Use, and tho' in every thing else their Avarice and Greediness after Lucre be glaringly conspicuous, in this affair, they are wholly divested from selfishness and have no Worldly Ends." Mandeville, of course, was being vastly ironic.

[64] Mandeville, *Fable*, "A Search into the Nature of Society," p. 337: "That boasted middle way, and the calm Virtues . . . are good for nothing but to breed Drones and might qualify a Man for the stupid Enjoyments of a Monastick Life, or at best a Country Justice of the Peace, but they would never fit for Labour and Assuidity, or stir him to great Achievements and perilous undertakings."

[65] Mandeville, *Fable*, "The Grumbling Hive, or Knaves Turn'd Honest," p. 64.

the sort of laborers it most needed. "No Body will do the Dirty, Slavish Work, that can help it. I don't discommend them but . . . the People of the meanest Rank know too much to be serviceable to us." Such unsuitable education led not only to laziness, but also to crime and riot. Mandeville claimed that the ringleaders of London riots and mobs had always been charitably trained youths.[66]

To sum up, Mandeville horrified his contemporaries by making the radical distinction between avowed principles and actual practice, between that which was espoused by the religious and that which governed the actions of men of commerce and of the world. And rather than follow up this description with a demand for mercantile reform and the reconfirmation of traditional Christian behavior, Mandeville sniggered that it was impossible to have one's cake and eat it. "Religion," he remarked, "is one thing, and Trade is Another."[67] While Mandeville was widely denounced as the "Man-devil" by the pious, his critics were particularly upset by the *Fable*'s continuing popularity. Thus, John Dennis, the literary critic, denounced Mandeville as "a Champion for Vice and Luxury, a serious, a cool, a deliberate Champion . . . and to make it further appear how widely Infidelity . . . [has] spread, the Work which this Champion has published in [its] Defense, has found great Success."[68]

MANDEVILLE'S CRITICS: COMMERCIAL CHRISTIANITY RESTORED

Mandeville's great historical importance rests not only on his popularity but also on the influence that he had on all subsequent thinking about human psychology and social structure. Some of the greatest minds of the age wrote refutations of his *Fable*, in an attempt to restore the system of Christian morality that he had so systematically attacked and ridiculed. These included two of the Anglican church's greatest eighteenth-century intellectuals, Bishop Joseph Butler and Bishop George Berkeley; William Law, mystic and author of *A Serious Call to a Devout and Holy Life*, one of the most influential religious tracts of the century; Francis Hutcheson, one of the principal philosophers of the day; and a host of prominent as well as popular writers, including Alexander Pope, John Dennis, and George Blewitt. *The Fable of the Bees* provided both the occasion and the necessity for a major and comprehensive rethinking of the relation be-

[66] Mandeville, *Fable*, "Essay on Charity," pp. 275, 307, 313. Nicholas Rogers, an authority on politics and riots in eighteenth-century London, tells me that there may be some substance in Mandeville's allegation of the riotous nature of charity-educated youths, especially Bridewell boys.

[67] Mandeville, *Fable*, "Nature of Society," p. 358.

[68] John Dennis, *Vice and Luxury Publick Mischiefs, or Remarks on a Book intitled "The Fable of the Bees"* (London: printed for W. Mears, 1724), p. xvi.

tween public morality and private practice, between the good of the commonwealth and the desires of individuals. That is not to say, however, that attempts had not already been made to reconcile traditional morality and the demands of a fast-growing commercial economy. We have noted piecemeal efforts at such a coming-to-terms with the compelling force of private interest. So, for example, Braddon explained why he felt it necessary to stress the economic benefits that would accrue to donors if they contributed to his charitable employment scheme by noting that

> notwithstanding [that] Public Blessings may be the probable Fruits of establishing this desir'd corporation, yet I can't expect that a sufficient Number of Gentlemen will be subscribers thereunto UNLESS they shall, by my probable Arguments, be convinc'd, that their own PRIVATE INTEREST shall be more advanced, by *such Subscriptions*, than by laying-out such Sums, in any Publick Fund or Private Trade.[69]

Charity was thus compelled to be "interesting," but the benefits it promised were not only of the material sort. One of the most widely read and often-quoted English divines, John Tillotson, described the sensual and emotional gratification that benevolence afforded. "To do good," he said, "[was] the most pleasant enjoyment in the world. It is natural, and whatever is so, is delightful."[70]

Despite these partial efforts to unite virtue and interest, it was Mandeville's attack on this union that compelled his opponents to provide a systematic and popularly accessible account of how Christian morality could be united with the practice of a worldly pursuit of wealth and power. Rather than deducing permissible human behavior from the nature and needs of the economy, these critics described an economy of human nature that allowed for the harmonious coexistence of motives and passions hitherto seen as necessarily in conflict. In doing so they formulated a complex moral code, which, while tacitly including many of Mandeville's premises, allowed for the congruence of a multiplicity of interests and challenged Mandeville's conclusions.

One element of Mandeville's system that was universally rejected was his repudiation of the analogy between the nation's good and well-being,

---

[69] Braddon, *Form of a Petition*, pp. 23–24.

[70] Tillotson, quoted in Curtis, *Anglican Moods*, p. 41. Between 1695 and 1757, fourteen editions of Tillotson's sermons were printed. Tillotson was also the favorite author of that diary-keeping grocer, Thomas Turner: see Dean Kirkman Worcester, *The Life and Times of Thomas Turner of East Hoathly* (New Haven: Yale University Press, 1948). See also Barrow, *Works*, 1:73. For a study of clerical thought of this period, which, although very different in approach, comes to many of the same conclusions, see Margaret C. Jacob, *The Newtonians and the English Revolution, 1689–1720* (Ithaca, N.Y.: Cornell University Press, 1976), esp. chap. 1.

and that of the individual member of that society. In other words, contemporaries did not accept the notion that the follies and vices of individuals, which inevitably led to loss and personal misfortune, could be conducive to the general good. All agreed on the coincidence of personal and national aims and aspirations.[71]

None of Mandeville's opponents, however, rejected as unchristian the view that a certain degree of material well-being, above the level of mere necessities, was an acceptable, even a desirable state of affairs. Spending, they all maintained, even spending on frivolous items, could not rightly be called vicious, so long as it was within the means and abilities of the spender. Self-denial alone, maintained William Law, does not make an action virtuous. The implication is clear: self-indulgence alone does not make it vicious. "An action," said Law, "is virtuous, because it is an Obedience to Reason and the Laws of God."[72] To be sure, prior to Mandeville, clerics had reasoned away the injunction that bade good Christians to give all to the poor for their souls' sakes. However, increased emphasis was now placed on the reasonable use of the goods of the world, and reason held that consumption was vital for the maintenance of good government: "That every thing which Reason approves of in our Manners of Living, is Temperance, is Virtue. That as for Equipage, Furniture, Apparel and Buildings, Reason will approve of just so much of them as is requisite for the Distinction of Rank and the keeping of that Subordination, which is absolutely necessary to Government."[73]

Thus, while accepting Mandeville's notion of the centrality of consumption to the prosperous state, these critics insisted that the widespread and moderate enjoyment of the pleasures of life would be more profitable to the state than the more narrowly based, intemperate forms of expenditure that Mandeville presented. Hutcheson noted that while, in the short run, the drunkard will consume more wine than the more moderate imbiber, "it may be justly questioned, whether that same number would not have consumed more in their whole lives, by being temperate and frugal; since all allow that they would probably live longer, and with better health and digestion." Not only would consumption be greater because of the longer duration of life, but because of the population increase that would occur as a natural result of that prolonged du-

---

[71] George Blewitt, *An Inquiry into Whether a General Practice of Virtue Tends to the Wealth or Poverty, Benefit or Disadvantage of a People* (London: R. Wilken, 1725), p. 19.

[72] William Law, *Remarks Upon a Work Entitled the Fable of the Bees*, in *The Works of William Law*, 9 vols. (London: Printed for J. Richardson, 1762), 2:44. Law (1668–1761), a nonjuring cleric and friend of Sherlock's and Tillotson's, was the eighteenth century's most influential English mystic. He was loved by the poor, although disliked by his local parish authorities, for his "excessive charity."

[73] Dennis, *Vice and Luxury*, p. 54.

ration. It is significant to note that Hutcheson did not rebuke Mandeville for considering the question of consumption or for assessing in pounds and shillings the value of morality versus immorality. Instead, he chastised Mandeville for his faulty and limited arithmetic, for not reckoning properly.[74]

Furthermore, by emphasizing the strength of reason, Mandeville's opponents were able to construct an alternative psychology, in which passion, self-interest, and social sympathy could all coexist and work toward the same goal. Bishop Butler, for example, used the term "self-love" not as Mandeville had, to refer merely to the selfish indulgence in pleasure, but to that rational and calculating faculty that weighed pleasures, and willingly sacrificed immediate or inadequate joys for future or more significant experiences. Given this new understanding of self-love, Butler could assert that "conscience and self-love, if we understand our true happiness, always leads us the same way." For Mandeville's critics, the pursuit of enlightened self-interest strengthened, rather than destroyed, those impulses aimed at the public good. The pleasures derived from socially valuable affections, from the practice of charity and religious observance, provided the individual with the most solid and durable of pleasures.[75] Butler noted that if men were truly concerned with the certain promotion of their private interest they would voluntarily limit their indulgence in acts of self-gratification to maximize their own long-term advantage.[76]

Not only were such social affections pleasurable, but also natural and inevitable. Reintroducing the image of the nation as a single organism or family, Hutcheson and other critics of Mandeville described society as united by an inborn, instinctive love and sympathy. "There is no mortal without some love towards others and desire of the happiness of some person as well as his own." Men were bound to one another by more than the machinations of clever politicians. Their bonds were social, "they feel for each other shame, sudden danger, resentment, honour, prosperity, distress." To assume, as Mandeville seemed to, that men feel interested in nothing but what pertains to the gratification of their immediate sensual desires was, therefore, "a speculative absurdity," like imagining "a hand

[74] Francis Hutcheson, *Reflections Upon Laughter and Remarks Upon the Fable of the Bees*, [1725–1727] (Glasgow: Baxter, 1750), pp. 61–62. Hutcheson (1694–1746), a follower of Lord Shaftesbury and an opponent of Hobbes, like Mandeville, whom he regarded as a Hobbesian, was one of the most important, and now most neglected, thinkers of the eighteenth century.

[75] Joseph Butler, quoted in E. C. Mossner, *Bishop Butler and the Age of Reason* (New York: Macmillan, 1936), p. 118; Hutcheson, *Reflections*, p. 46.

[76] Joseph Butler, *Works*, W. E. Gladstone, ed., 2 vols. (Oxford: Clarendon Press, 1897), "Dissertation on the Nature of Virtue," 1:332. See also Barrow, *Works*, "Of the Love of Our Neighbours," 2:327.

or any part to have no natural respect for any other, or to the whole body."[77]

In opposition to Mandeville, all his critics made benevolence and social affections, not narrow selfishness, the key to pleasure and happiness. But for them, as for him, it was happiness that was the only real goal of human life. "It is manifest that nothing can be of consequence to mankind or any creature, but happiness."[78] Thus, underlying the major disagreements between Mandeville and his critics was a basic agreement; both advanced systems that rested upon men's single-minded search for happiness. Both saw the goal of human life—happiness—to be set by the passions, with reason having the subordinate role of finding the means to achieve that state. While Mandeville pointed out what he believed to be the inevitable disharmony between virtue and national glory, taunting the public by demanding they chose one or the other, Butler, Hutcheson, and Law saw the harmony of virtue and national interest and reassured their contemporaries that no real sacrifices were necessary.

> It is manifest that, in the common course of life, there is seldom any inconsistency between our duty and what is *called* interest; it is much seldomer that there is an inconsistency between duty and what is really our present interest; meaning by interest, happiness and satisfaction. Self-love then, though confined to the interest of the present world, does in general perfectly coincide with virtue; and lead us to one and the same course of life. But, whatever exceptions there are to this, which are much fewer than are commonly thought, all shall be set right at the final distribution of things.[79]

Not only was there a transformation of Mandeville's general psychological, moral, and economic arguments, but, not surprisingly, another vision of the nature and function of charity emerged from this attempt to renew the foundations of Christian morality. For Mandeville's critics were forced to provide answers to those perennial questions—why do people give to charity, what is its character, and what are its effects—that not only accorded with traditional Christian teaching, but also took Mandeville's attacks into account and refuted them.

As we have seen, Mandeville believed that men were benevolent either out of a mistaken impression that "charity covereth sins," to gain power over their peers and over the poor, or to alleviate the personal distress caused by viewing misery. On the first of these points, most of Mande-

---

[77] Hutcheson, *Reflections*, p. 44; Joseph Butler, *Works*, "Upon Human Nature," 2:12, "Upon the Love of Our Neighbour," 2:167.

[78] Ibid.

[79] Ibid., "Upon Human Nature," 2:36, "Upon the Love of Our Neighbour," 2:150. See also Waterland, *Works*, "The Nature and Kinds of Self-Love," p. 449; Law, "Remarks," pp. 36–40.

ville's critics agreed with him that deathbed charity was no charity at all.[80] Posthumous giving was already on the decline, and Guy's Hospital, built in 1727, was the last major philanthropic venture to be erected by bequest in eighteenth-century London. The second of Mandeville's criticisms was indirectly answered by the insistence on the unifying and brotherly consequences of charitable cooperation. The third, that men give to alleviate their own pain, was accepted but stood on its head, not to prove, as Mandeville claimed, the basically egoistic and selfish nature of man, but to demonstrate the interconnectedness of all men in society, and to prove that though charity and compassion were appetites or desires, they were not merely such, but had as their providentially assigned goal the good of the whole. Law, for example, detailed the reasons that the desire to relieve the poor, though originating in the passions, was not therefore selfish or irrational: "As it appears, that in our rational Natures, we are naturally and complexionally formed to practice and delight in reasonable Actions, and that such a Tendency of Temper or Nature towards Virtue, no more lessens the Excellence of it, than the Rectitude of God's Nature, takes away the Excellence of his Actions."[81] Butler went even further. "Compassion," he said, "is a call, a demand of nature . . . to relieve the unhappy, as hunger is a natural call for food." Although the pangs of hunger are experienced as pain to be relieved, they serve an important function in reminding us to feed and care for our bodies, and though they make us uneasy, they are vital for our continued existence and good health. Similarly, the pangs of misery caused by the approach of distress compel us to relieve it, thus promoting the good of the object, our own pleasure, and the well-being of society as a whole. And, "in defect of that higher principle of reason, compassion is often the only way by which the indigent can have access to us."[82]

Thus, Mandeville's overly rigid definition of true charity as disinterested virtue was rejected. Charity was interested, indeed supremely interested. It embodied the conjunction of the satisfaction of all interests simultaneously—private, public, and spiritual. Thus, Butler noted that it was this "mutual coinciding" of interests "so that we can scarce promote one without the other [that] is equally proof that we were made for both."[83]

[80] Henry Waring, identified only as "a gentleman," was but one of the many authors predating Mandeville who argued against deathbed charity. In *The Rule of Charity* (London: printed for the author, 1690), pp. 35–36, he notes that "to Defer our Charity till Death, is to lose much of the commendation that is inseparable from holy PRACTICE; because then it appears a work of necessity, to give that away, which we cannot longer possess."

[81] Law, "Remarks," p. 44.

[82] Butler, *Works*, "Upon Compassion," 2:71, 62–63.

[83] Ibid., "Upon Human Nature," p. 6. See also ibid., "Upon the Love of our Neighbour," p. 150; Grey, *Sermon*, p. 7.

Not only did Mandeville's opponents criticize his separation of the beneficent and the pleasurable, they also took exception to his views on the dangers of charity for the national economy. We recall Mandeville's description of charity as one of the methods by which the consumers and producers of the nation were brought into too-close proximity. The effects of this frequent intercourse would lead, Mandeville asserted, to sloth and discontent among the laboring poor. Butler, however, clearly believed that charity, properly applied, would lead to greater productivity as well as greater morality in the common people. The intimacy established between rich and poor would moralize the working class, "restrain their vices, and . . . form their minds to virtue and religion."[84] Rather than promoting wants among the poor, charity and the inculcation of Christian resignation would teach the laboring classes to accept their lot, and not grieve for what they could not have. Butler, like many of his contemporaries, believed that though benevolence was an appetite, it was not necessarily irrational, not a "blind *propension* but a principle in reasonable creatures." As such, reason, though the servant of the charitable impulses, "will teach us how to produce the greatest good."[85]

Mandeville's objection that charity schools would overstock certain professions and leave none to do the requisite but distasteful labor was capably answered by Blewitt: "Besides, that there can never be a want of Hands in those Employments where there is so little Skill or Money required to set up with. The Refuse of other Trades, such as are defective either in their Capacity or Fortune for better Business, will always, it is feared, furnish a larger supply of such Offices than the Necessities of Mankind will ever require."[86] So the refutation of Mandeville served as the occasion for uniting Christian and mercantile views of the value and goals of charity into a new, revitalized tradition of benevolence.

THE TRADITION OF BENEVOLENCE: CONTINUITY AND CHANGE

The "tradition of benevolence" that swayed the philanthropists of the early eighteenth century was very complex. On the one hand, this tradition encompassed the enduring belief that charity was the very expression of Christian devotion, however broadly defined. The act of giving was an affirmation, an imitation of the life of Christ. At the same time a subtle change was occurring within this Christian understanding of charity. Charity derived from superfluities was no longer considered mere justice,

---

[84] Butler, quoted in William J. Norton, *Bishop Butler, Moralist and Divine* (New Brunswick, N.J.: Rutgers University Studies in Philosophy, 1940), p. 4.

[85] Butler, *Works*, "Upon the Love of God," 2:185, "Upon the Love of our Neighbour," pp. 166–67.

[86] Blewitt, *Inquiry*, p. 190.

but mercy. And, despite a surprisingly long life, the notion that charity was the rent on property payable to the only absolute proprietor was also fading from view.[87] More and more, religious thinkers stressed discrimination as a vital part of a sensible philanthropy. More and more clerics urged their audiences to give during their lifetimes, when they could direct and keep control over their donations, rather than give posthumously. Charity, it was felt, could and should address itself to change, to improvement. Rather than merely relieve, which was the purpose of most charitable bequests, the charity of the living, active philanthropist could direct and promote the course of such change. For, while clerics still blessed the Lord for "having the poor always with us," they began to believe that the number of such poor could be greatly reduced by efficiently managed charity and, above all, by the charitable provision of employment.

The political arithmeticians also held the employment of the poor to be a central social and economic concern. Employment of the poor, they believed, was the most effective as well as nationally beneficial form of aid: "What signifies the distribution of a little *broken meat* amongst a few Wretches, in comparison of the support of hundreds of thousands of Families" by the creation of jobs?[88] Although the enrichment of the nation and not its salvation was the goal of these early economists, in many ways their social vision was not incompatible with that of the clerics. Both relied heavily on the metaphor of the family to discuss and describe the proper operation of the state. Both wished for a society that was stable, hierarchical, and protected from excesses by the sovereign power. And, in the last decades of the seventeenth century and the first decades of the eighteenth, these two streams of thought were subtly and un-self-consciously merging.

Mandeville's *The Fable of the Bees* was a deliberate attempt to stop such a mixing together. A strong rationalist and antitraditionalist, Mandeville brought a wickedly ironic rhetoric to bear on this union of religion and trade, of virtue and interest. Demanding that contemporaries choose one or the other, he made conscious and explicit the process of merger that had occurred, without design, over the past forty years. In order to refute him, Mandeville's critics were forced to look seriously at the problems he raised and systematically to resolve them. This they did in part by tacitly accepting many of Mandeville's own insights—a belief in the primacy of pleasure, the "interested" aspect of even benevolent actions—but stood these on their heads to prove and reestablish a modified but still essentially Christian morality. Refusing to accept the imperative of

---

[87] See William Law, *A Serious Call to a Devout and Holy Life*, 6th ed. (London: printed for W. Innys and J. Richardson, 1753), p. 79.

[88] *Britannia Languens*, pp. 300–301.

Mandeville's declaration of choice, his opponents portrayed human psychology as containing overlapping motives, all leading to the same providentially ordained ends, the good of the individual and the good of the whole. It is for these reasons that philanthropists of succeeding decades were able to establish charities that they believed could serve charity and trade simultaneously. They were neither naive humanitarians, unaware of the personal and political goals they wished to advance, nor selfish manipulators who used the institutions they created to exploit and control the poor.[89] Believing that national prosperity would inevitably flow from the right ordering of personal actions and that personal interests, public welfare, and the relief of the poor were not only compatible but identical, gave them the remarkable energy that translated itself into the foundation of the many charities at which we will soon look. The direction of that energy, the concrete activities taken by this spirit, however, depended on the outcome of practical experiments and short-term influences to which we must now turn.

[89] The humanitarian argument is implicit in McClure's recent treatment of the founders of the Foundling Hospital: see *Coram's Children*. The more cynical view is well stated in Christopher Hill, *Reformation to Industrial Revolution* (Harmsworth: Penguin Books, 1969), p. 280: "The high ideals of Bacon, Vane, Milton, Bunyan, George Fox, had led to the South Sea Bubble and the workhouse test, to charity schools which applied the joint-stock principle to charity, once the holiest of the three. . . . The real horror of Swift's *Modest Proposal* . . . perfectly catches the smug note of detached benevolence in the literature of the voluntary societies." However, William Law was by no means alone when he reminded his contemporaries that "our *estate* is as much the gift of God as our *eyes*, or our *hands*, and is no more to be buried, or thrown away, at pleasure, than we are to put out our eyes, or throw away our limbs, as we please." *A Serious Call*, p. 79.

CHAPTER TWO

"Private Virtue and Publick Spirit Display'd": The Search for Charitable Forms

IN CHAPTER 1 we examined the origins and structure of opinion about poverty and charity that was to provide the backdrop to philanthropic activity through the mid-eighteenth-century. Now we must look at the practice of charity itself, in order to discover why new methods of organization and funding came to be associated with benevolent enterprises, and why the charities of the midcentury were directed to new goals. Finally, we will look at these new charities in some detail to trace their aspirations and successes or failures.

Before we can examine charitable practice, however, we must briefly consider the place of such aid in the larger system of poor relief. For the voluntary benevolence of individuals, often called private charity, was only one half of such care. The other half, public charity, the operations of the Poor Law, was by the eighteenth century both quantitatively more significant and much more contested.

From the late seventeenth century till the passage of the New Poor Law in 1834 every decade seemed to see at least one major proposal for an amelioration of the laws governing relief. In addition to the intentions of the Poor Law legislation of 1601–1603, which discriminated between the impotent, the unemployed, and the idle poor, suggesting domestic relief for the first, parochial provision of raw materials to employ the second, and salutory punishment as incentive to labor for the third, the Act of Settlement of 1662 made each parish responsible for the care of its properly entitled poor. Although this system was considered unsatisfactory by many commentators, few could agree on what should be done instead. Even when Parliament passed amendments to the Poor Law, like the Workhouse Act of 1723 or Gilbert's Act of 1782, there is little evidence that these acts either satisfied critics, or were widely enforced and changed parochial practice. For each proposed improvement in poor-law administration would have resulted in a change in the balance of power on the local level between parish officials, justices of the peace, and guilds or private executors of charitable bequests. A good example of this can be seen in William Hay's proposed Bill for the Better Relief of the Poor of 1736. This act would have given a newly created body, a Corporation of Guardians of the Poor, enormously enlarged powers of taxation and control. Contemporaries were quick to point out its problems. Some objected to the creation of "this Corporation . . . as dangerous to our Constitution, by giving Power to a new Body of Men, unknown heretofore," while others complained of the "superior Powers" that would accrue to the local justice of the peace "who is not always wise enough, often not honest enough, and never independent enough to be trusted with the extraordinary Powers." Furthermore, the act stipulated that constables would be able to make "a general privy Search in one Night . . . for the finding of Rogues, Vagabonds and Sturdy Beggars," raising the specter of local constables "with their rabble" endowed with the hated power of the exciseman. Thus, all attempts to improve poor-law administration and organization met with strong opposition. In contrast, charitable societies, properly constituted, could do good while fitting into existing local balances of power.[1] In some sense, as we shall see, the charitable experimentation of the early eighteenth century can be seen as an attempt by philanthropic, civic-minded citizens associated into societies, to find just such a role for themselves.

London Charity, 1680–1740

The outpouring of charitable efforts in the 1740s and 1750s, which we have mentioned briefly in chapter 1 and to which we will shortly return, was not, despite the opinion of some, sui generis, nor the unprecedented beginnings of a new humanitarianism.[2] The charities of the midcentury

---

[1] *Gentleman's Magazine* (February 1737), p. 92; *Grub Street Journal* (April 7, 1737), quoted in *Gentleman's Magazine* (April 1737), pp. 222, 223. The connection between Hay's bill and excise is strong though inferential. One of the strongest complaints of the above cited piece is that this act would give justices "a Power, first of *committing without Bail*, afterwards of *judging their own Proceedings*, and the Subject is *deprived* of that inestimable Privilege a *Jury*." On September 11, 1736, the *Country Journal of the Craftsman* objected to the "Excise Laws which subject the People to such heavy Penalties, without a Trial *by Juries*, entirely agreeable to the *Nature of our Government*, or *such a State of Liberty* as We were promised at the *Revolution*." Hay's bill obviously suffered from the fact that Hay was a strong supporter of Walpole and his regime.

[2] See Raymond G. Cowherd, *The Humanitarian Reform of the English Poor Laws from 1782 to 1815* (Philadelphia: American Philosophical Society, 1960); Dorothy Marshall, *The English Poor in the Eighteenth Century* (London: G. Routledge, 1926); A. W. Coats, "Changing Attitudes to Labour in the Mid Eighteenth Century," *Economic History Review*, 2d ser., 11 (1958), pp. 35–51. In "Economic Thought and Poor Law Policy in the Eighteenth Century," *Economic History Review*, 2d ser., 13 (1960), pp. 39–51, Coats uses the euphemism "generous thinking" to describe the intellectual climate at midcentury. Daniel Baugh, in an important critique of "Tawneyism," "Poverty, Protestantism, and Political Economy," in *England's Rise to Greatness, 1660–1763*, Stephen Baxter, ed. (Berkeley: University of California Press, 1983), pp. 63–109, calls this spirit "broad optimism." David Owen, *English Philanthropy* (Cambridge, Mass.: Belknap Press, 1964), calls his chapter on midcentury charity "The Philanthropy of Humanitarianism." Ruth McClure, *Coram's Chil-*

were rather the result of a combination of tradition and innovation. Arising in response to specific discontents and the needs of a rapidly urbanizing commercial center, they were not only part of a very long tradition of civic benevolence, but also the latest expressions of a fifty-year period of philanthropic experimentation.

London's philanthropic tradition has been well documented. In the period 1480–1660, W. K. Jordan has estimated that 34 percent of the nation's charity was given by Londoners, who numbered only 5 percent of the nation's people. Most of this charity was by bequest and was directed toward the care of the young, the impotent, and the elderly.[3] However, this period marks a sort of watershed for posthumous charity. An analysis of the 1819 investigation of London's charities reveals that over half (59.4 percent) of London's extant endowed charities originated in the period before 1649. The later seventeenth century showed a definite decline in the extent of such establishments, with only a brief upward flurry during the period of enthusiasm for charity schools, which we will examine shortly.[4] An investigation of late-seventeenth and eighteenth-century wills confirms this trend.

TABLE 2.1
The Decline in Charitable Bequests

	Number of Wills	Bequests to Charity (Percent)
1675–1699	10	70
1700–1719	76	63.5
1720–1739	107	53.2
1740–1759	149	39.3
1760–1779	127	38.5
1780–1799	152	40.7
1800–1850	42	29.9

Source: Author's evaluation of 663 wills of charitable donors.

The decline in the rate of posthumous endowment is also reflected in the changing patterns of aldermanic charity. Aldermen occupied positions of civic authority and responsibility and, therefore, it seemed only

dren (New Haven: Yale University Press, 1981), p. 80, says the new sensibility struck England between 1756 and 1758. Although the analysis of this book is substantially different than that of McClure, her scholarship is exhaustive and will be referred to often in this chapter.

[3] W. K. Jordan, The Charities of London, 1480–1660 (London: Allen & Unwin, 1960), p. 20.

[4] See Great Britain, Commissioners for Inquiries into Charities, The Endowed Charities of the City of London reprinted at large from seventeen reports of the Commission [1819] (London: H. Sherwood, 1929).

fitting that their charity be exemplary. While more than two-thirds of the surviving wills of members of the Court of Alderman, 1690–1719, have some provisions for posthumous aid to the poor, only one-third of the aldermen serving 1739–1778 left similar bequests.[5] Why did this age-old method of giving to the needy decline in the early eighteenth century?

There is clearly a tangle of reasons for this important change. Part of the explanation must lie with shifting but deeply held views about the nature of property, which we have touched on in chapter 1. Two further examples may illustrate the strength of these new beliefs. The first is the furor following the erection, by bequest, of Guy's Hospital in 1727. Thomas Guy, a wealthy bookseller, left his large fortune to create a hospital for the care of the poor. This seemingly unimpeachable act brought vilification on his memory; by giving posthumously, it was said, Guy stole from his heirs what was rightfully theirs.[6] It is not insignificant that Guy's was the last major charitable institution founded by bequest in London. A second instance of the growing priority of property rights over the claims of charity occurred with the passage of the Mortmain Act of 1736. This Act, though passed for a host of reasons unrelated to our discussion, explicitly made the same argument for the centrality of inheritance over benevolence. The act forbade charitable donations of land less than one full year before death. A correspondent to the *Old Whig* noted that "One great Intention of this Act was to prevent the mistaken Charity of Men" who, dying, cede away "the Riches which they can no longer enjoy and which are indeed the Property of their Heirs."[7] Thus, though one could

[5] In a comparative study of the bequests of City of London alderman to charity, more than two-thirds (67.4 percent) of the 46 aldermanic wills from the period 1690 to 1719 left charitable bequests. Of the 54 aldermanic wills which were available for the period 1739 to 1759, more than one-third (37 percent) left charitable bequests. Of the available aldermanic wills proved between 1759 and 1779, less than a third (29.6 percent) left anything to charity. My thanks to Professor Henry Horwitz, Department of History, University of Iowa, for information on aldermanic wills in the earliest period. All such wills were found in the Public Record Office, Chancery Lane, London.

[6] For attitudes against posthumous bequests, see Francis Atterbury, *Sermons and Discourses on several Subjects and Occasions*, 2 vols. (London: J. Bettenham for C. Bowyer, 1730), "Spital Sermon 1709," 2:227; Thomas Lynford, *A Spital Sermon* (London: Joseph Downing, 1712), p. 9. Owen, *English Philanthropy*, p. 87, citing Courtney Kenny, discusses the "many malicious rumours about disinherited kinfolk" that Guy's bequest gave birth to. See [John Dunton], *An Essay on Death-bed Charity Exemplified in the Life of Mr. Thomas Guy* (London: printed by D. L. for J. Roberts, 1728); and B. Kirkman Gray, *A History of English Philanthropy from the Dissolution of the Monasteries to the Taking of the First Census* (London: King, 1905), p. 127.

[7] *Old Whig*, no. 67, June 17, 1736, reprinted in *Gentleman's Magazine* (June 1736), pp. 336–37. *Old Whig* also noted that the issue was much larger than injustice to the heirs, for "whatever Persons may suffer by these kind of Donations, they will appear quite trifling Inconveniencies, if we compare them with those which the Publick must suffer if they are permitted to increase" (March 25, 1736).

still leave funds by bequest, it is clear that legislative, as well as popular, opinion found all such action suspect.

Yet another reason for the decline of benevolence by bequest may be related to the new courses of action that midcentury charity took. Though new charities promised important social benefits, they were rife with danger. While men and women in the past had felt at ease in leaving their monies to almshouses or hospitals, knowing that the old and poor would be a perennial problem, eighteenth-century donors, engaged in a more "timely" and socially relevant charity, hesitated to endow these agencies after their deaths. Though potentially useful, these charities could easily become misdirected or outmoded and thus agents for corruption, not benefit. Therefore, more and more eighteenth-century philanthropists retained control in their hands while alive, and encouraged their progeny to do the same after their deaths. This difficult point, the ambiguous nature of the new charities, is one to which we shall have to return later.

The last factor contributing to the decline of charity by bequest was a growing public perception of, and unwillingness to continue, the financial wastefulness and mismanagement that resulted from posthumous charity. The misapplication of funds, whether by parish officials or private executors, seemed particularly galling and dangerous. As early as 1700 an anonymous critic of the parish-controlled bequests urged the creation of a Commission of Charitable Uses because "there is scarce a parish of any Bigness in this Nation, but hath one way or some other Charitable Gift settled upon it; and it is very evident that diverse Charities are misemployed, contrary to the Intentions of the Donors, whereby the Poor are defrauded."[8] In 1715 Parliament instituted an investigation into the workings of the parish care of the London poor, choosing to examine the returns of St. Martin's in the Fields because, they claimed, it "Had been represented to the Committee as the most free from Fraude and Abuses and averred to be under the best Regulation of any Parish in London." The committee found massive wastage and fiscal irregularities. For one thing, though the books showed that only about 70 percent of the monies collected were ever disbursed to the poor, the committee, noting the "several Rasures [sic] in the Parish Books ... and that some Books of Accounts were freshly written," reckoned that not "much above One-half of the great sums aforesaid, which are collected by, and paid to the Churchwardens and Overseers yearly, are really expended on that pious and charitable Work of relieving the Poor."[9] Things had not improved by

---

[8] *Some Thoughts concerning the Maintenance of the Poor* (London: T. Goodwin, 1700), p. 5. I am not, however, suggesting that the concern over misapplied posthumous bequests was new to the eighteenth century; it has a long history of its own.

[9] 2 Geo. 1 (March 8, 1715), pp. 391–95. Despite the disinterested tone of the parliamentary committee in their recital of how they came to select a parish for study, Nicholas Rogers

1725 when Thomas Thwaites assured the king, Lords, and Commons: "That our Poor Rates and occasional Charities are misapply'd, is well known and believed by all Sober thinking people."[10] The cupidity, dishonesty, or sheer incompetence of parish and church officials undermined public confidence in the value of appointing them as agents for posthumous charity. From the 1690s onward, concerned philanthropic citizens searched for alternatives that would not suffer from the inadequacies of parish administration.

The answer for many seemed to lie in the joint-stock or "associated" charity. These new groups depended on public subscriptions for the bulk of their support, and were managed by committees of governors elected annually by subscribers from among themselves. Like their contemporaries, the great joint-stock companies of the metropolis, associating together for common action insured larger sums for ambitious projects, beyond the scope of any single individual. Neither the scandal of the South Sea Bubble nor its counterpart, the giant "Charitable Corporation" embezzlement, disillusioned the public with joint-stock enterprises.[11] It was hoped that committee direction and annual election would insure that the work of the charity would be skillfully managed and that the managers would be annually accountable.[12] Thus, the perceived inadequacies of parish officials as proper agents of charitable distribution, combined with the growing sentiment that posthumous bequests were selfish, unchristian, and wasteful, led the philanthropically inclined to associate. This new charitable form was used by three sorts of charitable endeavors: the charity-school movement, the workhouse movement, and, to some extent, the societies for the reformation of manners.[13]

---

informs me that there was more than a little political bias and self-interest involved in this choice.

[10] [Thomas Thwaites], *A Proposal Humbly Presented to the King . . . Setting Forth the Manner How We May Very Profitably Employ our Now Idle, Chargeable, Young, Weak, Feeble and Aged Poor* (London: 1725), p. 1.

[11] The joint-stock idea does not seem to have suffered as much of a blow from the fiasco of the South Sea Bubble as Ruth McClure suggests, *Coram's Children*, p. 20. The charity-school movement was fatally wounded by furious religious differences, not by the scandal.

[12] Thus, Bishop Warburton, in a 1760 sermon to the governors of the Smallpox Hospital, noted that as the "funds [of these new charities] consist chiefly of annual and voluntary contributions . . . it will be carefully and honestly administered . . . the Governors of the Hospital which so subsists being rather Stewards than Trustees to the Public": *The Works of the Right Reverend William Warburton*, Richard Hurd, ed., 12 vols. (London: Luke Hansard for T. Cadell and W. Davies, 1811), 10:248–49.

[13] For charity schools, see M. G. Jones, *The Charity School Movement: A Study of Eighteenth-Century Puritanism* (London: F. Cass, 1964). For the societies for the reformation of manners, see Dudley Bahlman, *The Moral Revolution of 1688* (New Haven: Yale University Press, 1952); and A. G. Craig, "The Movement for the Reformation of Manners" (diss., University of Edinburgh, 1980).

These three charitable projects shared some common features. All were largely urban movements that began in the 1690s, and all aimed at the improvement of the physical and moral plight of the lower orders. Both the societies and the charity-school movement also had waned quite noticeably by the 1730s. The techniques and specific aims of these three movements, however, were quite distinct. The goal of the societies was for the purification of the nation's morals and the reintroduction of Christian restraints through the imposition of existing legal penalties on wrongdoers. Using paid informers, the societies attempted to enforce laws against blasphemy, gambling, prostitution, obscene publications, and breaking the Sabbath. They saw the promulgation of a revitalized morality as essential to the nation's best interests. William Simpson, preaching to the London society at their annual meeting in 1738, expressed this worldly hope by noting that their work would "make our Nation glorious and prosperous . . . [and] introduce that which exalted a nation, which gives them a Name amongst their Neighbours, who will always be afraid to injure or invade a People whom Virtue inspires with Unity and Courage."[14] Although David Owen has called these societies "aberrant examples of associated philanthropy," insofar as they reveal a deep concern for the nation's purity and a recognition of the importance of virtue for the practical and political future of the state, these societies were in fact pioneers in the history of eighteenth-century charity. However, because of their involvement in the pursuit and prosecution of blasphemers, they ran afoul of local peacekeeping authorities, and ultimately disappeared.[15]

At the same time as the societies were pursuing malefactors, the charity-school movement was attempting to eradicate the sins of society by providing a Christian education for the children of the poor. The historian of the movement, M. G. Jones, has characterized it as the attempt of a Christian utilitarian ethos to grapple with the problems of poverty and profanity. Under the aegis of the newly founded Society for Promoting Christian Knowledge (SPCK), charity schools spread over most of Great Britain. By 1732 London alone had 132 such schools. In the years since 1688 more than twenty thousand students had benefited from their tutelage, three-quarters of whom either were apprenticed or went into the armed services.[16] Not surprisingly, in London these schools were set up

---

[14] William Simpson, *A Sermon Preached to the Societies for Reformation of Manners* (London: Printed 1738), "The Great Benefit of a Good Example," p. 24.

[15] Owen, *English Philanthropy*, p. 21. Although these organizations are not as humane as the other charities Owen discusses, there seems to be no convincing reason to call them aberrant.

[16] Gray, *History of English Philanthropy*, p. 107. According to *An Account of Several Workhouses for Employing and Maintaining the Poor . . . also of Several Charity Schools,*

in the greatest numbers in the poorest outlying districts and continued their strongest growth there. (London's poorest areas had a total of ten charity schools in 1704 and twenty-one in 1732).[17] In addition to benefiting the poor and the nation, supporters of the schools were promised all the spiritual and pleasurable benefits of an active piety, with little expense of energy, time, or money.

However, by the 1720s, the impetus to found new schools and expand the work of the movement in the metropolis seems to have peaked, and by the 1730s to be in a major decline. In the first two decades of the eighteenth century, the average number of new schools founded yearly in London was forty. Between 1730 and 1740 only five new schools were established.[18] It is difficult to say why this fall from popularity should have occurred. M. G. Jones stresses the disruptive effects of religious dissension in which the charity schools became pawns. The growing fear that these schools were promoting dissent was one reason for their loss of popularity and support. B. Kirkman Gray and others have suggested that the Workhouse Act of 1723 gave parliamentary encouragement to the erection of workhouses as cheaper alternatives to the educative care of the schools. Even Jones sees the charity schools and workhouses as clearly alternative ways of "disciplining the infant poor."[19] Other than the chronological coincidence, however, there is no solid evidence connecting the decline of the charity-school movement with the growth of workhouse schemes. It may have been that workhouses were seen as supplementary, not alternative, institutions to the existing charity schools. Much more work on the parish level is needed before this can be established. Whatever the influence of the workhouse, however, it is clear that the movement was shattered and lost its impetus because of sectarian divisions and distrust.

Though workhouses were widely advocated, little is known of the cre-

---

2d ed. (London: J. Downing, 1732), p. 36, of 20,832 children taught, 15,235 were apprenticed or put out to domestic service.

[17] These conclusions are based on D. V. Glass, *London Inhabitants within the Walls* (London: London Record Society, 1966), p. xxiii. The poorest parishes are those in which less than 10 percent of the heads of households have personal estates worth not less than £600 and/or real estate worth at least £50 per annum.

[18] See *An Account of the Charity Schools in and about London and Westminster* with Josiah Tucker, *A Sermon . . . for the Charity Schools* (London: J. & W. Oliver, 1766); and Gray, *History of English Philanthropy*, p. 107.

[19] See Jones, *Charity School Movement*, chap. 4, also pp. 31–34; Gray, *History of English Philanthropy*, p. 116. Gray talks of "slackness of interest . . . in the actual work of education," pp. 107–8, and of "the dying away of the High Church movement." See also a very fine study of the London Workhouse by S. M. MacFarlane, "The Care of the Poor in Late Seventeenth Century London" (diss., Oxford University, 1980); and another by T. V. Hitchcock, "The English Workhouse: A Study in Institutional Poor Relief" (diss., Oxford University, 1985).

ation or day-to-day operations of such institutions in the eighteenth century. The first workhouse founded in London in this period was at Bishopsgate Street, established in 1698. The plan of the institution was that children were to be "taught to spin wool and flax, to sew and knit, to make clothes, shoes and stockings in addition to learning how to read and cast accounts."[20] While it was hoped that private charity and money levied from the city wards would fund the institution, neither sort of income seems to have been forthcoming. In 1704 the author of "A True Account of the Foundation, State and Design of the Workhouse" complained that "the Undertaking is now reduced to great Streights and Necessities" because of "want of a suitable Supply" of funds.[21] In 1714, when the wards were taxed for the institution's support, many refused to contribute. In December 1732 the London Magazine reported that no money had been raised on behalf of the workhouse since 1720.[22]

With the passage of 9 Geo. 1, c.7, the overseers of the poor of each parish were enabled and instructed to erect publicly supported workhouses for the indigent and unemployed poor. From what can be gathered from the published accounts of these institutions, such workhouses had checkered and varying histories. All tried to employ their inmates at such things as carding and spinning wool, but most were reduced to employing their poor at picking oakum. Some even made a virtue of this sad necessity. "They that pick oakum," said one advocate of such workhouse labor, "are continually refresh'd with the Balsamick odour of it."[23] Many, like the Moor Lane workhouse, or that in St. Mary Whitechapel, soon lost even this "work" aspect and came to resemble the older types of almshouses or poor houses. Thus, the workhouse set up in Ayliffe Street in 1724, "which for some time promis'd to answer the Expectations of the Projectors of it, but since then the Officers of the Parish have thought fit to turn it into a House for Lodging only such Poor as are not otherwise provided, who go out daily for Work where they can get it, and return in the evening." Even in the workhouses that retained internal employment for their residents, many must have resembled that of Limehouse Hamlet, Stepney, where "The Number of Poor now [1725] in it is about 30, most of whom are unfit for Labour, but about a Dozen of them are employed in picking oakum." The work of these twelve inhabitants had to supply their own needs as well as those of their eighteen impotent coresidents

---

[20] John Stow, A Survey of the Cities of London and Westminster, Brought Down from the Year 1633 . . . to the Present by John Strype. At the End is Added Certain Tracts Concerning the State of the City of London (London: printed for A. Churchill, 1720), pp. 197–203.

[21] "A True Account of the Workhouses," ibid. (1704), appendix.

[22] London Magazine (December 1732), p. 485.

[23] An Account of Several Workhouses for the Poor, p. 7.

and the house's children, who were "all young and helpless, and therefore ... sent to a school in the neighbourhood, at the publick Charge."[24] Workhouses, it is clear, did not provide a completely satisfactory solution to the problem of caring for the poor.

In addition to the three major charitable enterprises we have discussed, another much smaller endeavor occurred simultaneously, but unlike the others, and despite its own slow and small start, it continued to grow and prosper. This was the establishment of general hospitals for the care of the sick and injured. Following the opening of the Public Infirmary at Petty Lane in 1719 (later to become the Westminster Hospital), three more general hospitals were created in the following decades: St. George's (1733), the London (1740), and the Middlesex (1745). These institutions attracted a great many subscribers and flourished and grew through most of the century.[25] These are the charities that Owen has characterized as springing from a humanitarian motive, namely, the care of the sick and injured. Though their main purpose was, no doubt, the cure of illness and the treatment of injuries, it would be wrong to see these hospitals as concerned only with the improvement of their patients' physical health. The title of one of Josiah Tucker's early sermons, *Hospitals and Infirmaries considered as Schools of Christian Education for the Adult Poor, and as Means Conducive toward a National Reformation in the Common People*, provides a clue to some of the larger social and religious purposes of these institutions. In fact, the governors of St. George's stressed the great benefits derived from bringing the poor into the "regular Society" of the hospital ward.

> There is yet a farther Benefit received by the Poor. . . . It regards no less than their eternal Welfare. . . . Immediate Application is made to the Patients . . . both in Matters of Instruction and Devotion; and a Perseverance in this Care, enforced by the awakening Terrors of Death, or the First Openings of Gratitude for Mercy received, . . . produces extraordinary Effects upon the most Ignorant and Abandoned. . . . And others . . . have been softened into such a state of Penitence and Reformation, or by their exemplary Behaviour when discharged . . . promises . . . an increase of True Religion and Piety amongst the Common People.[26]

The London, whose first purpose was to care for local workers injured

---

[24] Workhouse information for 1725 in *An Account of Several Workhouses* (1732), pp. 7, 4, 6.

[25] See Owen, *English Philanthropy*, pp. 36–50; Gray, *History of English Philanthropy*, pp. 127–31.

[26] *An Account of the Proceedings of the Governors of St. George's Hospital* (London: n.p., 1737). See also Owen, *English Philanthropy*, pp. 36–50; Gray, *History of English Philanthropy*, pp. 127–31.

on the job, promised, in addition to religious reformation, solid savings to the rate-paying public. By treating disabling wounds quickly and effectively, workers who might have died or been unable to work were returned to their families as productive breadwinners. Thus, the nation not only saved the future labor of the workman, but avoided the outflow of poor relief that would have had to have been spent on the needy family. The general hospitals thus hoped to advance the reformation and amelioration of manners, while increasing the nation's productive resources, no less than had the charity schools or workhouses. By limiting their aid to only one category of need, and that only for a short period, the hospitals could demonstrate impressive and efficient use of subscribed funds. This combination of effectiveness and efficiency proved irresistible to London's many philanthropists. Here, finally, was a type of charity that was neither subject to religious bickering nor interfered with poor-law officials or with officers of the law. Created as nondenominational, nonpartisan organizations, the general hospitals found a lasting role for themselves in the care of London's poor.

CHARITY AND WAR: THE POPULATION PROBLEM

In the 1740s and 1750s London's charitable community seemed to be taking a new tack. Having virtually abandoned education and provision of employment as suitable areas for charitable involvement, benevolent Londoners instead turned their attention toward charities that they hoped would increase the nation's population and improve its morals. Why, we must ask ourselves, did organized charity take this turn? Why did the benevolent turn from provision of work and education to these newer concerns?

Like much else in this study, the answers must be both tentative and complex. In some sense, philanthropic funds had been "freed" by the passage of the Workhouse Act of 1723, which took employment out of the sphere of the charitable and placed it into the hands of the civil authorities. Since workhouses were being paid for out of parish poor rates, the philanthropic citizen could look for other outlets for his donations. Thus, the public assumption of responsibility for the provision of employment may have made charitable involvement in this field seem less necessary. Voluntary involvement in the charity-school movement was fatally weakened by internal religious and social antipathies by the 1730s, as we have already noted. And, by the late 1730s, two new sets of problems appeared that forced charitable Londoners to redirect their attention. These were the shocking ill health and mortality of London's population and the pressing needs of a nation at war.

The period from 1730 to 1750 seems to have been a particularly fatal one for many Londoners. While London's population was kept relatively stable by constant in-migration from the countryside, its natural or indigenous population constantly fell. Few Londoners of the 1730s could have missed the implications of the disastrous figures displayed in the monthly bills of mortality, which were widely available in the popular press. While almost 150,000 babies were christened in London during this decade, almost 110,000 children under five years of age simultaneously were buried.[27] Of the almost one-quarter of a million people interred between 1731 and 1750, 50 percent of them were children five years old and under. Few would have disagreed with Corbyn Morris's assessment in 1751 of the bad influence that London exerted on the population, and therefore on the general wealth, of the kingdom.

> The loss within so short a term, within the memory of thousands living, at present, of no less than 600,000 people, who might now in themselves, and their children, have subsisted in this nation, will at length be viewed with horror and amazement; a loss wholly owing to the continual destruction of infants and adults in this slaughter-house of London.[28]

In addition to these anxieties, the wars of the midcentury must be accorded an important place among the factors responsible for the changed direction of philanthropic activity. Many saw the War of Jenkins's Ear (1739–1741), the War of the Austrian Succession (1739–1748), and the subsequent Seven Years' War (1756–1763) as crucial in deciding England's destiny. The outcome of the first two of these wars had left people unsatisfied, and though the Treaty of Aix-en-Chapelle temporarily ended the fighting between the French and the English, many felt that the peace was not real. Nothing, they said, had been resolved in the last round of conflict, and new warfare, they were certain, must soon break out. People

---

[27] The bills of mortality, as published in the *Gentleman's Magazine*, show that in the decade 1730–1739, 143,102 babies were christened in London and 119,538 children under six years old were buried. Furthermore, of the 234,199 people buried in London from 1730 to 1739, 51 percent were under six years old. According to the figures quoted by Deane and Cole in *British Economic Growth, 1688–1758* (London: Cambridge University Press, 1967), the estimated natural change in the population of London, 1701–1751, was minus 451,276. The city managed to maintain its population through those fifty years only because of an even larger net gain by immigration of 463,626. Mabel Craven Buer, *Health, Wealth, and Population in the Early Days of the Industrial Revolution* (London: G. Routledge, 1926), p. 33, suggests that 10,200 immigrants per year to London during this period were needed merely to maintain a constant population. See M. Dorothy George, *London Life in the Eighteenth Century* (New York: Capricorn Books, 1965), pp. 109–11, for an interesting discussion of London migration.

[28] Corbyn Morris, *Observations on the Past Growth and Present State of the City of London* (London: n.p., 1751), p. 108. Again, I am not suggesting that concern about high mortality rates was new, but only that mortality rates during the "Gin Age" skyrocketed, and that the condition of war exacerbated fears about high infantile mortality.

hoped that these wars, like the wars between Rome and Carthage, would decide conclusively which nation would become the world's premier imperial power. With the outbreak of a war of such consequence only a matter of time, preparation for war became a vital objective of national policy.[29]

In addition to making national preparedness more obvious, war may have also removed the pressing need for the charitable to provide employment for the needy. There is a good bit of evidence to suggest that, beginning with the War of the Austrian Succession, and even more during the later war, England's economy expanded enormously. Wars against the French seemed to be particularly beneficial for the expansion of industry and the employment of those previously without work. England's internal and increasing overseas demand for products, as well as the forcible employment of many of the idle in the armed services, undoubtedly eased the problem of unemployment.[30] The concerned and charitably minded citizen could therefore turn his mind away from the need to provide jobs, and increasingly involve himself in those charitable activities that were most suited to aid national policy, in this case, toward the needs and pressures of war.

The second effect of the wars was to intensify public concern about the size of the population, especially about the availability of adequate numbers of men to serve in the armed forces, especially in the navy. While it was possible to hire foreign mercenaries for the land forces, English seamen filled the ships that were considered a vital part of England's fighting force. Thus, the existence of a large pool of potential soldiers and sailors was a crucial wartime need. Not only were numbers important, but the good health and good spirits of the forces was equally important. It was believed, however, that soldiers and sailors did not marry, and thus did not aid in the general procreative effort: "Another cause of the want of people, is the great number of soldiers in modern armies, among whom there are few who marry, and by whose means so many women were debauched, and venereal distempers spread so wide and so fatally."[31] Promiscuity, it was said, was nongenerative: "beaten paths are always barren." Furthermore, the widespread prevalence of sexual license was considered to be very harmful to a martial nation. First, it was seen as sapping

[29] "The Issue of this War," held the anonymous author of *An Enquiry into the Nature, Foundation and Present State of Publick Credit* (London: Printed for H. Carpenter, 1748), p. 4, "determines the fate of Europe, and entails Liberty or Slavery upon this Island."

[30] The beneficial effects of war on the problem of unemployment during the first half of the eighteenth century are suggested in A. H. John, "War and the English Economy, 1700–1763," *Economic History Review*, 2d ser., 7 (1955) pp. 329–44; and Douglas Hay, "War, Dearth, and Theft in the Eighteenth Century: The Record of the English Courts," *Past and Present*, no. 95 (May 1982), pp. 117–60.

[31] Robert Wallace, *A Dissertation on the Numbers of Mankind in Ancient and Modern Times* (Edinburgh: Archibald Constable & Co., 1753), p. 304.

the health and vigor of England's fighting men by turning them into lascivious idlers: "And certain if this Lustful Fire be not quench'd, or else be
timely restrained, 'twill soon emasculate the Age, consume the Strength,
and melt down the Courage of the Nation . . .' If we design to maintain
our Martial Vigour, for which we are now renown'd thr' the World, we
must keep at a Distance from Venus' tents."[32] Thus, license among soldiers and sailors would be triply harmful in that it was enfeebling, unhealthy, and unproductive.

It was also feared that the war might have crippling aftereffects on the
general state of the nation's economy. Many who might productively
have contributed to the nation's wealth would be lost in the conflict; in
addition, many more would be drawn away from their proper occupations to swell the ranks of the military forces. In the short run, trade
would be impoverished by the impressment of merchant sailors into the
fighting navy. In the long run, this might result in reduced international
trade and a weakened nation. Therefore, it became an important goal of
national policy to encourage population growth in order to man the
armed services and to maintain the normal functioning of the economy.[33]

However alarmed many were by the threat of population decline at the
very time when growth was most needed, philanthropically minded citizens did not feel this to be an unsolvable dilemma. In fact, in many varied
ways they organized themselves to tackle this problem, for the involvement in war seemed to mobilize the charitable community in a highly
effective manner. Under its impetus, and relieved of the problem of providing employment, London's charitable donors attempted to increase
population through agencies designed to encourage marriage, to provide
better care for lying-in women and their babies, to rescue orphaned and
abandoned children, and to aid in the rehabilitation of the doubly unproductive, the prostitutes.

THE FOUNDLING HOSPITAL: ITS EARLY HISTORY

I cannot however conclude this, without paying a compliment to the present
Age for two glorious Benefactions, I mean that to the Use of Foundling Infants
and that for the Accommodation of poor Women in their Lying-in.
—Henry Fielding,
The Covent Garden Journal (1752)

[32] *An Essay on Conjugal Infidelity, Shewing the Great Mischief that Attend Those that
Defile the Marriage Bed* (London: T. Warner, 1727), pp. 12–13. See also [Charles Dave-
nant], *An Essay Upon the Probable Methods of Making a People Gainers in the Balance of
Trade* (London: printed for James Knapton, 1699).
[33] A Seaman, *An Infallible Project for the More Effectual, Speedy and Easy Manning of
the Navy of England without that Intolerable and Unparrall'd Practice of Pressing, Plainly
Demonstrated* (London: sold by M. Cooper, 1745), intro.

Both of the charities that Fielding lauded owe much of their initial popularity, as well as their continued support, to the needs of an expanding economy and a state at war. The idea behind the foundation, in 1739, of the first of these institutions, the Foundling Hospital, was that the preservation as well as the education of abandoned and illegitimate children was an important aspect of national policy. Although not a novel idea in 1740, this attempt to preserve infant lives was nevertheless fairly new in the history of English charity. The first mention of such an idea that I have been able to find is in William Petty's writings. In the 1680s Petty suggested some sort of institution, supported through public taxation, that would care for and rear illegitimate children in order to preserve their lives and guarantee a continuing and expanding source of labor for the nation. Thus, from the first instance that such a scheme was proposed, programs to save infant lives were intimately connected with the belief that increased numbers were fiscally valuable to the nation.[34] In so far as a large supply of men became valuable and desired, children increasingly came to be seen as a national resource too precious to be wasted. It was in this spirit that in 1718 Joseph Addison proposed the establishment of foundling hospitals and pointed out that "many who are by this means preserved . . . do signal service to their country . . . But do pass by the greatness of the crime [of letting innocent infants die] . . . if we only consider it as it robs the commonwealth of its full number of citizens, it certainly deserved the utmost application and wisdom of a people to prevent it.[35] However, it was not until 1739 and the outbreak of war that the desire to save infant lives was given practical expression in the establishment of the Foundling Hospital. The early aims of the hospital were to save as many lives as possible, to offer mothers of illegitimate children, who had no means to support themselves or their children, a more fitting alternative than infanticide or prostitution, and to "supply the Government plentifully with useful Hands on many Occasions; and for the better producing good and faithful Servants from amongst the poor and miserable cast-off Children or Foundlings, now a Pest to the Publick, and a chargeable Nuisance within the Bills of Mortality."[36]

The man most responsible for the foundation of the hospital, Thomas Coram, a retired sea captain, was representative of charitable donors of the midcentury in his fusion of Christian benevolence with patriotic and mercantile zeal.[37] A good example of this complete union of the practical

[34] William Petty, quoted in K. R. Kuczynsky, "British Demographers' Opinions on Fertility, 1660–1760," in Lancelot Hogben, *Political Arithmetic* (London: G. Allen & Unwin, 1938), p. 318.

[35] Joseph Addison, *The Guardian* [1713], 2 vols. (London: J. Tonson, 1714), 2:125–26.

[36] *An Account of the Hospital for the Maintenance and Education of Exposed and Deserted Young Children* (London: printed by order of the governors, 1749), p. 4.

[37] See Richard Brocklesby, *Private Virtue and Publick Spirit Display'd in a Succinct Es-*

and religious, the benevolent and the interested, can be seen in one of Coram's earlier projects—a program of conversion and education for Indian girls in America. Of this program he said, "This would be a refined Stroke of Policy; for he is the wisest and ablest of all Politicians, who, by prompting the Glory of God, interests the Divine Providence in extending the Power of any Nation."[38] In a tract written in behalf of the creation of the Foundling, his friend, Dr. Thomas Bray employed the same admixture of elements. On the one hand, Bray could plead for the tender care of the abandoned and illegitimate infant out of a purely benevolent and Christian regard:

> God forbid that in a Christian Nation, so enlightened with the bright Beams of the Gospel, as Ours is, that the Innocents themselves should be punished for their Parent's Sins, and be left to starve or exposed to Violence, for want of due Care to preserve their Lives, which cannot otherwise be secured effectually than by such Provision, as is here proposed. And in the Midst of Judgement we are to remember Mercy.

But, in the same work, he also remarked on the countless practical advantages to be derived from such an institution, among which the most important was that "by being withal put out to Service and honest Occupations, they would be moreover rendered useful Members of the Commonwealth, and not left to remain like Warts and Wens, and other filthy Excrescencies, to the defacing and weakening of the Body Politick."[39]

That philanthropists of this era saw that economic advantages could arise from the promotion of charity in no way belittles their motives, nor does it cast doubt on the sincerity of their religious convictions. The beliefs and piety of many of the early and important supporters of the Foundling were broadly latitudinarian: they were not so much concerned with dogma as with the practice in daily life of what they saw to be the primary duties of Christians. Thus, although Owen is right in saying that the fathers of the Foundling had "none of the characteristic evangelical concern for the souls of their charges," he is perhaps unjust in concluding that "unlike the charity schools and unlike nineteenth century societies for reclaiming children, there was little religious inspiration, other than

---

say on the *Character of Captain Thomas Coram* (London: J. Roberts, 1751); John Brownlow, *The History and Design of the Foundling Hospital* (London: W. & H. S. Farr, 1850); H.F.B. Compston, *Thomas Coram: Churchman, Empire Builder, and Philanthropist* (London: SPCK, 1918); and McClure, *Coram's Children*.

[38] Brocklesby, *Private Virtue*, pp. 23–24.

[39] [Thomas Bray], *A Memorial concerning the Erecting in the City of London or the Suburbs thereof of an Orphanotrophy or Hospital for the Reception of Poor Cast Off Children or Foundlings* (London: 1728), pp. 31, 16.

of a formal sort, among the builders of the Foundling."[40] While their emphasis was this-worldly and on the practical value of the charity, the religious element was not absent. In this spirit an anonymous correspondent of the *Gentleman's Magazine* suggested that, in contrast to the false charity of Catholic countries, which was "vain, selfish and superstitious," institutions like the Foundling were the best expressions of the true and untainted Christianity of England.

> But since the Reformation has banished ignorance, and restored Christianity, we have nobly distinguished ourselves by donations of another kind, such as are truly stiled *charities*; . . . Among these the raising of a fund for maintaining and educating exposed and deserted young children, appears to be the most excellent, with respect to its objects, its motives and its use.[41]

The advocates of the hospital saw no inconsistency or hypocrisy in noting that the fulfillment of the demands of religion would be rewarded by material prosperity and in assuring the public that their charity would be financially, as well as spiritually, profitable. In addition, it must be remembered that without these assurances, the Foundling would probably never have raised the necessary funds. For the Foundling Hospital, probably more than many other charities of the century, encountered repeated and severe criticisms, both for its alleged effects on public morality and for its doubtful efficiency. Early proponents and supporters of the hospital were often personally attacked, and it was a common insinuation that their great interest in such a hospital sprang from a desire to dispose, cheaply and conveniently, of their own illegitimate offspring.[42] Indeed, Coram and his friends had to work for seventeen years before they could overcome such public objections and get the hospital established. In a letter to a friend, Coram explained some of the difficulties he had encountered: " 'Many weak persons, more Ladies than Gentlemen, say such a Foundation will be a promotion of Wickedness . . .' and he instanced one such man who wished his wife to hand over some money to the Hospital, 'but she would by no means encourage so wicked a thing.' "[43] It was popularly believed that the mere existence of the Foundling, by providing a possible shelter for illegitimate children, would serve as an encouragement to thoughtlessness and increased licentiousness. Young men and women, no longer having to worry about the shame or difficulty of rear-

---

[40] Owen, *English Philanthropy*, p. 53.

[41] *Gentleman's Magazine* (April 1747), pp. 163–64.

[42] See, for example, *Joyful News to Bachelors and Maids* (1760); or C.A., *Candid Remarks on Mr. Hanway's Candid Historical Account of the Foundling Hospital* (London: printed for C. Henderson, 1760).

[43] R. H. Nichols and F. A. Wray, *History of the Foundling Hospital* (London: Oxford University Press, 1935), p. 21.

ing a child out of wedlock, would, it was feared, indulge in a life of heedless and abandoned sensuality: "the possibility of concealing Shame, or of an easy Provision for a spurious Issue, is an Encouragement to Vice, and a Means of Seduction of innocent Women."[44]

Allied to this criticism was the notion that the long-term efforts of this charity would in fact run opposed to its avowed objectives. Though it aimed at population increase, it would, it was said, result in the contrary effect, through the disincentives it gave to marriage. If the Foundling, by allowing unwed mothers and fathers to dispose of their illicit issue rather than marry, acted as "an encouragement to celibacy by being an open asylum for illegitimates . . . the community is so far from being increased, that the very foundation of its strength is undermined by it . . . therefore, in this view, the charity is hurtful."[45]

Even those who rejected the charge that the Foundling would hurt the nation's morals were troubled by other objections involving the management of the hospital. It is clear that from the beginning it was both an expensive and an uncertain undertaking. Thus, a reviewer of a pamphlet hostile to the Foundling, while dismissing all of the author's moral objections to the hospital, nevertheless conceded that if "THE EXPENSE OF EVERY CHILD, SO PUT OUT, IS MORE THAN £1,500 sterling, this was a very serious charge indeed."[46]

The question of why the Foundling was so expensive to run and produced so few concrete results in its first fifteen years of operation is difficult to answer. We have some reason to believe that the figure quoted by this author was exaggerated. While he maintained that the hospital had received more than £166,000 from its commencement to December 1757, the published records reveal that it had received only £107,568.12.8 to December 1756. Second, it can be shown by a closer examination of expenditures that a much smaller percentage of total receipts went to the actual care of the infants admitted. If we look at the accounts of the hospital to December 1752, we see that more than £27,000, or 32 percent, of its total revenue had gone into building the hospital and its chapel. A further £25,000 had been invested in land and in stocks. Of the total revenue, only about £30,215 had been spent on child care. When one considers that in these twelve years the hospital had admitted more than one thousand children, most of whom it had to maintain for that whole period of time, the amount expended, though large, seems less staggering. Of course, it is unlikely that many members of the

---

[44] *Some Considerations on the Present Method Used for the Relief and Employment of the Poor* (London: n.p., 1759), p. 8.

[45] *Gentleman's Magazine* (Supplement 1759), pp. 622–23.

[46] Ibid. (February 1759), p. 55.

public, on reading the alarming report of the institution's expenditures, would have bothered to analyze them in a careful or systematic manner.[47]

Along with the large expenses, the Foundling's mortality figures, though much better than those for babies cared for in parish workhouses, were still high. By 1756 the hospital had admitted 1,384 children, of whom between 40 percent and 55 percent had died before the age of two. Care of infants, especially of crippled or malnourished infants, was by its very nature a difficult and expensive business. Initially, the governors had hoped to lessen the expense by hiring nurses to hand-feed the babies. After a short trial of this method of feeding, it became clear that children so nourished had a far higher mortality rate than children who had been suckled. The governors then determined to find suitable wet nurses in the country with whom the children could live until they were three years old. In the beginning, the governors paid these nurses a lump sum per child for its care, but when many of the babies died soon afterward, under suspicious circumstances, the policy was changed and the nurses were paid yearly, with a premium at the end of the first year if they kept the infant alive. When a nurse lost two children successively, she was struck off the list and denied further employment. Not only was it difficult to find suitable nurses for the children, but the Foundling's governors encountered equal difficulties in finding reliable staff for its London quarters. Many of its early employees were fired for drunkenness, accepting bribes, or other improprieties. The governors felt that these irksome changes in personnel were necessary in order to establish a reputation with the public for integrity and efficiency.[48]

While the charity encountered many difficulties in this early period, its governors still felt able to express a guarded optimism about the society's future. Though expensive at present, "in process of time, a regular succession of children taken in and put out will render the good effects of this hospital more conspicuous to the publick."[49] In the meanwhile, the governors tried to keep down expenses by severely limiting the number of infants admitted. The evidence on this point is unclear, but no more than two hundred and forty babies, and probably only one hundred, were admitted per year in the period between 1739 and 1756. The charity's directors also stressed the extent to which the institution was self-supporting. Thus, in addition to pointed announcements in popular magazines stating the sums made by the children's work, in 1753 the governors converted one of their kitchens into a shop "where the children might

---

[47] McClure, *Coram's Children*, Appendix 5, p. 265. McClure's figures are derived from the 1756 *Account of the Hospital*.

[48] On early difficulties, see McClure, *Coram's Children*, pp. 52, 87.

[49] *Gentleman's Magazine* (July 1753), p. 324.

work in public for all passers-by to see the virtue and utility of the experiment."[50]

In addition to all the other criticisms leveled against the hospital, there were also those who objected that the children were being coddled and were not being instilled with a sufficiently humbling or complete religious education. In 1748 the governors attempted to refute the first of these charges by publishing their intention to change the occupation of the Foundling boys from the manufacture of silk, which was deemed too effete, to the manufacture of hemp and flax into twine and fishing nets. This occupation was seen as being more "consistent with their destination to Navigation and Husbandry," since it could be conducted in the open air and the boys would become hardened to weather changes. The girls would receive practical training in "all sorts of Household Work in the Kitchen, Laundry and Chambers, to make them fit for Service, and also in sewing, knitting and spinning." Lest it still be thought that the children were being treated too softly and spoiled for the life of labor, which was to be their lot, the general committee recommended that "their Bread be good, but coarse and made of different sorts of Corn, as Wheat, Rye, Barley, Pease, Oats, Etc. occasionally, that they may be inured to these accidental changes." In regard to the adequacy of the children's religious training, the governors reminded the public "that the children do constantly attend Divine Service in the Chapel on Sundays, to often remind them of the Lowness of their Condition, that they may early imbibe the Principles of Humility and Gratitude to their Benefactors; and to learn to undergo, with Contentment the most servile and labourious Offices."[51]

However, despite their attempts to assure the public of the propriety and good consequences of their project, even the charity's governors and supporters seemed aware of the novelty and possible danger of their enterprise. There are two indications of this awareness. The first is the surprising absence of female subscribers among the published subscription lists. Although earlier twenty-one gentlewomen had sent a petition to the king, pleading for a charter of incorporation for the charity, not one of them gave publicly, that is to say in her own name, to the charity once it became incorporated. Of these twenty-one women, however, eighteen had husbands or other near male relatives who were active early subscribers.[52] Since women were commonly held to be the arbiters and bastions

---

[50] According to McClure, *Coram's Children*, Appendix 3, p. 261, 136 children were admitted 1741–1742, an annual average of 87 from 1742 to 1752, and an annual average of 69 from 1752 to 1756. For the children's work, see John H. Hutchins, *Jonas Hanway, 1712–1786* (London: SPCK, 1940), p. 21.

[51] *An Account of the Hospital for Young Children* (1749), pp. xvii–xviii, 70. See also Thomas Secker, *Fourteen Sermons* (London: J. F. Rivington, 1777), pp. 164–65.

[52] McClure, *Coram's Children*, pp. 21–22; Ruth K. McClure, "New Channels of Benef-

of public morality, they may well have been hesitant to allow their names to appear in support of an institution that could possibly be thought to be "improper" or conducive to sexual immorality. The second indication we have of the sentiment that, though the institution was important and valuable, its workings must be carefully administered lest it exceed itself and cause harm, is the seeming unwillingness of some of its leading and charter members to leave bequests to the charity in their wills. Robert Nettleton, for example, a bank director and governor of the Russia Company, who was on the board of governors of the Foundling in 1745, left nothing at all to the charity on his death. He did, however, bequeath considerable sums to other, less controversial London charities (£4,000 to the Hospital for Innoculation and Smallpox, £1,000 to the London Infirmary, £500 each to St. Thomas's and to the Society for Encouraging Arts and Manufactures), as well as more traditional bequests of £50 for marriage portions for poor maidens, and £40 to the poor of Bromley. Similarly, Peter Delme, another important and wealthy contributor, left nothing in his will to the hospital. Although bequests to the Foundling were not unknown (John Milner, for example, a vice president of the charity, left it £100 in his will), the relative infrequency of such bequests suggests that there was a hesitancy to support this institution blindly or posthumously, and a preference to donate to its coffers when the direction and use of those funds could still be influenced and controlled.[53]

In its first fifteen years of operation, despite the hesitation, the difficulties, and the criticisms, the Foundling did not suffer from lack of funds or support. The large financial resources of the hospital, plus the cautious direction and eminence of its governors, convinced many people that the charity was, on the whole, a useful and worthy institution. By 1745 the Foundling had not only managed to double its original number of members, but had convinced peers, gentry, and important merchants and directors to serve on its governing committees and lend the weight of their names and experience to its administration. While the peers and gentry may have played a less active role in the actual work of the charity, their

---

icence: A Portrait of Pre-Evangelical Associational Charity, 1739–1758" (thesis, Columbia University, 1968).

[53] Wills of all donors mentioned can be found in the Public Record Office, London, under their probate number: Robert Nettleton, PROB 11/999/277, Peter Delme, PROB 11/956/138, John Milner, PROB 11/802/182. Of the thirty-eight men who were directors of the Foundling in 1745, only four left anything by bequest to this charity: Joseph Fawthorpe, Dr. James Mead, John Milner, and Thomas Strode. Strode's bequest was contingent on his heir, his niece, either predeceasing him or marrying without his consent. Despite this, the Foundling received 174 direct legacies worth almost £36,000 before 1759: see *The Legacy Book of the Foundling Hospital*, Greater London Record Office, Foundling Hospital Papers. Most of these bequests, however, were not from the active and involved charitable community of the day.

names and support lent the charity important prestige. Furthermore, about half (eighteen of thirty-eight) of the governing committee in 1745 were prosperous merchants and financiers. These included four directors of the South Sea Company, an important government contractor, a governor of the Royal Exchange Assurance Company, a fair sprinkling of city politicians, and seven past and five current members of Parliament. These men undoubtedly provided the financial know-how to run the charity as well as a practical understanding of the fiscal and political importance of preserving the lives of the infant poor. The presence of these important merchants and financiers as subscribers and committee members seemed to accompany, and perhaps was responsible for, the charity's popular success. Not only were such men able and willing to contribute money and financial expertise to the operations of the charity, but their large circle of business and personal acquaintances included many potential subscribers, who could be persuaded to contribute and serve the charity in times of need.[54]

CHARITY AND MATERNITY: LONDON'S LYING-IN HOSPITALS

In addition to the Foundling Hospital, Henry Fielding praised the Lying-in Hospital for poor married women (later called the British Lying-in Hospital), started in 1749. This charity, like the Foundling, had the advantage of combining aid to the needy with the advancement of national policy. In addition, this hospital, and other lying-in charities subsequently established, played an important part in the advancement of the science of obstetrics and gynecology. As in the case of the Foundling, too, the need for such an institution had long been recognized and advocated, and only little acted on. Although Sir Richard Manningham, an early practitioner and teacher of obstetrics, had opened a ward for lying-in women in the parochial infirmary of St. James's Westminster in 1739, and the Middlesex had opened a similar ward in 1747, the British Lying-in Hospital for poor married women was the first specialized institution in London dealing only in the delivery of children.

This hospital and its counterpart, the City of London Lying-in Hospital, founded in 1750, owed their start, in some part, to the increasing interest in a scientific understanding of the birth process. These hospitals marked and initiated the great advances that had been and were being made in obstetrical theory and practice. Well into the early years of the eighteenth century, childbirth had remained a mysterious process, outside the scope of scientific inquiry, and fit only for the ministrations of un-

---

[54] *The Royal Charter Establishing An Hospital for the Maintenance and Education of Exposed and Deserted Young Children . . . and a List of Governors* (London: Thomas Osborne, 1746).

trained midwives. Yet, by midcentury much was being attempted to ease the dangers of childbirth and to further a scientific understanding of the processes involved. Although forceps had been invented in the seventeenth century by Peter Chamberlen, they remained a family secret and consequently were not used in general practice until the mid-eighteenth-century. The first cesarean section in England was performed in the 1730s. In the 1740s and 1750s a flood of midwifery manuals appeared, including Manningham's *Artis obstetricariae compendium*, Burton's *Essay toward a Complete New System of Midwifery*, Smellie's *Treatise on the Theory and Practice of Midwifery*, and *Collection of Cases*, and Benjamin Pugh's *Treatise on Midwifery*. In addition to the manuals, both Manningham and Smellie gave classes in obstetrics to the growing number of male midwives wanting to enter this practice. Doctors, like philanthropists, seemed suddenly to become anxious to overcome the dangers of and loss of life at birth.[55]

There were those, however, who considered male interest in this field to be scandalous and improper. Many agreed with Hanway that childbirth should be returned to the sole charge of the female midwife.[56] In addition to charges of impropriety, there was a wider debate going on over the relative value of female midwives versus "accoucheurs," as the male obstetricians liked be called. It is entirely to this dispute that Aveling attributed the simultaneous appearance of so many lying-in hospitals: "The contest, however, undignified as it was, had the effect of interesting the public and concentrating their attention upon a subject which had too long been neglected. A practical indication of this interest is to be found in the fact that about the same time five of the most important lying-in hospitals in London were established."[57] There is no doubt that the hospitals benefited from the support and patronage given to them by many concerned and famous surgeons, physicians, and apothecaries. In the 1750s, for example, the British Lying-in Hospital had between twelve and fifteen medical men, four of whom were midwives, on their subscription lists. At the same time the City of London Lying-in Hospital had between six and eight, and the Middlesex Hospital about ten doctors and druggists. Still, it seems fairly clear that this debate, and the public attention it

[55] For excellent notes on the history of obstetrics, see M. C. Versluyen, "Midwives, Medical Men, and 'Poor Women Labouring of Child' " in Helen Roberts, ed., *Women, Health, and Reproduction* (London: Routledge & Kegan Paul, 1981), pp. 43–49. For the City of London Lying-in Hospital, see Ralph B. Cannings, *The City of London Maternity Hospital* (London: J. S. Forsaith, 1922).

[56] Jonas Hanway, *The Defects of Police, the Cause of Immorality* . . . (London: J. Dodsley, 1775), pp. xx–xxi.

[57] James Hobson Aveling, *English Midwives: their History and Prospects* [1872] (London: Elliot, 1967), pp. 124–25.

aroused, was not the only, and probably not even the greatest, reason for the foundation of these hospitals. In one of them at least, the training aspect was discounted; just three years after the opening of the City of London Lying-in Hospital, Thomas Church, in his benefit sermon for the charity, commended the hospital for "the utter exclusion of all pupils of surgery whose presence might shock the modesty of some and give offense to others." Furthermore, most babies born in these hospitals were delivered without instruments by female midwives.[58]

Other interests besides the desire to understand and improve the process of birth contributed to the support for lying-in hospitals. The theme of the pregnant woman in danger of death was seen to be ripe with possibilities for eliciting charitable donations. This picture appealed to the sentiments, touched the heart, and aroused a desire to relieve the anguish of those who bestow life. One should not underestimate the genuineness or strength of this sentimental benevolence. The early eighteenth century witnessed the rise of appeals to "sentiment," with the exaltation of the emotional aspect of personality. Chief among the sentiments lauded, and held as constituting the truest and best element of human character, was benevolence.[59] The importance and primacy of this passion was stressed by both clerics and deists, and, most notably, in the writings of the third earl of Shaftesbury. These writings prepared the way and lent force to appeals to the emotions made by most charities of the day. Like the Foundling's appeal to religious benevolence, these claims, when combined with more practical ones, which we shall look at in due course, appeared irresistible. The eloquence of the preacher, therefore, though perhaps extravagant and long-winded, and designed to extract funds from recalcitrant givers, should not be dismissed as totally unfelt or entirely manipulative. "And when we consider, that we all came in the same manner into the world, we may be thought forgetful of our very original and unthankful for our being, if we overlook their miseries, and neglect their wants. . . . O let it not be said, that we are unmindful of their anguish, to whom we have such continual and enduring obligations."[60]

It is clear that these maternity charities owe their beginnings to a combination of the desire to advance science, the sentimental appeal of the pregnant woman, and the more practical advantages promised by these

[58] Thomas Church, *A Sermon Preached . . . before the President and Governors of the City of London Lying-in Hospital for Married Women* (London: Chas. Say, 1753), p. 20; J. S. Lewis, "Maternal Health in the English Aristocracy: Myths and Realities, 1790–1840," *Journal of Social History*, 17 (1983–1984), p. 108, notes that few babies were delivered by forceps in eighteenth-century maternity hospitals.

[59] R. S. Crane, "Suggestions towards a Genealogy of the 'Man of Feelings,' " *English Literary History* 1 (1934), pp. 205–38.

[60] Church, *Sermon*, p. 9

hospitals. The first of these practical advantages was that by freeing poor laboring people from "all uneasy fears, that in times of sickness or calamity, they may, notwithstanding their labours, be left abandoned to want,"[61] a more cheerful and active laboring class would emerge. The recognition that the poor often could not provide for such care in times of childbirth, no matter how they labored, led to the view that it was the obligation of the well-to-do to secure this provision for them. Furthermore, aid to pregnant women was seen as especially effective in work promotion. Women who were helped through their "greatest exigencies [will] redouble their labour, will work more cheerfully, and return to labour with better health."[62] In addition to industry, religion would be promoted by the work of the maternity hospitals. Women were provided with Bibles and visited regularly by clergymen who exhorted them to prayer and reflection. Children born in the hospitals were baptized in the attached chapels, and were thus started off as proper Christians. At least one lying-in hospital also demanded a public show of gratitude from women they had accommodated, and threatened exclusion from further benefits if this was not forthcoming.[63] Finally, the hospitals claimed that, while increasing and improving public morality through the promotion and reward of marriage, they were also aiding in the increase of England's population by the successful delivery of more babies, as well as by the conservation of many women as future productive and reproductive citizens.

With few exceptions, most of the lying-in hospitals insisted that the clientele they were interested in aiding was poor *married* women, and they often demanded written proof of marital status before providing care. Both the British and the City of London lying-in hospitals made it quite clear that they were in no way encouraging licentiousness, that the women they were treating were truly deserving, and that their institutions were examples of "an open testimony borne in favour of the first ordinance of Heaven [i.e., marriage]; on which not only the comfort, but the very support of human life so greatly depends; which is the foundation of families and government."[64] It was the avowed and often repeated purpose of these institutions to strengthen marriage, families, and government. Insofar as marriage was seen as being conducive to population growth, and thus to the expansion of commerce and empire, these institutions served primarily national purposes. The grand aspirations of these

---

[61] Ibid., p. 21.

[62] John Lawson, *Occasional Sermons* (Dublin: J. Fisher, 1765), pp. 299–300.

[63] Calvin Woodward, "Reality and Social Reform—the Transition from Laissez-Faire to the Welfare State," *Yale Law Journal*, 72 (1962), p. 302.

[64] Church, *Sermon*, pp. 18–19.

hospitals is well illustrated by the following excerpt from a prologue read for the benefit of the City of London Lying-in Hospital:

Each hardy son, whom this night's alms shall raise,
Will to Great Britain consecrate his days;
Her arts, her commerce, her domain extend,
Or force her haughty enemies to bend;
Whilst the fair daughters of this genial day
Shall serve their country—in a gentler way;
If doom'd as humble spinsters to grow old,
Shall spin our envy'd fleeces into gold;
If wedded, shall with Hymen's magic chain
From foreign climes our artizans refrain,
From foreign climes recall the wandering tar,
With hearts of oak supply the wastes of war
And with sons' sons enrich our future store,
Till time, and this great empire, are no more.
    (Theatre bell rings)
But lo! the laughing muse comes tripping on,
And by her herald warns me to be gone;
Yet hence this great moral understood,
That *private virtue* leads to *public good*.[65]

THE LOCK HOSPITAL AND THE TREATMENT OF VENEREAL DISEASE

The third charity to be started in the 1740s, the Lock Hospital for the treatment and cure of venereal disease, established in 1746, was not mentioned by Fielding. Perhaps even more than the Foundling, the Lock had great difficulty in convincing the public of the necessity of its existence. There was a widespread belief that since venereal diseases resulted from sexual promiscuity, it would be wrong to alleviate well-deserved punishment. This kind of aid, it was feared, by making venereal disease less dangerous, would lead to an increase in sexual impropriety. In addition, the colorful, though eccentric, career of one of its founders, the Reverend Martin Madan, cast some doubts on the soundness and good sense of the institution. In his younger days, Madan had lived a rakish and dissolute life, but renounced the sins of the flesh, it was said, under the influence of John Wesley's sermons, and dedicated the rest of his life to aiding victims of vice.[66] Undoubtedly, his character and religious and moral views, as

[65] *Gentleman's Magazine* (December 1769), pp. 601–2. See also Lawson, *Sermons*, pp. 294–96.

[66] Martin Madan's antecedents and connections were all highly respectable. His father was an M.P., his grandfather a judge, and his younger brother, Spencer Madan, became

well as the absence of a concerted effort to show the practical and national advantages of such an institution, lost the hospital the support of the most active and involved of London's charitable donors.

On the other hand, Madan's gentle birth and connections doubtlessly aided him in soliciting support for the society among the nobility and gentry. In addition to support from the upper classes, the charity also received aid, either in the form of subscriptions or services, from nineteen doctors and apothecaries, who had obvious scientific and professional interests in the treatment of venereal disease, as well as from a significant number of military men. The presence of this last group in the ranks of the subscribers supports the view that the problem of venereal disease had reached significant proportions in the 1740s. Although the evidence is lacking, it seems likely that the increased military and naval activity in this period served to spread and intensify the effects of these diseases. London must have been especially hard hit, since it was both the depot for soldiers and sailors and the home base of a large maritime fleet. These men would have been the perfect subjects for, and carriers of, all sorts of venereal infections. While venereal disease was spreading, the causes and treatment were largely unknown or misunderstood, even by doctors and surgeons of the period. It was known, however, that persons afflicted with certain venereal diseases were often unable to bear or engender children. It was feared that the spread of these diseases hindered the procreation that seemed so necessary from a national point of view. Not only did it take its toll in the ill health of its victims and have national consequences in the reduction of the population, but it ruined the health and lives of many innocent children and potentially useful citizens. The public of eighteenth-century London must have been shocked to read the following communiqué from the governors of Lock:

> As several children from two to ten or twelve Years old, have become Patients in this Hospital, from Ways little suspected by the Generality of Mankind, the Governors think it their Duty, out of Regard to little Innocents, to publish the Motives of *Wicked People* to so vile an Act, and to assure them of the Fallacy of it. It is received Opinion of many of the lower Class of Mankind, both Males and Females, *that when infected themselves, if they can procure a sound Person to communicate the Disease to, they certainly get rid of it.* And from this Principle the most horrid Acts of Barbarity have frequently been committed on poor

---

bishop of Peterborough. Madan himself is reputed to have been a man of great personal charm and a witty and amusing conversationalist. His public image, however, must have been considerably tarnished by the protracted debates he engaged in over the rectory of Aldwinkle, an entirely insignificant incident that, before it was resolved, brought him into conflict with the *Monthly Review* and with Selina, countess of Huntingdon. His defense of polygamy in 1780 did nothing to restore his image.

Infants; tho' *these vile Wretches* have by Experience been convinced of the Absurdity of such vulgar Notions, yet this requires the utmost Publication to prevent such unheard of Cruelty, and Inhumanity for the future.[67]

The governors of the Lock, however, unlike those of the Foundling or lying-in hospitals, did not stress the practical benefits of their charity, but merely mentioned these as an afterthought or bonus. In the main, their appeal was to a spirit of Christian forgiveness and charity.

> But if any notwithstanding, should say, what too many have said, that no Hospital should be supported, which is to relieve persons who willfully bring a disease upon themselves, through their own wickedness and abandoned life. To this I answer, 1st. It bespeaks a far better sense of our love of our neighbour, to be finding reasons for doing him good, than inventing, or even admitting excuses for withholding our charity from him.[68]

That the reliance on this sort of appeal alone was ill conceived can be seen from the small number of subscribers the charity attracted (only 165 by 1749), the absence of subscribers who could bring administrative talent and experience as well as financial backing to the charity, and the limited amount of financial support it received in its first several years.[69]

LONDON CHARITIES OF THE 1740S

Of the three sorts of charity that arose in the 1740s, those like the Foundling and lying-in hospitals that combined appeals to sentiment and religion with illustrations of the social usefulness of the institutions were assured of public support in their endeavors. Both the child-care and maternity charities stressed the utility of their work primarily in terms of the numbers of soldiers, sailors, laborers, and colonists they would add to the national stock. That charity that did not stress its practical usefulness, and relied only on disinterested appeals, found it much more difficult to attract public aid.

[67] *An Account of the Proceedings of the Lock Hospital from its First Institution, July 4, 1746 to September 29, 1749* (London: n.p., 1749), n.p.

[68] Martin Madan, *Sermon for the Opening of the Chapel at the Lock Hospital* (London: E. Dilly, 1762), "Every Man our Neighbour," p. 21. See also Joseph Butler, "Sermon Upon Compassion," in *Fifteen Sermons Preached at the Rolls Chapel* (London: G. Bell, 1949), pp. 102–3; and Warburton, *Sermon, London Hospital*, p. 264.

[69] Within the first several years of its foundation, the Lock had to dismiss two larcenous preachers. During its first five years of service, its annual income was little more than £700. Of the sixty-two men who are listed as attending directors' committee meetings before 1751, only two gave to more than one other charity (John Beard to six and Nathaniel Curzon to two). Three others subscribed to one other charity. An additional twelve may have given themselves or had a close relative subscribe; the information is too scanty to be more certain.

In all three types of charity, the absence or presence of female subscribers can be taken as an indication of the "reputation" of the charity, that is, of its supposed tendency to increase or decrease vice while relieving affliction. Both the Foundling and the Lock hospitals listed no female subscribers, though the former had sent a petition signed by a host of noblewomen to the king, and the latter indicated that they had received donations from women who had requested that their names not appear on any public lists. Only the two maternity charities, both of which made a strong point of aiding only married women, had many female supporters. In fact, 33 percent of all the listed subscribers to the British Lying-in Hospital in 1751 were women, while the City of London Lying-in Hospital's female subscribers constituted between 14 percent (in 1753) and 28 percent (in 1759) of its total number of subscribers in its first ten years of operation.[70]

Another interesting point about all the charities started in the 1740s is the apparent importance of members of the upper classes, of "well-connected" men and women of birth or reputation, on the lists of supporters. All four of these charities had a good number of such subscribers, whose names enhanced the social standing of the charity, and, presumably, served to attract smaller, less well-connected donors who wished their names to appear publicly in the same list as a famous duke or even an important city politician. Further, it can perhaps be inferred from their relatively large numbers that these peers and politicians were more willing to gamble on a new charity than some of the more prudent and cautious merchants and company directors. The peer was perhaps more susceptible to appeals made to his disinterested benevolence and humanitarian sentiment, and more easily convinced to contribute some sum, even to dubious charities like the Lock, than was the merchant, who was used to appeals made to his purse, and accustomed to considering the security and size of the return before he committed himself or his money to any investment.

[70] Sixty-five, or 33.9 percent of the 192 subscribers to the British Lying-in Hospital in 1751 were female. By 1757 the percentage had gone up to 39 percent. There were twenty (20 percent) female subscribers to the City of London Lying-in Hospital in 1753 and fifty-five (29 percent) in 1759. F. K. Prochaska, in his excellent *Women and Philanthropy in Nineteenth-Century England* (Oxford: Oxford University Press, 1980), ignores the high proportion of women in these earlier charities and overvalues the innovativeness of early-nineteenth-century female involvement. See also *An Account of the Rise and Progress of the Lying-in Hospital for Married Women from its First Institution in November 1749 to July 25, 1751* (London: n.p., 1751); *An Account of the Rise, Progress and State of the British Lying-in Hospital for Married Women from its Institution . . . to December 25, 1757* (London: n.p., 1758); *An Account of the City of London Lying-in Hospital for Married Women* (London: Say, 1753); *An Account of the City of London Lying-in Hospital for Married Women* (London: n.p., 1759).

Yet, despite this, any charity that hoped to have continuing success needed the support and involvement of merchant and financier philanthropists. Unlike the work of parish officials, who were generally "persons, who engage in the office with regret, have no turn for the employment, act only for one year, and have seldom anything else in view than putting themselves and the parish to as little expence as possible in their maintenance," the activities of philanthropists "have the thing at heart, are disinterested, and serve voluntarily."[71] Annual subscription combined with business management would insure philanthropic efficiency. Once this was assured, once citizens felt confident that their monies would not be lost nor spent recklessly, they could indulge fully in the many pleasures of charity.

> Self-love shall learn to taste of social joy,
> And public works the miser's hands employ;
> Folly inform'd, converted Vice shall own,
> That Wisdom, Pleasure, VIRTUE gives alone;
> Deists shall scorn the Christian name no more,
> And atheists God, as love immense adore.[72]

[71] *Gentleman's Magazine* (July 1761), pp. 291–93.
[72] *Gentleman's Magazine* (October 1746), p. 553, "To Mr. Layng on his Sermon on Mutual Benevolence."

CHAPTER THREE

Charity and the Charitable Community at Midcentury

IF, IN CHAPTER 2, we heard the fanfare, the prologue, as it were, of both the City of London Lying-in Hospital, and the proud beginnings of a new associational charity in the 1740s, the 1750s and 1760s are definitely the play itself, the full-blown drama of eighteenth-century London benevolence. It is, however, a Janus-headed drama—looking both backward and forward. The charities of the 1750s and 1760s, while agreeing fully with the ends of the earlier charities, such as population increase, promotion of public virtue, and the maximization of national productivity, began to look for new, more efficient methods to achieve those ends. So, while there seems to have been a turning away from institutional forms, there was, if anything, an increase in fervor, in the conviction that charitable intervention was necessary to get England through a difficult period.

The decades of the midcentury saw not only a remarkable flowering of charitable activity, but the emergence of a fairly well-defined group of major charitable donors. Many of these donors were also directors and governors of these charities, responsible for successful fundraising, publicity, and the management of the organizations' operations. In this chapter we will attempt to build a "snapshot" of this group, to provide a "still life" picture of these important and active philanthropists. In the process it will be necessary to anticipate ourselves somewhat, and, in order to appreciate the magnitude and complexity of their charitable involvement, to mention some charities not yet discussed, but introduced in subsequent chapters.[1] However, now it is time to draw the curtains, and meet the actors.

---

[1] These charities are the Magdalen House for penitent prostitutes, established in 1758; the Marine Society to send boys to sea; the Asylum for Orphaned Girls; and the Lying-in Charity for Delivering Poor Married Women in their own Habitations, all established in the late 1750s, and all discussed in chapter 4. The General Lying-in Hospital is discussed in this chapter and not elsewhere in greater detail since only two of its printed subscription lists exist. However, since some of their papers still exist, I have used these to cast light on the daily workings of a midcentury charity. The Society for Bettering the Condition and Improving the Comforts of the Poor and the Philanthropic Society are examined in chapter 6.

JONAS HANWAY AND LONDON'S PHILANTHROPIC COMMUNITY

The hero of the drama is Jonas Hanway, philanthropist, traveler, and indefatigable pamphleteer and publicist for a host of charitable societies.[2] The other actors in this play are less well known and speak more often through their actions than their voices or written opinions. Hanway served with many personal acquaintances on a variety of governing boards, as we shall soon see. His old business partner in the Russia trade, Robert Dingley, was the man who suggested the foundation of the Magdalen House, for which Hanway was to be so active. John Thornton, Jacob Bosanquet, and Robert Nettleton were also major charitable figures whom Hanway had met in his travels, with whom he had conducted business, and with whom he was to be intimately involved in a multitude of philanthropic schemes. Beyond the foreground of the stage, however, were the many supporting actors, faceless donors whose contributions made these charitable experiments possible. Though there was a good deal of continuity with the sorts of people who had given to the charities of the previous decade, and who also took part in the newer charities of midcentury, changes were also occurring within London's philanthropic community. The midcentury charities depended more heavily on the merchant community and less on aristocrats for money and support. There was also a steady growth in donors giving to multiple charities in the 1750s and 1760s than had been the case in the 1740s.[3] The world of London charity was becoming more concentrated and more mercantile. Let us leave the community for a short time, however, and return briefly to our hero.

Hanway spent much of his youth abroad, returning to England in 1750 from travels in Russia and elsewhere. A small legacy enabled him to "retire" from business and find another field of activity. Hanway first came

[2] A need exists for a complete prosopography of Hanway and his circle. For existing biographies see John Pugh, *Remarkable Occurrences in the Life of Jonas Hanway* (London: printed by J. Davies and sold by Payne & Son, 1787); R. Everett Jayne, *Jonas Hanway: Philanthropist, Politician, Author, 1712–1786* (London: Epsworth Press, 1929); John H. Hutchins, *Jonas Hanway, 1712–1786* (London: SPCK, 1940); and James Stephen Taylor, *Jonas Hanway: Founder of the Marine Society* (London: Scolar Press, 1985).

[3] By comparing the interlocking memberships of the contributors to the British and City of London Lying-in hospitals, the Foundling, and the Lock for the 1740s and 1750s, we see that 31 out of 850 donors (3.6 percent) gave to more than one of these. During the 1750s and 1760s, when a similar comparison was made of the donors to the Magdalen, the Marine, the Asylum for Orphaned Girls, and the Lying-in Charity, we see that 132 out of 1,283 (10.3 percent) of the donors gave to multiple charities. There are few intact lists for the 1740s but Ruth McClure contrasts the aristocratic membership of the Foundling (19 percent) with the smaller noble involvement in the Magdalen, the Marine, and the Asylum, three charities started in the 1750s: see "New Channels of Beneficence: A Portrait of Pre-Evangelical Associational Charity, 1739–1758" (thesis, Columbia University, 1968), p. 66.

to the public notice as a writer of travel books, but this did not seem to offer him the active commitment he desired. In many ways, these early years back in England can be seen more as the conclusion of his traveling, mercantile youth than the work of his mature manhood. It was really in his involvement with London's charitable community that Hanway fully matured.

Hanway's writings and philanthropic activities display the entire range of interests and concerns of many charitable givers. For Hanway was nothing if not extraordinarily representative of his time and class. He stands out only in the fact that he, unlike most of his fellow donors, wrote voluminously about, and for, the charities with which he became involved. So when we look at Hanway and examine his writings, we are also getting a glimpse of the unarticulated, unrecorded views of many of his contemporaries and friends. What sorts of men and women were these? What do we know of them, and what can we infer? We know surprisingly little. We learn of them mainly through their work activities— through their involvement with the Bank of England, with the Russia Company, through trade directories and company records, and through their wills. Many of them knew each other in a multiplicity of ways— through connections of profession, friendship, similar interests, and family. Thomas Edwards Freeman, a South Sea Company director and colleague of Hanway's on the governing committee of the Magdalen House, was elected to Parliament through his relation to Sir John Honywood, father of Frazer Honywood, banker, fellow Magdalen House committee member, and director with Hanway on the Marine Society's board. Robert Dingley was a Russia merchant and London silk merchant who served with Hanway on the committees of the Foundling, the Magdalen, and the Marine. Dingley's interests in art and archaeology and his membership in the Royal Society linked him both with Sir Hans Sloane, another fellow of the Royal Society, art collector, and contributor to the Foundling, and Lady Betty Germain, patroness of Hanway to whom he dedicated his book *Account of the British Trade*, whose fame as a collector was more than matched by the vast number of her philanthropic interests.

The evidence available suggests that many of these key London philanthropists were, like Hanway, in vigorous early-middle age.[4] These men and women were old enough to have made many valuable business and charity "connections," old enough to have the time to devote to charity, yet young enough to have the physical and mental stamina needed for the work involved in organizing, overseeing, and running these concerns.

[4] The average age for thirty-one donors who sat on governing boards with Hanway in the late 1750s and early 1760s (including Hanway) was almost forty-six. All governing board members were male.

What one is particularly struck by, however, when reading the records of their business careers and their bequests, is the two-sided nature of their personalities. On the one side was commercial adventurousness and ability: James Crockatt, for example, started life as an India trader and ended it as the leader in the South Carolina trade; Thomas Fletcher left the haberdashery trade for tea dealing and retired thirty years later worth £100,000; and Saunders Welch, whose parents were paupers, became a successful grocer and respected London magistrate.[5] On the other side was prudence in charitable matters, a definite unwillingness to commit oneself to a charity when one was no longer there to oversee it. This reluctance to leave bequests to charity in general, and to the charities of the midcentury specifically, is particularly clear when we look at the wills of thirty-five of the most charitably involved citizens of this period.[6] These were men who not only donated money to charitable causes, but perhaps more importantly, gave of themselves, of their time and energy, to serve on various philanthropic governing bodies. Of these thirty-five, twenty-one left nothing to any charities at all, though Jonas Hanway did leave money to three girls whom he had "fostered" in the Foundling Hospital. Of the remaining fourteen, five left bequests entirely to "traditional" charities. Thus, Thomas Fletcher, an active philanthropist and prominent dissenter, left funds for St. Thomas's Hospital, for an orphan working school in London, and for the establishment and maintenance of a number of dissenting charities. Andrew Thom[p]son left his executor £500 to distribute to the poor and another £200 to found a new college in Edinburgh. Robert Nettleton, Hanway's fellow committee member on the Foundling and Magdalen boards, and active with him in the attempt to eradicate the evils of chimney sweeping, while leaving more than £10,000 to charity, left nothing to any of the more controversial ones of which he had been a governor.[7]

Even those who did leave bequests to the newer London charities left more, both in number and amount, to older, more conservative concerns.

[5] See Patrick Pringle, *Hue and Cry: The Story of Henry and John Fielding and the Bow Street Runners* (New York: Morrow, n.d.), p. 148.

[6] I have read the wills of 35 of the 174 men who served on the various governing committees of the Magdalen, the Marine, and the Asylum for Orphaned Girls in the late 1750s and early 1760s.

[7] Wills of all donors mentioned can be found in the London Public Record Office under their probate number: Jonas Hanway, PROB 11/1145/478; Thomas Fletcher, PROB 11/1226/607; Andrew Thomson, PROB/11/1258/216; and John Delme, PROB 11/1016/63, did leave money to the newer charities, but they seem to have done so *pro forma*, leaving £50 to each hospital on whose board each had been at his death. Michael Adolphus, PROB 11/1126/61, who left the British Lying-in Hospital and the Marine each £10, left £200 to help an illegitimate great-nephew to become a lawyer. Few donors left any of these newer charities more than 20 percent of their entire charitable bequests.

Timothy Waldo, a wealthy London attorney, on the governing committees of the Magdalen House and the Asylum for Orphaned Girls, and a
contributor to the Marine, the London Hospital, and the Society for the
Discharge and Relief of Persons Imprisoned for Small Debts, left £600 to
the Salters Guild to help apprentice and clothe poor members, and £100
to the Asylum for Orphaned Girls. Interestingly, Waldo also left £10 to
his parish to provide clothes for those poor not on alms. This stipulation
was also made in the bequest of John Dorrien, banker and Russia merchant, who, in addition to leaving money to the London, the Smallpox
Hospital, and the Magdalen charity, left bequests to those poor of the
parish of Allhallows, London, who were not in receipt of alms.[8] Perhaps
the most interesting of all the wills, however, is that of Thomas Edward
Freeman, subscriber to most of the important charities of his day, member of Parliament, financier, and company director. His will is more personal than most and contains a clear expression of his principles and beliefs. These, like his politics (which Namier has described as independent
and self-contradictory), were dual natured. Though he was one of the few
philanthropists known to have left money to the Lock Hospital, most of
his other charitable bequests were very traditional: £100 to the Society
for Improving the Comfort and Bettering the Conditions of the Poor,
£100 to the Middlesex Hospital, and £100 to the Society for the Discharge and Relief of Persons Imprisoned for Small Debts. He appears in
many ways to have been a model paternalist, leaving money for the upkeep of his "family place of residence to the End that persons living in the
neighbourhood, particularly those of the lower classes in it, may by their
employments, professions and labour continue to derive some benefit and
support to themselves and their families from the abundance which it has
pleased God most graciously to bestow upon their opulent neighbour."
Neither did he forget his servants, commenting that "it has always appeared to me right and proper, that the faithful and diligent service of
attentive domestics should be properly noticed and that the latter part of
their lives should be rendered comfortable by a suitable provision whenever it has pleased God to grant the ability." Yet, his generosity was tempered by prudence, his philanthropy by public concern. Thus, when he
left funds to a local school for "instructing the Children of the poor in
Religion and Morality and in promoting habits of Industry," he instructed his executors that if these objectives were not fulfilled, the funds
were to be cut off.[9] Freeman's will, like those of Dorrien and Waldo,

   [8] T. Waldo, PROB/11/1138/52; John Dorrien, PROB 11/1124/637.
   [9] L. Namier and J. Brooke, *The House of Commons, 1754–1790*, 3 vols. (London:
H. M. Stationary Office, 1964), 2:383; T. E. Freeman, PROB 11/1475/195.

while continuing posthumous charity, attempted to direct and curb even traditional giving to conform with important social considerations.

The charitable world of London in the 1750s and 1760s was even more active than that of the 1740s, as we shall see. Of the eighty-five committee members of this period for whom I have information, more than half of them contributed to four or more charities, with eighteen donating to six or more.[10] While actively philanthropic and concerned to promote most of the same ends as those who gave to the earlier charities, the donors of midcentury were more wary and cautious about the means employed.

DONORS AND DONATIONS

How did these charities find the money so essential for their operation? Many, if not most, of the techniques employed had been practiced by earlier philanthropic societies, especially self-advertisement and the use of personal connections. These methods were even more intensively and extensively exploited in midcentury. I would now like to look at the process of fundraising and ask a series of interrelated questions about the nature of monetary support for midcentury charities. First, how did directing committees go about convincing people to donate subscriptions, benefactions, or contributions? Second, what were the occasions of such giving and how much was generally given? Finally, who were these donors and why did they give?

First, after having disparaged the role of posthumous charity, we should reconsider the importance of bequests. For, though bequests could not be counted upon to sustain charitable activity, and though increasingly those most intimately involved in charitable direction were not leaving their money to the institutions posthumously, the importance of such "free" grants should not be underrated. One of the main jobs of the secretaries of each of the charities was soliciting and recording such gifts. Charities like the General Lying-in Hospital were even prepared to go to court to secure such deathbed bequests. This kind of donation was especially welcome by the directors. Free from scrutiny, or from attached strings and stipulations, bequests were often invested in annuities and stocks and provided the charity with a regular income in good times, and a source of quick capital in bad. Legacies accounted for about 20 percent of the annual income of most charities. It is scarcely a wonder, therefore, that many charities provided blank forms for such bequests at the end of

---

[10] This, of course, refers to donations over their life's course of giving, and not merely during the 1750s and 1760s. Ten gave to one charity, thirteen to two, seventeen to three, fifteen to four, twelve to five, five to six, seven to seven, three to eight, two to nine, and one to eleven.

their printed charity sermons, and made executors responsible for such donations perpetual governors of their societies. [11]

If the charities could not rely solely on bequests, how then did they go about finding funds? Though the great charity balls and bazaars, so lovingly described by F. K. Prochaska, were money-raising devices of the nineteenth century, the mid-eighteenth century was not without its equivalents. Benefits at theaters and operas, charity sermons and dinners, and contributions following stirring exhortations or choral works in the chapels often attached to the charities were just some of the methods. Even composers as famous and widely patronized as Handel welcomed such occasions for benevolence combined with publicity; in addition to his many well-known concerts and gifts to the Foundling, Handel promised the Lock Hospital an oratorio on March 1753, and he told the Marine in March 1758 that not only could they present his oratorio gratis but that he would perform in it himself. Not all charity performances were so chaste and refined. The governors of the Marine Society planned for an opera to be presented at Ranelagh, one of London's most famous pleasure resorts, and enjoyed the income that David Garrick promised them from the staging of the play *Lara*. The income derived from such events was clearly welcome, even if it was not crucial. The General Lying-in Hospital, for example, reaped £163.11.0 from its benefit day at Covent Garden in 1759.[12]

In addition to such events of pure entertainment, a variety of other pleasurable fundraisers took place. Thus, usually on the anniversary of the establishment of the charity, the society would invite a prominent or popular clergyman to address present and potential donors, and a collection would be taken afterward. Following such a sermon, the governing committee of the Asylum for Orphaned Girls congratulated itself on July 9, 1762, well pleased with a collection of over £226 "and many new sub-

[11] General Lying-in Hospital, *Weekly Minute Book, 1769 to 1777*, July 5, 1774; the charity went to court to secure the £150 bequest of the Hon. William Molesworth. The papers of the General Lying-in Hospital are located at the Greater London Record Office, London. The amount of legacies and their significance in the total finances of each charity varied enormously. Furthermore, several charities lumped legacies with benefactions in their annual reports, or made peculiar reckonings. Thus, the Magdalen, in its 1776 report, noted the legacies of two subscribers who were not yet dead. I have averaged the known legacies of the charities of this period to arrive at the 20 percent figure.

[12] F. K. Prochaska, *Women and Philanthropy in Nineteenth-Century England* (Oxford: Oxford University Press, 1980), chap. 2. Lock Hospital, *General Court Book #1* (July 4, 1746, to May 29, 1762). All of the Lock's records are held by the Royal College of Surgeons, Lincoln's Inn Fields, London: The Marine Society, *The Fair Minutes of the Committee of the Marine Society*, MSY/A/1, p. 348. All Marine Society material is held by the library of the National Maritime Museum, Greenwich. General Lying-in Hospital, *Weekly Minute Book* (1766–1777). For more on the General Lying-in Hospital see Philip Rhodes, *Dr. Leake's Hospital* (London: Davis, Poynter, 1978).

scribers added." The chapel adjacent to the society's buildings was the site of such annual events and was also an ongoing source of revenues. For the Lock Hospital, a charity that suffered from a dearth of subscription and mercantile support, as we gave seen, such income was particularly vital. Thus, the earnings from its chapel (from fees paid for pews and prayer books, for example) amounted to between one-third and one-half of its annual income through the 1780s. Any decline in this necessary income resulted in serious problems for the institution and grave concern among the governors. Thus, in January 1785, due to "the Select Committee having with great concern beheld the very great declension in the Congregation of the Chapel of this Hospital, and consequently a considerable deficiency in its Income, to the great Detriment of the Charity," an inquiry was launched into the reasons for this failure and measures taken to restore the congregation.[13]

Attending an anniversary sermon, and contributing often did not end the charitable day. The sermons were usually followed by charity dinners, convivial occasions that both reaffirmed the solidarity, significance, and worthwhile nature of the enterprise, and allowed one and all to enjoy a hearty meal, for a relatively small sum, in the company of the aristocrats and honored guests who were its presidents and vice presidents. Thus, an important activity of each of these charities was selecting stewards with some care: charitable members who had the financial resources to insure that an event would bring in more income than it cost and the personal resources to attract many diners and potential members to the feast. For, after an evening of fellowship would come the inevitable collection plate, and people, moved by appeals to their good sense made by the speakers at dinner, or by their good spirits, were given the opportunity to publicly pledge.[14]

In addition to whatever money charities derived from such occasions, there were a number of other small but interesting ways that philanthropic societies added to their funds. Perhaps one of the earliest and soonest to disappear was the donation of money as a means of atonement or as penalty. Thus, the contribution of £21 by an anonymous lady to the Asylum for Orphaned Girls on March 24, 1758, under the pseudonym of

[13] Asylum for Orphaned Girls, *Minute Book for the Gentlemen*, March 11, 1761 to April 4, 1765. This is the only surviving record book for the Asylum in the eighteenth century. It is now held by the Royal Shaftesbury Society, London. Lock Hospital, *General Court Book #3* (April 1773 to May 1789).

[14] The annual dinner at the Marine cost 5 shillings and included a pint of wine, *Fair Minutes of the Committee of the Marine Society*, MSY/A/1, May 1, 1760, p. 383. On April 15, 1796, the Philanthropic Society invited that "superstar" of the world of charity, Count Rumford, to attend their annual dinner: see Philanthropic Society, *Minute Book*, 2271/2/2. The papers of the Philanthropic Society are held by the County of Surrey Record Office, Kingston-upon-Thames.

"The Fruits of Repentance," was clearly an example of someone trying to atone for past fault. A similar donation was given to the Marine Society in 1769 to mark the reconciliation of a quarrel, or the £5 donation made to the Magdalen House in 1761, which the anonymous donor had received as the satisfaction for a public injury. Corporations and guilds also found charitable donation an appropriate channel for the fines and penalties they imposed. The Asylum for Orphaned Girls was given £3.7.6 by the Bakers' Company on May 6, 1761, which was a fine laid on one of its members for selling underweight loaves. The Marine was similarly given £6 in fines from the Guildhall and Mansionhouse in February 1774.[15]

Both the Asylum and the Magdalen House benefited from the bequest of the famous Dr. Ward. On his death, Ward left these two charities a certain proportion of the profits from his immensely popular cure-all. The Asylum was so grateful for this additional revenue that it made Robert Dingley, Hanway's old friend and an executor of Ward's will, a perpetual governor on October 13, 1763. Between 1758 and 1768 the sales of Ward's medicine netted the Asylum more than £628. And, though posthumous legacies were increasingly scarce, at least one charity thought it worthwhile to pay a clerk in the Registry Office to keep an eye open for such bequests, lest through inattention or peculation they disappear. Potential donors and executors were soon quick to find out and exploit this desire for bequests. Thus, in 1762 a George Green offered the Asylum £200 that his sister had left him, if, and only if, the orphanage agreed to care for a young girl of his nomination.[16]

The sermons and the dinners, the benefits and the assorted fines, then, were important but secondary sources of income. Of central importance to the economic health of the organization and its ability to manage its functions efficiently was the ability to attract donors and directors who would give each year and shoulder the responsibilities of overseeing the charity's operations and expanding its role and funds simultaneously. Two main methods were employed to entice such people.

---

[15] *An Account of the Institution and Proceedings of the Guardians of the Asylum or House of Refuge . . . for the Reception of Orphaned Girls* (London: n.p., 1763); Marine Society, *Subscription Lists, Donations, Legacies, and Cash Received, 1769–1772*, MSY/u/1; *A List of the Subscribers and a General Account of the Society* with William Dodd, *A Sermon Preached at the Anniversary Meeting of . . . the Magdalen Charity* (London: W. Faden, 1762); Asylum for Orphaned Girls, *Minute Book for the Gentlemen*, May 6, 1761.

[16] Asylum for Orphaned Girls, *Minute Book for the Gentlemen*, October 13, 1763, August 25, 1762; *An Account of the Proceedings of the Guardians of the Asylum* with George Horne, *A Sermon Preached . . . the Anniversary Meeting of the Asylum for Orphan Girls* (London: Harriot Bunce, 1774). The Magdalen charity paid the clerk of the prerogative court £2.12.6 for bringing bequests to their attention: see John Butler, *Sermon for . . . the Magdalen Hospital* (London: H. & R. Causton, 1786).

The first attraction that a charity could offer, one especially important with new or relatively untried charitable ventures, was the presence of the "great," those leaders of the social world whose names on a charity list gave it a certain *éclat*. The value of such pillars of the worlds of fashion and power can be clearly seen when one examines the massive efforts that charities made to secure such names as vice-presidents of their institutions. Thus, the General Lying-in Hospital, using the name of one of its current supporters, Sir Edward Astley, tried to convince Sir John St. Aubyn to act as one of its vice presidents. After writing to him several times, and waiting personally upon him three times, the hospital finally gave up. Similarly, the Lock Hospital sent Thomas Quarme to visit and solicit the marquis of Granby, Lord Monson, Lord Carpenter, and Colonel Lyttleton to act as its vice presidents. Not only was the presence of their names on subscription lists and their attendance at annual dinners guaranteed to attract new support, but they each had a large personal interest, that is, a retinue of dependents and hangers-on who would thus be drawn into the charitable sphere. Thus, on November 5, 1771, application was made to the vice presidents of the General Lying-in Hospital appealing for benefactions and begging them "to honour the Charity with their *Interest*." This "interest" was both personal and territorial; the directing committee of the London Hospital, for example, "at a General Court held Jan 27, 1745, . . . thought [it] proper to add another Vice-President, whose Residence should be at the other End of Town, to support the *Interest* of this Charity there."[17]

The second, and perhaps most important, method for attracting supporters was the constant solicitation that went on in behalf of the charities through networks of acquaintance, friendship, family, and business. It was Hanway's personal contact with Rich, the proprietor of Drury Lane Theater, that was responsible for the Marine benefit of 1758. Fielding's acquaintance with David Garrick enabled the Marine to benefit from the performance of *Lara*. Friends and directors of particular charities used their "interest" with groups with whom they were associated to enhance their organizations' fiscal standing. The Society of Artists in the Strand decided to send the Asylum £50 on June 1, 1761, "through John Blake's *interest*." The Marine sent a letter to Robert Dingley in 1757, "asking for his kind offices with the Dilettanti Club." Sometimes one con-

---

[17] General Lying-in Hospital, *Weekly Minute Book* (1769–1777), April 23, 1771, to April 30, 1771, emphasis added; November 5, 1771; Lock Hospital, *General Court Book Number 1* (1746–1762), October 1750, emphasis added. For the London Hospital, see Matthew Audley, *Sermon Occasioned by the Death of the Duke of Richmond* (London: H. Woodfall, 1751). For this sense of "interest," see Norma Landau, *The Justices of the Peace, 1679–1760* (Berkeley: University of California Press, 1984), p. 21.

tact was not enough; on March 23, 1758, Hanway waited on the marquis of Granby, who also promised his aid with the Dilettanti. Even friends of friends were contacted in the ongoing effort to secure income. The secretary of the Asylum was instructed on September 15, 1763, to send a letter "to Mr. Lane, Castle Yard, Holborn, [asking him] to use his *influence* with the gentleman, who, through his Means, has been a Benefactor to the Magdalen House." The Marine Society asked its current subscribers to send in lists of possible new donors, and the General Lying-in Hospital, on May 26, 1772, sent letters asking each governor to find at least one new subscriber. Little more than two years later, the secretary of the General Lying-in Hospital was told to cannibalize other hospital lists to make up a roster of charitable ladies whom they might approach.[18]

The strength and importance of this web of personal relationships and networks of influence can be seen most clearly in the manner in which provincial subscriptions were generated. In October 1757 a Mr. Littlehales acted as the charitable conduit between the Drapers' Company of Shrewsbury and the Marine Society. Both Michael Adolphus and a Mr. Nash agreed to solicit for the Marine, perhaps while taking the waters, in Bath in November 1757. Contacts, perhaps the Thorntons, netted the Marine £58.5.0 from a group of Hull gentlemen in February 1758. The indirect "stretch" of such personal contacts is well illustrated by Robert Nettleton's 1757 offer to deal with subscriptions from Sussex on the Marine's behalf. In practice, his responsibility ceased when he turned the job over to a Mr. Gideon, who in turn said he would raise the matter with Lord Gage. Nettleton may have known Gideon through their shared involvement in London's banking and financial circles; Gideon's connection with Lord Gage, who came from an old Sussex family, was more intimate—Gideon's daughter had married Gage's son. But despite the value of such indirect connections, much of the actual fundraising demanded personal attention. Hanway, in his efforts in behalf of the Marine in 1758, stressed "the necessity of personal application" and offered to visit the duke of Newcastle and the Honorable Legge himself.[19]

In addition to advertisements in the newspapers appealing for funds and announcing committee meetings, dinners, and elections, no opportunity for publicity was missed. Hanway had the boys of the Marine Society march in proper formation, cleanly dressed and stepping in time to

---

[18] For a good discussion of the centrality of networks, see Ruth McClure, *Coram's Children* (New Haven: Yale University Press, 1981), pp. 22–23. Asylum for Orphaned Girls, *Minute Book for the Gentlemen*, June 1, 1761, emphasis added; Marine Society, *Fair Minute Book*, MSY/A/1, December 22, 1757, March 23, 1758, October 7, 1756. The General Lying-in Hospital, *Weekly Minute Book* (1769–1777), May 26, 1772, January 25, 1774.

[19] Marine Society, *Fair Minute Book*, MSY/A/1, October 6, 1757, November 1757, February 2, 1758, January 19, 1758, October 5, 1758.

fife and drum, through the City of London and over Westminster Bridge on their way to Portsmouth. And in February 1759, when a Captain Palliser, who in the course of his sea campaign, had recaptured the *Winchelsea* and donated some of the prize money to the Marine Society, Hanway was quick to act. Ordering letters to be written to all other naval commanders informing them of Palliser's noble gift, he spurred them on to emulate such munificence by similar donations.[20]

All the charities for which records survive reveal massive problems in collecting the funds that had been pledged. Different charities came up with different solutions. The Marine paid the secretary of the Society for Promoting Christian Knowledge, a Mr. Lane, eight guineas for recovering subscriptions for them. The General Lying-in Hospital hired another man of mercantile acquaintance, a Mr. William Davis of Grocers' Hall, as their collector, offering him 6*d*. on every annual donation of £5.5 or more submitted. At these rates, it is no wonder that many collectors short-circuited the process and kept all the collected funds for themselves. Perhaps that is why the Lock, in the hope of keeping its collector honest, offered the grander sum of a shilling on the pound. A dishonest collector could not only lose the charity vital funds, but create problems for years afterward through court costs and general nuisance.[21]

Subscribers also had to be placated and honored, lest they withdraw support. When a subscriber to the Lock Hospital, a Mr. William Spinnage, offered to paint the hospital for free, the governors gladly accepted, but were unpleasantly surprised when Spinnage sent them a bill for £22. Asked about this, he complained of the "lack of public thanks." Several cases also exist of donors suddenly getting qualms about some particular part of an institution's operations, or being aggrieved at the refusal to admit their sponsored objects, and having to be soothed, visited, and spoken to. There was also the possibility that a governor or exgovernor would do something embarrassing and have to be helped out. Thus, in 1772 the Lock Hospital decided to give an impoverished exsubscriber, Carolina Williams, a weekly annuity of 2*s*.6*d*. for life if she would stop publicly selling (lottery?) tickets and thereby lowering the reputation of the charity.[22]

[20] Marine Society, *Fair Minute Book*, MSY/A/1, March 23, 1758, February 1, 1759.

[21] Lock Hospital, *General Court Book #2* (October 1762 to January 1773), May 1761, April 1769; Marine Society, *Fair Minute Book*, MSY/A/1, September 16, 1756; General Lying-in Hospital, *Weekly Minute Book* (1769–1777), March 28, 1769; Lock Hospital, *General Court Book #1* (1746–1762), May 1762.

[22] Lock Hospital, *General Court Book #1* (1746–1762), February, May 1762; *General Court Book #2* (October 1762 to January 1773). Not untypical was the case of a Miss Tynte, a subscriber to the Philanthropic Society, who formed some unspecified objections to the Female Reform. A governor of the charity, Mr. Coxe, was sent to see her and convince her to continue her support: Philanthropic Society, *Minute Book*, 2271/1/1, February 16,

Having looked at the processes and problems of soliciting revenue for associated charities, let us look at the methods of donation in more detail. Subscribers to the various charities mainly donated in one of two ways. They could either pledge large, lump-sum contributions, ranging from a single or cumulative gift of between ten guineas (for life membership in the Lying-in Charity) to fifty guineas (for life membership in the Lock Hospital), or give smaller sums that would entitle them to vote annually (between one guinea to the Lying-in Charity and ten guineas to the British Lying-in Hospital). In each case, such a gift entitled the giver to vote for the yearly board of directors, and in this way to influence policy, and also allowed donors to recommend recipients for aid to the charity and to fill posts within the charity itself. As we shall see, the interest and activity surrounding the appointment of applicants for charity positions was spectacular and ongoing. Some clearly gave to secure for themselves or their friends valuable positions as charity officers, either administrative (matrons, clerks, secretaries), medical (doctors, surgeons, apothecaries, druggists), religious (preachers), or supply (food, drink, coal, clothes). In the young field of obstetrics especially, hospital practice was essential in order to establish a reputation and attract wealthy clients. Similarly, many young clerics looked upon an appointment as preacher to a popular charity as an important step up the ladder of preferment.

The value of the charitable society as a provider of jobs is well illustrated in the records of attendance at general meetings. The only occasion when one could be certain of almost complete attendance and full and protracted discussion at these meetings was when there was an appointment to be made. Winning such jobs often required more than just friends among the governors. *The Aurora and Universal Advertiser* noted that

> It is to be lamented . . . that the officers of public charities are seldom bestowed on the most meritorious candidates, particularly those where medicinal knowledge is requisite. It is not the man who can be of the greatest utility from his abilities who is most likely to succeed, but he who will spend the most money in procuring proxies.

Doctors often became subscribers so they could be appointed to serve as the charity's physician and then let their donation lapse. This became such a problem that the General Lying-in Hospital governors decided that, since "Gentlemen holding ostensible Offices under the Charity have withdrawn their Subscriptions," it would be necessary for medical officers to subscribe at least three guineas annually throughout the term of their appointment. Donors who were also suppliers to their charity could

---

1798. See also subscribers' withdrawal threats if their objects were not admitted: ibid., February 3, 1797, February 20, 1801.

be every bit as troublesome as manipulative physicians. Thus, when one of the General Lying-in Hospital's suppliers, a Thomas Hammond, sent the charity his bill, they took the occasion to request that "he will pay in the remainder of his subscription money." The same Mr. Blake persuaded the artists of the Strand to donate to the Asylum, and then convinced the charity to rent him part of its premises for his fish manufactory, with the charity paying the rates and taxes on the property. Similarly, Mr. J. Middlemarsh, who donated £5 to the Asylum in 1762, also supplied it, one expects with some profit, with coal. Less crassly, donation for some was clearly an act of corporate benevolence. Thus, "the nobility at the Cocoa Tree" donated the princely sum of £100 to the Marine in 1756, the Antigallicans contributed £21 to the Magdalen House in 1761, the Society of Bucks of Liverpool, a high-living drinking club, proved their patriotism by their £50 gift to the Marine in 1757, and the radical Robin Hood Society matched their zeal, if not their wealth, with a contribution of ten guineas to the same charity.[23]

Not surprisingly, different charities had varying numbers of subscribers. We have already noted, in chapter 2, the wide discrepancies in support between the Foundling and the Lock Hospitals, for example. In the broadest terms, however, all of the charities we consider had more than one hundred and less than five hundred subscribers at midcentury. There was also a wide range of aristocratic and female involvement, as we have already noted. The charities dedicated to maternity had the highest and fastest growing proportion of women subscribers on their lists. While only 15 percent of the City of London Lying-in Hospital's donors in 1753 were female, six years later women doubled their participation rate to 29 percent of the subscribing population. The British Lying-in Hospital and the Lying-in Charity followed similar patterns. Other charities seem to have been much more consistently male dominated. While a few women gave large sums, by and large in every charity there were considerably fewer large-scale female than male donors. In the great majority of charities of this period most male and female subscribers donated less than £10 on average, and probably less than £5. Charitable giving was an activity not only of the very wealthy, but also of the frugal, though comfortable, mercantile classes.[24]

---

[23] *The Aurora and Universal Advertiser*, February 22, 1781, p. 2. In an open letter to the London Dispensary, Henry Haskey said he would not attempt to have himself chosen as their physician because election expenses would amount to about £500. General Lying-in Hospital, *Weekly Minute Book* (1769–1777), March 14, 1775; Asylum for Orphaned Girls, *Minute book for the Gentlemen*, November 18, 1761, February 3, 1762; Marine Society, *Fair Minute Book*, MSY/A/1, December 8, 1757, November 11, 1760.

[24] The total number of City of London Lying-in Hospital subscribers in 1753 was 137, 114 males and 23 females; by 1757, of 147 subscribers, 108 male and 39 female; in 1759,

Aristocratic donation to these charities seems to fall into three distinct types. First are those charities that received relatively little such donation, like the Marine Society and Lying-in Charity, both of whose lists are less than 10 percent nobility. The second group consists of charities like the Foundling Hospital, with a fair sprinkling of nobility, and, finally, those that had many noble donors, like the British Lying-in Hospital, almost a third of whose subscribers by 1770 were aristocrats. As we have seen, however, even when relatively scarce, their importance to a charity was greater than their numbers. At this crucial period in charity formation, aristocratic donation and support was still quite significant.[25]

There were thousands of Londoners who gave at one time or another to one of the charities under review. Most people undoubtedly gave to one charity and considered their duty done. Some, however, gave again and again. It is this much smaller group that we must now examine. These 138 donors who were active between 1740 and 1770, averaging involvement in 5 charities, were by no means typical. In order to qualify for inclusion in this sample, each had to contribute to at least half (three) of the major foundations of the midcentury. However, their atypicality may perhaps most boldly illustrate the importance of several of the factors we have been considering. What then was this group of super givers like and what ties, if any, bound them together?

Fifteen of these major donors were female and twenty were upper class. While this is not an enormous involvement of either group, it is also not trifling. While some, like Sir Charles Asgill, left estates of £160,000 at their death, or, even more impressively, the fortune of £500,000 that Sampson Gideon left to his heir or the £900,000 that Sir Samuel Fluyder was reputedly worth at his death, several others experienced bankruptcy

of 189 subscribers, 134 male and 55 female. The British Lying-in Hospital went from 35 percent female subscription (64 of 181) in 1751, to 42 percent (127 of 304) in 1757. The Lying-in Charity went from 21 percent female subscription (79 of 380) in 1767, to 22 percent (135 of 603) by 1770. In the Marine Society of 1756 only 4.5 percent (20) of its total number of subscribers (444) were women. The Magdalen went from 17 percent female representation (62 out of 361) in 1759 to only 11 percent by 1768 (53 of 463). Fifty-eight percent of male and 80 percent of female subscribers to the Marine Society in 1757 gave less than £10; in 1770 more than 80 percent of male and almost 90 percent of female subscribers to the Lying-in Charity gave sums of less than £10; 66 percent of male and 82 percent of female donors to the British Lying-in Hospital in 1757 gave less than this sum, while the Magdalen had the highest percentage of larger subscribers, with 44 percent of male and 54 percent of female donors giving less than £10 in 1759.

[25] In 1757 the Marine had 34 upper class donors (out of 444), while the Lying-in Charity had only 28 such givers in 1770 (of a total of 603 contributors). Of the Foundling's 959 governors in 1767, 145 were gentle. The British Lying-in Hospital had 15 percent upper class subscribers in 1751; by 1757 this had climbed to 23 percent, and by 1770 was up to 28 percent.

at some time in their careers. Even charity, it seems, could not stave off this most dreaded of commercial occurrences.[26]

One important network of interest bringing potential major donors together was the lively artistic and scientific life of London, as we have seen in looking at Hanway's own circle. In this group of major givers we have both one of the century's best known writers, Samuel Richardson, and the model for one of his last heroes, Sir Charles Grandison. At least eighteen of these men belonged to one or more of such societies as the Royal, the Dilettanti, the Society of Antiquarians, or the Society for Encouraging the Arts. Drawn from a broad range of social circumstance, from different religious and ethnic groups, these cultural societies were one of the many foci for the enlistment of charitable donors and directors.[27]

In keeping with Owen's comments on the relative lack of committed religious motivation among this group is the moderate number of donors (nineteen) who either belonged to an organization like the Society for Promoting Christian Knowledge or had a reputation for piety, like William, second earl of Dartmouth, "who wears a coronet and prays." While these are very rough indicators of religious sensibility, it will be interesting to note changes even in these as the century progressed. As important, perhaps, was the significance of charitable giving and direction for men involved in municipal or national politics. Twenty-five members of Parliament and six City politicians were among these major givers. Although their charitable activities often preceded their political involvement, both kinds of activity have similar elements. Both depended on connection and interest, both sought simultaneously to improve the public condition and their personal position, and both derived from a conception of political authority with important, though only implied, social obligations.

I have read fifty-eight (or more than 40 percent) of their wills. Of these fifty-eight people, who were so involved in their lifetime with charity, more than half (53.4 percent) did not bequeath any money for benevolent purposes. However, this is still a larger proportion of charitable bequests than was found among the larger, undifferentiated sample discussed in chapter 2, of whom two-thirds left nothing. On closer examination of the wills, however, we notice that eleven of these posthumous donors left funds for other than the time-honored gifts of gloves or money to the poor at one's funeral. These eleven are very interesting. As far as I can

---

[26] The major donors who went bankrupt were George Colebrooke, Alexander Fordyce, S. T. Janssen, and Henry Shiffner.

[27] The members of these societies were George Colebrooke; Richard Dalton; the earl of Dartmouth; Robert Dingley; Sir John Fielding; Thomas Fluyder; Jonas Hanway; Thomas Hollis; Edward Hooper; the earl of Northumberland; Robert, Lord Romney; Joseph Salvador; Sir George Savile; the Honorable Charles Townshend; the duke of Bedford; the duke of Portland; and Earl Cardigan.

tell, eight were bachelors or childless; perhaps since they couldn't leave the charities to their sons to direct, bequests had to do instead. Of the twenty-seven donors who were also committee members whose wills I have read, eighteen left nothing by bequest to any charity. It seems, therefore, that these givers and directors preferred not to leave money to charity, but that when they did it was because of a lack of heirs.[28]

Neither upper-class nor female participation was out of line with the general findings: almost one-fifth were nobles, more than a tenth were female. Much more significant, however, was mercantile involvement. Comprised of financiers, stockbrokers, company directors, foreign and domestic merchants and manufacturers, these seventy-one men in many ways controlled charitable finance and spending. Of the entire group, ninety (65.2 percent) gave as part of a family pattern, that is, not only they, but at least one other (and often many other) family members also contributed to charity. Of the business community, fifty-three of the seventy-one (74.6 percent) had such family connections. Brothers especially abounded. There are seven sets of brothers in this group of major givers, as well as several men who had brothers who were charitably involved, but not on the same scale, including Sir George Colebrooke, member of Parliament, stockbroker, and banker, and his brother James; Benjamin Mendes da Costa's brothers Isaac and Moses; Robert Dingley's brother Charles; John Fielding's literary half-brother Henry; and Alexander Fordyce's respectable clerical brother. There is at least one uncle-nephew and two husband-wife sets in this group. There were several other interesting familial and business connections: Peter Delme and his sister Lady Ravensworth both were major givers. Isaac Akerman, china merchant, married his daughter to the banker William Noble, another major donor. Sir John Barnard's daughter married Sir Thomas Hankey, brother of Sir Joseph and uncle of J. C. Hankey, both major donors, while one of Barnard's executors, John Small, a Russia Company merchant, was also one of this select circle. Peter Gaussen, a Huguenot silk merchant, married the daughter of another Huguenot major giver, Samuel Bosanquet, the brother of Jonas Hanway's old friend and major contributor Jacob. Jacob's daughter, in turn, married Gaussen's son Samuel Robert. Three of Stephen Peter Godin's daughters married men in this group, or their near

---

[28] The eleven who left money to the newer charities were Michael Adolphus (left £10 to the British and £10 to the Marine), Sir John Barnard (£50 to the Foundling), Peter Gaussen (£100 to the Foundling, £100 to the Magdalen), S. P. Godin (£5 to the Foundling and £50 to the Magdalen), Thomas Hanson (£500 to the Magdalen and to the Foundling), Thomas Hollis (left money to endow libraries all over the world), Vansittart Hudson (£100 to the Foundling), James Matthias (£50 to the Marine), John Smith (£80 to the Marine), Barlow Trecothick (£500 to the City of London Lying-in Hospital), and John Whiston (£50 each to the Asylum for Orphaned Girls, the Magdalen, and the Lying-in Charity). As far as I can tell from their wills, Adolphus, Hanson, Hollis, Hudson, Smith, and Whiston were unmarried and Matthias and Trecothick childless.

relations. The first wed John Cornwall, ropemaker, Russia Company member, and director of the Bank of England; the second married Godfrey Thornton, cousin of John Thornton, also a Russia Company member and major giver; and the third married John, brother of Henry Shiffner, yet another Russia Company merchant. Henry Shiffner's father, Matthew (a relation of the Grenvilles), had been a business partner of Samuel Holden, the husband of another large donor, Jane Holden. When Shiffner's firm became insolvent in 1761, John Thornton, friend and ally of Hanway's in Russia Company business and charity work, and almost-relation of Henry's, called on Shiffner's knowledge and expertise to salvage what could be saved of the wreck. The centrality of the Russia Company link, mysterious as it is, continued to hold even further. Thomas Hanson, merchant of Crosby Square, was one of the executors of the will of Benjamin Longuet, Bank of England and South Sea Company director and member of the Russia Company. When Hanson died in 1770, James Matthias, Hamburg merchant, London Assurance director, and Russia Company member, was one of his executors. Matthias and Hanway, much of an age, must have known each other well, if not through the Russia Company then as directors of the Marine Society in the 1750s.

Before discussing the Russia Company further, we should examine other interconnections. Hanway, who had dedicated the third volume of his *Historical Account* to the naval hero and husband of another major donor, Lady Anson, also knew Barlow Trecothick, North America merchant and Trecothick's partner in sending food and funds to North America, Sir George Colebrooke, from their time together as directors of the Marine Society. Thomas Fluyder, whose brother Samuel Hanway knew from their involvement as directors of the Magdalen charity in the 1760s, appointed Trecothick as one of his executors. Thus, the dense mix of family, business, and charity was both potent and tremendously useful for the recruitment to, training of leaders for, and stability of philanthropic societies. Furthermore, to get ahead of ourselves, we can see that this web continued over the next two generations or more. Of these 138 donors, 19 were familially related to the major donors of the years between 1790 and 1820.[29]

To return to the puzzling role of the Russia Company in this process.

---

[29] There were twenty-five aristocrats (17.9 percent) and fifteen women (10.8 percent) among this sample. Mercantile men composed 51 percent of the total sample. The seven sets of brothers are the Bosanquets (Samuel and Jacob), the Fluyders (Samuel and Thomas), the Franks (Aaron and Naphtali), the Hoares (Henry and Richard), the Hornes (Samuel and John), and the Stanhopes (the Honorable Charles and Phillip). James Colebrooke contributed to the Smallpox Hospital, the Foundling, and the London Hospital. In addition to the brothers mentioned were Edwin Lascelles's brother Daniel, John Lefevre's brother Peter, Joseph Martin's brothers John and James, and Henry Shiffner and his brother John. The uncle and nephew were Isaac and Abraham Henckell; the two couples were the Honorable and Mrs. Southwell, and the Honorable George and Mrs. Grenville.

While it was undoubtedly the case that an undue number of significant charitable donors belonged to it, as yet no really adequate explanation exists for why this should have been the case. Perhaps the hardiness required or the distances from England made this type of merchant more willing to undertake the difficult task of aiding the nation while aiding the poor. Whatever the reason, it remained a narrow but tight focus for charitable leadership. At least nine of its members appear among the major subscribers to charitable efforts in this period. Of the eight of these Russia Company directors who were also major donors, seven were directors of charities to which they contributed. Whatever the reason for the overrepresentation of this particular company, among the major charitable donors, it seems clear that shared business interests led to and reinforced shared charitable concerns.[30]

THE MENTAL WORLD OF THE MIDCENTURY DONOR

This discussion of the charitable world of midcentury London began with Hanway and his central role in it. We must now return to Hanway to understand the continuity and change that occurred in charitable institutions of this period.

Hanway's thought and prose are full of ambiguities: alternately very prolix and very muddled, optimistic and wildly fearful, resigned and constantly urging to action. This is perhaps an accurate reflection of the mind and spirit of his generation, for in many ways Hanway shared the problems and prejudices of his contemporaries. In some respects their work, like his, was a jeremiad, full of condemnation of modern luxury and corruption.[31] Decrying urban living because "vice and lewdness, in all their variety of shapes, revel in cities and flourish among the votaries of elegance,"[32] condemning the voluntary childlessness of many of the upper classes who disdained marriage from "a mean avarice, and an ambitious vanity"[33] and the involuntary inability to marry of their servants and many of the poor,[34] Hanway and his contemporaries often seem to be

[30] For the involvement of Russia Company merchants, see the explanation offered by J. S. Taylor, *Jonas Hanway*, pp. 59–60. See also David S. Macmillan, "The Russia Company of London in the Eighteenth Century," *Guildhall Miscellany*, 4 (1973), pp. 222–36.

[31] A good example is the Cambridge University prizewinning essay by William Bell, *A Dissertation on . . . Causes . . . Contribute to Render a Nation Populous* (Cambridge: J. Bentham, 1756), p. 15.

[32] Ibid., pp. 18–19, 15. See also John Brown, *An Estimate of the Manners and Principles of the Times*, 2 vols. (London: L. Davis & C. Reymer, 1758), 2:186–88; Samuel Fawconer, *An Essay on Modern Luxury* (London: James Fletcher, 1765), pp. 6–7.

[33] Bell, *Dissertation*, pp. 12–13.

[34] Jonas Hanway, *Letters on the Importance of the Rising Generation of the Labouring Part of Our Fellow-Subjects*, 2 vols. (London: A. Millar & T. Cadell, 1767), 2:159. See also Bell, *Dissertation*, p. 10.

advocating a return to earlier, simpler times. In keeping with this bucolic nostalgia was the common proposal to give allotments to the rural poor, to attach them to the land, to increase national procreation, and to recreate a race of hardy and patriotic peasants,[35] ready to defend their land and their lords from foreign depredations. Thomas Short's paean of praise for the conditions and values of the simple country life was typical: "a rural Life was the first State of Mankind, and as it is still the healthiest and affords the truest and most innocent natural Pleasures: For there . . . still remains such Vestiges of Virtue, Sobriety, Regularity, Plainness and Simplicity of Diet Etc. as bears some small Image or Resemblance of the primeval State."[36] To return to such a state of virtue, Hanway proposed the reestablishment of truly paternal bonds, bonds of affection and trust between servants and masters. This he thought could only be accomplished through the abolition of vails, or tipping. This modern, degenerate practice, he believed, intruded between masters and servants, introducing the cash nexus into the sheltered world of the home and dividing loyalties and obligations. "I am morally certain," said Thomas Trueman, Hanway's alter ego, "that the *Abolition* of *Vails* will be the *restoration* of the *harmony of families*, as much as the reformation of any Abuse can be. . . . We should probably find more indulgence in *Sickness*, and *Old Age*; greater *promotion* and *Assistance* in case of *Wedlock*; and there would be more *conjugal Faith* in our rank of life."[37]

In many ways, then, Hanway seemed to speak for the values of an earlier time, a time before the growth of commerce, the growth of luxury, and the growth of an unattached, uncared-for poor. John Brown also portrayed this idyllic, rural past as a time when "the *great* People of course mixed with their *Neighbours* in the Country: This generous Communication naturally created or improved in them a Spirit of Benevolence toward their Countrymen, though their inferiors."[38] We seem to hear in Hanway, and in many others of this period, the echoes of earlier thinkers and earlier themes. Like many of the seventeenth-century clerics we have noted in chapter 1, Hanway claimed that when the rich enjoyed the superfluities of life and the poor starved, this was an act of political injustice. "Luxury," noted Samuel Fawkener, "is an injustice to the poor de-

---

[35] Hanway, *Letters*, 2:207. See also Bell, *Dissertation*, p. 16; *Observations on the Number and Misery of the Poor, on the Heavy Rates Levied for Their Maintenance, and on the General Causes of Poverty* (London: T. Becket and P. A. Dehondt, 1765), pp. 43–44; Wallace, *A Dissertation on the Numbers of Mankind in Ancient and Modern Times* (Edinburgh: Archibald Constable, 1753), p. 19.

[36] Thomas Short, *New Observations Natural, Moral, Civil, Political, and Medical, on City, Town, and Country Bills of Mortality* (London: Longmans, 1750), p. 1.

[37] Jonas Hanway, *Eight Letters on . . . the Custom of Vails-Giving* (London: C. Henderson, 1760), pp. 29–30. See also Hanway, *Reflections, Essays, and Meditations on Life and Religion* (London: J. Rivington, 1761), pp. 48, 116–17.

[38] Brown, *Estimate*, 1:73–74; Hanway, *Letters*, 2:110.

frauding them of that portion, which reason and religion give them a right
to expect."[39] Furthermore, like the earlier opponents of Mandeville, Hanway asserted that true self-love was identical with the fulfillment of social
duties, and thus best pursued in the improvement of the public realm. The
purpose of "that first and strongest passion of [human] nature," remarked Bishop Warburton, "is to assist the heart to awaken Virtue, and
to push out and develop the great principle of BENEVOLENCE."[40]

Like the political arithmeticians, thinkers of this period held that national wealth arose from the number and work of the common laborer.
"For were it not for the incessant drudgery of the Poor, we should soon
be brought back again, even amidst our largest accumulation of fortune,
to a condition of distress."[41] Like the earlier political calculators, Hanway
and his contemporaries continued to employ the language of political
arithmetic, speaking often of the pecuniary value of human life. Hanway,
however, remarked that the nation benefited by the mere employment of
the poor, and not only by the profits derived from their labor.[42] This view
resembles the proposal made in the late seventeenth century by Sir William Petty that a pyramid should be built on Salisbury plain, for no other
reason than to keep the poor working. Yet Hanway often spoke glow-
ingly of the importance of utility. And, unlike the earlier arithmeticians,
Hanway emphasized the economic value of popular consumption. Employment then was important because it "primed the pump," got people
working, and their consumption created more work. Unlike the arithmeticians as well, Hanway stressed the importance of a large population to
maintain England's new imperial destiny, to provide soldiers, sailors, and
settlers for its worldwide dominions. Petty and his contemporaries would
have had no disagreement with Hanway about the four ends of national
policy: increasing the numbers of the laboring poor, provision of cheap
necessities, low prices of goods destined for export, and a thriving, widespread religious observance.[43] They would also have agreed that the role
of government was to preserve both the rich and the poor, to bolster and
create the circumstances for the practice of proper subordination and
concern.[44] For such subordination was providentially ordered:

[39] Fawconer, *Essay on Modern Luxury*, pp. 37–39. See also Hanway, *Letters*, 2:102;
Samuel Squire, *A Sermon for the London Hospital* (London: Woodfall, 1765), p. 12.

[40] William Warburton, *The Works of the Right Reverend William Warburton*, Richard
Hurd, ed., 12 vols. (London: Luke Hansard for T. Cadell and W. Davies, 1811), "The Love
of God and Man," 9:57; Hanway, *Letters*, 2:2.

[41] Warburton, *Works*, 9:21. See also Hanway, *Letters*, 2:88.

[42] Hanway, *Letters . . . Rising Generation*, pp. 97, 93.

[43] Ibid., pp. 27, 246, 129, 162, 122–23.

[44] Hanway, *Letters . . . Rising Generation*, 2:19, 168. See also John Thomas, *Sermon
before the Governors of the the Middlesex Hospital* (London: John Whiston, 1750), pp. 7–
8; Lawson, *Occasional Sermons*, pp. 87–88; Warburton, *Works*, "Sermon . . . before the
Governors of the London Hospital" (1767), 10:259.

He could certainly have provided for all his Creatures without any of our Assistance: He could have *open'd his Hand and fill'd all Things Living with Plenteousness*: But this Dispensation affords Room for trying and proving us in a Manner suitable to his Wisdom and our Reasonable Nature: The *Rich* and *Poor* now *meet together* and may both be the wiser and better for that Diversity of Circumstances, in which his Providence has plac'd them.[45]

However, while Hanway and many of his generation employed the language of political arithmetic, and often analyzed society in an arithmetical manner, they never entirely accepted the implications of commercial society, or believed that God and Mammon were reconciliable.[46] Brown warned that although "it seems to be the ruling Maxim of this Age and Nation, that if our Trade and Wealth are but increased, we are powerful, happy and secure," in fact, "There never was a more fatal Error more greedily embraced by any People."[47] Hanway railed against the desire for profit, unchecked consumption, emulation, and modern manners. In their place he recommended hard work and massive charity, heroic thrift and public service, and, above all, marriage and family living.[48] Like Hanway, William Bell believed "that whatever is calculated to preserve a frugal simplicity of taste and manners, to regulate the luxurious fancies, and restrain the fruitless indulgencies of a people; is so far adapted to increase the populousness of a nation."[49] Yet, at another moment, Hanway recognized the realities of contemporary life. He realized that England's economy was caught between the older regulated model and the unregulated free market. Commenting on the older laws controlling buying and selling, he said that the enforcement of such laws in his own day would create "something more of terror than of any law which comes new from the hands of the legislator." While accepting as self-evident that trade required freedom, he still could not accept the unrestrained liberty of the marketplace.[50] Similarly the author of *Political Speculations, or an Attempt to Discover the Causes of the Dearness of Provisions*, who commented on the deleterious effect of London's great size and growth, felt that "to forbid people coming to reside in the metropolis by any law

[45] John Thomas, *Sermon . . . before Governors of the Middlesex Hospital* (1752), pp. 7–8.

[46] Hanway, *Letters*, 2:157. See also John Forster, *Sermon to the Northampton Infirmary* (Cambridge: Stamford & Co., 1757), p. 47.

[47] Brown, *Estimate*, 2:150–51; John Sekora, *Luxury: The Concept in Western Thought* (Baltimore: Johns Hopkins University Press, 1977).

[48] Hanway, *Letters*, 2:228, 118, 184, 249. See chapter 4 for a contrary view. See also Thomas, *Sermon*, pp. 3–4; Brown, *Estimate*, 1:59.

[49] Bell, *Dissertation*, p. 5. See also Brown, *Estimate*, 2:186–88.

[50] Hanway, *Letters*, 2:223–24. Hanway adds, "trade, though founded on liberty, which enriches, has also a tendency to enslave and impoverish. And it requires a skillful management to ward off this consequence" (ibid., 121).

would be falling heavy upon the liberty of the subject."[51] Hanway was a realist. He saw, unlike many other contemporary writers who romanticized the rude but robust health of England's laboring classes, that the children of the rich were well fed and thus more likely to live than those of the working poor.[52] Advocating the importance of national religion, he was not above bribing the poor to read and study their Bibles.[53] Recognizing the potential political threat that a large and dissatisfied body of poor posed, he did not recommend repressive measures, but instead pointed out how imperative it was that they be made happy. Arguing for a system of care that would make the poor feel deep repugnance for any trace of dependency, he applauded the poor law that tamed the laborer enough to preserve his wealthier neighbor from his wrath, but left him ferocious enough to fight against England's enemies.[54]

Many of Hanway's contemporaries, however, thought that charity more effectively cared for the needy than the poor law. The anonymous author of *An Essay on the Causes of the Decline of the Foreign Trade* (1744), for example, blamed the poor law for general idleness and high wages among working people. If they only, he mused, had "nothing to depend upon but their industry, or the character of it to recommend them to the charitable in their misfortunes," they would be better laborers and citizens. Bishop Warburton concurred, lamenting "that beneficent, but ill-judged policy, of providing for the Poor by law." Instead, he argued that the erection of voluntary hospitals, "though it can operate but slowly," might one day replace the need for legal assistance, and thus "put some stop to the growing mischiefs of that provision." In the creation of a wide variety of philanthropic institutions "charity and policy will then go hand in hand," England's domestic police and international position would improve, and commerce and trade would flourish.[55]

What gives much of the writing of this period a sense of immediacy and urgency was the feeling that Hanway shared with his contemporaries of imminent and important changes in the political and social structure of

[51] *Political Speculations, or an Attempt to Discover the Causes of the Dearness of Provisions* (London: J. Almon, 1767), pp. 8–9.

[52] For example, see Henry Fielding, *A Proposal for Making an Effectual Provision for the Poor, for Amending Their Morals, and for Rendering Them Useful Men* (London: printed for A. Millar, 1753), pp. 4–5. In contrast, see Hanway, *Letters,* 2:86.

[53] Ibid., 2:79.

[54] Ibid., pp. 63, 163. For Hanway's view on ferocity and dependency see *Letters to the Guardians of the Infant Poor* (London: A. Millar & T. Cadell, 1767), p. 13; Warburton, *Works,* 10:62.

[55] *An Essay on the Causes of the Decline of the Foreign Trade* in John R. McCulloch, ed., *A Select and Valuable Collection of Tracts* (New York: A. M. Kelley, 1966), p. 201; Warburton, *Works,* 10:255, 258; William Dodd, *A Sermon before the President, Vice President, Treasurer, and Governors of the Magdalen House,* 2nd ed. (London: W. Faden, 1759), p. 4.

the nation. Some feared an impending war between the haves and have-nots: "Something however must be timely resolved on before affairs come to a fatal crisis and the Poor snatch the remedy themselves."[56] Others feared God's judgment against a wicked England in the shape of earthquakes and natural disasters: "And lo! the most terrible of God's judgments *hath been abroad in the earth* . . . strange and astonishing agitations of the sea were seen and felt; our own shores trembled."[57] And others, noting a probable war, reminded Britons of those "towering heights of Glory" to which the "greatest Empires of the World, now no more, fell successive sacrifices" because of irreligion, vice, and libertinism.[58] No one, however, knew what it was that might happen, or even whether it was likely to turn out for good or ill. Most felt it was a time to gird ones loins, to look into the concerns of the nation, to do whatever could be done by private citizens or societies to turn the impending crisis into triumph.[59] Like many others, Hanway saw charitable practice as having an important role to play in this upcoming struggle. The role of charity was central; only charity could mediate between rich and poor and act as a counterbalance "to all the evil passions of envy, covetousness, revenge, so frequent, so pernicious."[60] Only charity, "which, in the absence of FAITH, and during the loss of HOPE, may supply their place and restrain the madness of a desperate people,"[61] offered a possible remedy for "the hunger of the poor, crying aloud."[62]

[56] *Observations on the Number and Misery of the Poor*, pp. 33–34.

[57] Lawson, *Sermons*, pp. 96–97.

[58] John Forster, *Sermon*, p. 47.

[59] Note the anxiety that the outbreak and early reversals of the Seven Years' War caused Mr. Urban, in the introductory poem for 1756 in the *Gentleman's Magazine*: "O could thy Hand, with honest Pride record, / Still as of old the Feats of Britain's Sword!— / Vain wish!—'twas giv'n thee once with Joy to tell, / What Palms brave Vernon won at Porto-bell; / . . . Reluctant now; by Truth and Sorrow led, / You shew Minorca lost, and Braddock dead; / . . . Rise! Britain rise! by Arms her Peace restore, / And yet again be what thou wast before; . . ." See also Hanway's encomium to the heroic benignity of the mercantile world, *Letters . . . the Rising Generation*, 2:231–32. A more balanced account can be found in Wallace, *Dissertation*, pp. 238–40.

[60] Lawson, *Sermons*, pp. 93–94.

[61] Warburton, "Sermon . . . London Hospital," *Works*, 10:262.

[62] Hanway, *Letters . . . Rising Generation*, 2:223–24. "Nor is an occasional effort of benevolence sufficient to answer the great ends of virtuous liberty: it must be a permanent principle of action: it must be in *politics* what charity is in *religion*. . . . Indeed in the same view that the exercise of humanity is an essential part of religion, succor to a distressed countryman is an essential part of liberty" (ibid., 110). See also Samuel Squire, *Sermon . . . before the Governors of the Smallpox Hospital* (London: H. Woodfall, 1760), "The Support of Smallpox Hospitals Recommended," p. 3.

CHAPTER FOUR

Charitable Foundations, 1750–1770

COMMENTING IN 1854 on the incorporation of the major London charities of the 1740s and 1750s, Sir George Nicholls noted that

> The above six Acts [of incorporation] passed in the early part of the reign of George the Third, possess much interest as exhibiting the spirit by which the public of that day was actuated. They were all expressly designed to aid and give permanent and increased effect to institutions originating in private benevolence, supported by private charity, and carried into operation by the exertion of private individuals, who thus became, as it were, the pioneers of legislation, enabling it to proceed on assured grounds, tested by time and proved by experience.[1]

As we have seen in chapter 3, a number of midcentury writers on charity and poverty hoped that benevolence might replace legal care for the poor. Nicholls, however, was not incorrect in thinking that the foundation of the midcentury societies was part of a larger effort to reform both voluntary and public relief. Hanway, writing just two years after the simultaneous outbreak of the Seven Years' War and a rash of new charitable societies, as usual, voiced the hopes of his colleagues in philanthropy: "If we can thus introduce [through the establishment of innovative charities like the Marine and Magdalen] some kind of *police*, though under a private management, we may in time awaken the attention of our fellow-subjects; and if the laws already provided are . . . really insufficient, some amendments may be made to them."[2] We must look at the progress of these charities then, to see how attempts to aid the war effort and to promote an improved police found concrete expression.

THE FOUNDLING HOSPITAL, 1750–1770

Given the new level of national urgency, all existing charities were scrutinized with an eye to making them more useful and more productive. Initially, this concern merely led to an expansion of existing charities. Thus, the Foundling, like many of the institutions of the 1740s, continued

---

[1] Sir George Nicholls, *A History of the English Poor Law*, 2 vols. (London: John Murray, 1854), 2:73.

[2] Jonas Hanway, *Letter to Robert Dingley* (London: R. & J. Dodsley, 1758), pp. 27–28.

to grow in its second decade. As early as 1747 pamphlets and letters in popular magazines appeared urging the government to aid the Foundling financially. The form that this aid was to take varied from proposal to proposal. One suggested doubling and diverting each Sunday's London turnpike tolls to the hospital, thus augmenting the charity's funds by £1,600 per annum. Another proposed that private gambling be outlawed, and public gambling taxed for the support of the hospital.[3] The outbreak of war in 1756 seemed especially to enliven philanthropic experimentation. As Hanway remarked, "The nation is upon a trial of experiments, and it is a noble and useful, not a wanton trial; and the more necessary, as war consumes our people."

The Foundling was one of the first of the charities to be brought into public discussion. The hospital seemed a kind of exemplar of popular charity, a model of how organized philanthropy should operate. Thus, Hanway, in the guise of "an English country gentleman," commented that he could "by no means acknowledge the FOUNDLING HOSPITAL to be a LOCAL CHARITY, 'tho confined to the bills of mortality. London is but the magazine of the three Kingdoms, and of the world, and it receives every body; like the SUN it absorbs all lesser fires; but then it again emits its beams, and invigorates the whole."[4] However, when Parliament did act in 1756, it adopted none of these suggestions,[5] but voted that £100,000 be given to the Foundling on the condition that it admit any and all infants brought to it who were under two months of age. Both contemporaries and subsequent historians have judged this donation to have been a consequence of the outbreak of war. Hanway noted that "it was not till the last Spanish war broke out that Mr. Coram broached his scheme of a Foundling Hospital and it was not until the present French war that the parliament protected it."[6] The results of the open admissions policy were staggering. In the three and a half years from June 1756 to December 1759, the hospital admitted over 13,600 children. By the time the government had decided to withdraw its support in 1760, the hospital had admitted almost 15,000 infants, of whom only about 4,400 lived to be apprenticed. Even before the terrible mortality rates of children admitted during these four years became clear, and before the government had withdrawn, popular opinion had turned against the program of universal

[3] *Gentleman's Magazine* (April 1747), p. 164; Citizen of London, *The Vices of the Cities of London and Westminster* (London: Charles Corbett, 1751), p. 32.

[4] *The Genuine Sentiments of an English Country Gentleman, upon the Present Plan of the Foundling Hospital*, 2nd ed. (London: G. Woodfall, 1760), pp. 33, 24.

[5] For an account of the charity's petition to Parliament, see *Gentleman's Magazine* (March 1756), p. 147.

[6] [Hanway], *A Candid Historical Account of the Hospital . . . for Exposed and Deserted Children*, 2nd ed. (London: G. Woodfall, 1760), p. 25.

admissions, though not entirely against the hospital. Symbolic of this, perhaps, is the fact that in 1756 Hanway became a governor of the Foundling, and from then to the end of his life intimately involved himself with its management. However, Hanway was also one of the hospital's most outspoken critics. He felt that the institution had veered from its true purpose and that he was helping to return it to its original intentions, getting it "back on the tracks."

Hanway was not the Foundling's only critic; there was usually a passage in one of his works that echoes many contemporary views.[7] Among the charges was the old one that the institution encouraged celibacy and immorality. F.Y., in a letter to Mr. Urban in the *Gentleman's Magazine*, commented that "tho' this charity may be productive of the aforementioned good [of the preservation of a great number of lives] may it not at the same time be looked upon as an encouragement to celibacy by being an open asylum for illegitimates."[8] As well, the program called forth a host of new minor and major criticisms. One interesting charge was that illegitimate children would make bad soldiers and sailors, and thus fail to fulfill one of the hospital's major social goals. For how, asked the author of *Considerations on the Bill for Obliging all Parishes in the Kingdom to keep Registers of Births, Deaths and Marriages*, could children who had never known parental acknowledgment and affection ever be valuable or loyal soldiers?

> Are these foundlings when they grow up to manhood, to be the men to fight in defense of their country? Alas! what country have they, who have no relations, who have been abandoned in their infancy by their own parents, and have known nothing of the effects of natural affection exercised toward themselves. How shall they love their country, who have never had any love shewed them by parents or relations?[9]

This difficulty was set aside both by Hanway and by the reviewer in the *Gentleman's Magazine*, who replied that the absence of parental affection in no way prevented a foundling from becoming an excellent soldier.

> But if this gentleman would look into our fleets and armies he would soon be convinced that they consist at present of such as parental care has not trained to that or any other service, and such as derive no motives to discharge the

---

[7] One of the more radical and unusual attacks on the hospital suggested that money should be given directly to the babies' mothers for their support. "This," said the anonymous author of the pamphlet *Populousness with Economy, the Wealth and Strength of a Kingdom* (London: J. Brickland, 1759), "would soon put all partial, unnatural pretended charities out of countenance; here every mother is the nurse of her own children" (p. 27).

[8] *Gentleman's Magazine* (Supplement 1759), pp. 622–23.

[9] [F. Maseres], *Considerations on the Bill for Obliging all Parishes in the Kingdom to Keep Registers of Births, Deaths, and Marriages* (London: M. Cooper, 1759), p. xx. See also *Gentleman's Magazine* (February 1759), p. 55.

duties of their station from filial affection. Every foundling born in *England* is an *Englishman*, and has as much the honour of *Old England* at heart, as if he knew of what particular *Englishman* he was the son.[10]

A much more serious criticism hurled against indiscriminate admission was that it would encourage the married poor to cast off their legitimate children so as not to have to support them. Since the necessity to support their children was one of the few incentives the poor had to labor at all, the guaranteed admission of the children of the poor would remove this most vital motive. "To take in the children of the Poor indiscriminately might not only tend to weaken parental affection, a circumstance well worthy consideration; but it might also tend to increase the general idleness universally complained of by masters in most manufactures."[11] Another striking criticism of open admissions was that the policy perverted the original aims of the institution, which were directed only to the care of London's illegitimate and deserted infants. Hanway and his friends believed that unrestricted admissions would have widespread ill consequences on the morals of hitherto innocent country people.

> I am of the opinion, that the original intent of the Foundling Hospital was for the reception of the exposed, within the bills of mortality only; and not designed as a publick nursery of illegitimates for the community. An intention certainly of the greatest good, and will always remain so, whilst under proper restrictions: for it is the abuse of any thing that renders it pernicious and culpable. To provide for deserted innocents, is not only becoming the dignity of human nature, but is the greatest of charities: But then to encourage parents to desert their children must be allowed to be the greatest of evils. I am therefore so far from thinking this hospital a moral benefit to society under its present extension, that it appears to me to be quite the reverse.[12]

The force of popular opinion made itself clearly felt—the hospital had exceeded its original and proper purposes and overextended the scope of its operations. Thus, in 1760 Parliament withdrew its support for further admissions, while agreeing to maintain those children admitted under its aegis during the previous four years. When this support ceased in 1771, the Foundling drastically cut back the numbers of places available and adopted a more restricted admissions policy. Only the orphans of sailors and soldiers were admitted, and, in 1767, illegitimate or parish children were also allowed to apply.

The critics of government assistance have been characterized in a recent

[10] *Gentleman's Magazine* (February 1759) p. 55.

[11] Saunders Welch, *A Proposal to Render Effectual a Plan to Remove the Nuisance of Common Prostitutes* (London: C. Henderson, 1758), p. 33. See also *Six Concluding Letters on . . . the Tendencies of the Foundling Hospital in London* (London: C. Henderson, 1760), p. 36.

[12] Hanway in *Gentleman's Magazine* (February 1760), p. 87.

history of the Foundling Hospital as "strongly sympathetic to commercial enterprise," a description that certainly fits Hanway perfectly. It further notes that "the pamphleteers . . . measured the value of a life by its potential productivity, not by its intrinsic worth as a human soul." Again, Hanway exactly. It concludes with the view that "they could and did weigh children's lives in the balance against the costs of preserving them."[13] Yet again, Hanway. So there is much truth to these charges. And yet the essential point has been missed. For, as we have already noted, this way of computation and reasoning, this commercial concern, was present at the foundation of the hospital. And, even more importantly, Hanway realized, probably instinctively, that if the Foundling was to be kept viable and receive the dedicated voluntary direction and funding that made it different from poor-law institutions,[14] it would need the support, guidance, and approval of commercially minded gentlemen who were also Christian philanthropists. For Hanway, the Christian merchant was no contradiction. It merely proved God's providence that charity that aided the country and promoted trade also cared for the poor.[15]

LYING-IN AND MATERNITY, 1750–1770: HOSPITALS VERSUS HOME DELIVERY

The lying-in hospitals, like the Foundling, continued to grow and to expand the care they offered. This expansion occurred in both the British and the City of London lying-in hospitals. Along with strong and contin-

[13] Ruth McClure, *Coram's Children* (New Haven: Yale University Press, 1981), p. 111. So, for example, Hanway asks "may we not consider a child as we do a *calf*, a *lamb*, or a *colt?*" concluding, "it is gross ignorance of the value of a human life, that makes us so careless about the infant parish poor": see *An Earnest Appeal for Mercy to the Children of the Poor* (London: sold by J. Dodsley, 1766), p. 72. Hanway computes that the cost of raising an average number of children (allowing for three out of five to die before the age of apprenticeship) to the age of thirteen to be £85.16.0 each, while the worth of their labor, assuming an average life span of only thirty-six years, would be £269.19.3, "a gain of £184.3.3" (ibid., p. 73).

[14] Thomas Alcock remarked on the superiority of voluntary hospitals over poor-law institutions; "under an Institution that depends chiefly upon voluntary Contributions, the Managers are always on their good Behavior and know nothing can continue their Supports to them, but Honesty, Skill and Integrity in their Administration": *Remarks on Two Bills for the Better Maintenance of the Poor* (London: printed for R. Baldwyn, 1753), p. 30.

[15] See *Rules, Orders, and Regulations of the Magdalen House* (London: n.p., 1759), pp. 3–4. John Massie, in *A Plan for the Establishment of Charity-Houses for Exposed or Deserted Women and Girls, and for Penitent Prostitutes* (London: T. Payne, 1758), said of one of his own proposals "Thus might CHARITY, HUMANITY, PATRIOTISM AND OECONOMY be made to go Hand-in-Hand; and the ways to form this quadruple Alliance are so obviously proper and so easily practicable that one can scarcely help wondering how so much Good can be obtained from such simple Means" (p. 9). See also *Some Considerations on the Present Method Used for the Relief and Employment of the Poor* (London: n.p. 1759), p. v.

uing support from its members (in 1757 almost one-third of the active subscribers to the British Lying-in Hospital of six years before still appeared in an active role), the hospital continued to increase the numbers of women it delivered. In the decade 1749 to 1758 it had delivered 2,933 babies; in its second decade of operation (1759–1768) it delivered half again as many babies (4,773) as it had in its first. The City of London Lying-in Hospital also delivered substantially more babies in the 1760s (3,146) than it had in the 1750s (2,866).[16] However, since the City of London was a smaller institution with fewer subscribers, neither the number of deliveries, nor the rate of increase could be as great as its more prestigious counterpart. Also, unlike the British Lying-in Hospital, its membership tended to be less active and to have more continuity, that is, fewer new subscriptions from list to list. Thus, in 1759, while 50 percent of the subscribers from 1753 reappeared on the lists, only 11 percent of these repeaters seem to have been active.[17] Part of this seeming lack of involvement stems, no doubt, from the ambiguity of the lists. Unless a donor gave annually, or in repeated, small amounts, it is impossible to guess whether or not he was more actively involved in the charity. Having given enough to become a life subscriber entitled one to have one's name appear, regardless of further interest or activity, on the lists of the charity until one's demise (and sometimes even afterward). However, given all these difficulties, one can speculate that the solid preponderance of male life subscribers on the City of London lists may have indicated a certain desire for public notice without too much effort or interest. Still, it must be noted that some members of the City of London Lying-in Hospital had broader charitable interests, as revealed by their support of the British Lying-in Hospital as well as the Foundling.[18]

[16] The figures are drawn from *An Account of the Rise, Progress and State of the British Lying-in Hospital for Married Women* (London: 1770), and *An Account of the City of London Lying-in Hospital* with John Nicols, *A Sermon Preached . . . before the President and Governors of the City of London Lying-in Hospital* (London: 1767).

[17] Since it is impossible to know if life subscribers were active in the charity after their first donation, only annual subscribers are considered as active in this computation.

[18] In 1753 nine subscribers to the City of London Lying-in Hospital also subscribed to the Foundling and six City of London donors also contributed to the British Lying-in Hospital. In 1759 fifteen City of London members belonged to the Foundling Hospital and nine to the British: see *An Account of . . . the City of London Lying-in Hospital* with Thomas Church, *A Sermon Preached . . . before the President and Governors of the City of London Lying-in Hospital* (London: Charles Say, 1753); *An Account of the City of London Lying-in Hospital* (London: n.p., 1759); *An Account of the Rise and Progress of the Lying-in Hospital for Married Women from its first Institution . . . to July 25, 1751* (London: n.p., 1751); *An Account of the Rise, Progress and State of The British Lying-in Hospital . . . to 1759* (London: n.p., 1759); *The Royal Charter . . . together with . . . accounts of the [Foundling] Hospital, since its commencement till 25 March 1745* (London: Thomas Osborne, 1746).

The continued expansion of services of these two hospitals can be seen as a response to both long-term and short-term needs. Through the 1750s and 1760s, the needs of a nation at war and of a growing imperial power demanded an ever increasing population. We have already seen why large numbers of men were held to be a crucial resource during the war years; by the end of the Seven Years' War, the new international situation increased still further the demands for additional population. As Beer pointed out, the treaty ending this war marked and "revealed an important change in the economic theory of colonization."[19] Whereas colonies had previously functioned mainly as suppliers of raw materials that would be manufactured into finished goods in England, the new view of colonies favored their role as markets for the manufactured goods of an economy increasingly geared to colonial export. Since colonies were to take on the role of consumers as well as producers, the greater their population, the more effective their consumption. The choice of retaining Canada and the Ohio Valley while ceding Guadeloupe and Martinique made this new role of the colonies even more prominent. The costly acquisition of this enormous tract of land seemed to demand settlers and colonists to make it worthwhile. Therefore, each infant life lost in London's back alleys meant the death of a potential colonist, consumer, or tamer of England's new territory. This vast increase in unsettled lands greatly increased the potential economic value of each human life and influenced London's charities to do even more to save lives and promote the growth of population. And, the charitable were reminded, "all this is produced at an expense very small. A trifle, such as many of us throw away every day, saves one, perhaps two lives. . . . And it is a just recommendation of a charity, that the greatest good is done at the lowest cost."[20]

There are also reasons for thinking that during the 1750s and 1760s the hospitals performed more deliveries following times of economic distress. Though the price of bread is a very rough and inaccurate indicator of economic distress, especially for London, the trends in bread prices tended to coincide roughly with the trends in the number of deliveries. When the price of bread rose in the late 1750s, the number of deliveries also rose; when bread prices started rising again in the late 1760s, deliveries again tended to follow the same pattern. In addition to the effects of distress on the willingness of the hospitals to increase the amount of aid offered, the rise in the number of deliveries performed at the hospitals

[19] G. L. Beer, *British Colonial Policy, 1754–1765* (New York: Macmillan, 1907), p. 133.
[20] Hanway, *Letters . . . Rising Generation*, 2:128; Lawson, *Sermons*, pp. 294–96, 299–300.

may have been influenced by an increased demand for lying-in accommodations as the general London birthrate rose in the mid 1760s.[21]

Through the 1760s the hospitals continued to pursue their objectives with greater zeal and support than they had even at their inception. The City of London Lying-in Hospital, for example, averaged receipts of £1,085 per annum in the years 1753–1759, while it had only averaged £599 in the years 1749–1753.[22] However, in the late 1750s, an alternate scheme of lying-in care was begun, a scheme that would overshadow the work done by the hospitals. The proponents of this new form of lying-in care claimed that it could realize the goal of the hospitals, that is, a safer and more painless childbirth, while eliminating the dangers that the hospitals invited of an overgenerous or misplaced charity. This new approach found its first concrete manifestation in the formation of the Lying-in Charity for Delivering Poor Married Women in Their Own Habitations in 1757. This charity served the same sort of women as the hospitals, that is, women who were married but too poor to afford private aid in childbirth. It proposed to send out midwives, as well as to lend linens, to women who had their babies at home. A doctor, the public was assured, was always standing by if needed, but in most cases a midwife could as adequately, and far more cheaply, do the job. The Lying-in Charity supporters gave five reasons why their form of relief was preferable to that offered by the hospitals.

The first criticism of the hospitals was that they could not serve some of the worthiest of the poor. These, the Lying-in Charity claimed, were loath to ask for relief at a hospital, for that would be a public declaration of their poverty. On the other hand, these self-same proud but poor folk would greatly benefit from the sort of aid the new charity could offer, aid discreetly administered in the privacy of their own homes. Rather than refusing assistance out of a commendable pride, they could "accept of this commodious relief, so easily provided and studiously adapted to their circumstances."[23]

The second, and much more important, advantage of the Lying-in Charity over the hospitals was that home care was much cheaper. And it was undeniably true that the charity could deliver many more women for less money than either of the two hospitals. If one ignored fixed costs, and simply divided the amount expended by the different agencies by the number of women delivered, the British Lying-in Hospital spent almost £4.10 on each woman delivered and the City of London Lying-in Hospi-

[21] See E. A. Wrigley and R. H. Schofield, *The Population History of England* (London: E. Arnold, 1981), pp. 499, 640.

[22] See *An Account . . . of the City of London Lying-in Hospital*, 1753, 1759.

[23] Brownlow North, *Sermon For the . . . Lying-in Charity* (London: J. Robson, 1771), pp. 15–16.

tal almost £5, while the Lying-in Charity spent only 10 shillings. Thus, on a smaller budget, the Lying-in Charity could deliver far more women than either of the hospitals. In the decade 1760–1769, for example, the charity averaged 1,200 women delivered yearly, while the two hospitals only averaged 431 women delivered yearly for the decade 1759–1768.[24] In terms of operating efficiency, the Lying-in Charity was clearly superior.

Not only did the Lying-in Charity show that it was doing more good for less money than the hospitals, but it further claimed that home delivery was safer than hospital confinement. Certainly the writings of medical men familiar with the hospitals suggest that they were unhealthy places. Much of this unhealthiness was due to ignorance; little, if anything, was known about antiseptics, the causes of childbirth fevers, or the necessity to separate the ill from the well. In some of the lying-in hospitals the patients shared beds, and this no doubt encouraged the rapid spread of disease. Dr. Aiken, in his *Thoughts on Hospitals*, remarked that he had "been assured from the best authority that they [puerperal or childbirth fevers] have proportionally raged more in lying-in hospitals, than in private practice, which is a strong argument . . . of the tendency of these hospitals to produce them."[25] One must bear in mind, however, that the degree of ignorance about sanitation and hygiene was no less in the hovels of the poor than in the public hospitals, while other circumstances, such as the quality of food available for mother and child, as well as the likelihood of insufficient rest, might tend to make the birthing experience even more precarious in the home.

The evidence of the doctors is suspect too, since often when they discussed the ill effects of hospitals on the health of the women admitted, they were not only concerned about their physical well-being but also their moral state. Thus, Dr. Aiken complained that in the hospitals

> Nursing, confinement and unaccustomed diet, are more oftener carried to pernicious excess than deficient in a hurtful degree to the very lowest class of women. *Nature rather chooses to be confined within mere necessaries, than burthened with superfluities*, and though these may seem to contribute to the ease and comfort of patients, they scarcely will to their safety.[26]

Since women were commonly admitted to the hospitals a week or two before their expected delivery, during their stay they probably did eat bet-

---

[24] See North, *Sermon* (1771) with *An Account of the Charity for Delivering Poor Married Women in their Own Habitations; Account of. . . the City of London Lying-in Hospital* (1767); and *An Account . . . of the British Lying-in Hospital* (1770).

[25] John Aiken, *Thoughts on Hospitals* (London: Joseph Johnson, 1771), p. 62.

[26] Ibid., p. 40.

ter and work less than they would have had they remained at home.[27] This reputedly over-rich diet and lack of exercise may possibly have had some adverse effects on the health of the women. What is more likely, however, is that the complaint about ill health was an indirect method of making an oft-repeated complaint, the fourth weighty charge brought against the hospitals, that by providing too much food, too little work, and in general a mode of living unsuited to their station, the hospitals were spoiling the very women they sought to aid.

In contrast, the Lying-in Charity promised that it would encourage labor in both the husband and the lying-in wife herself. By removing the wife from her home, the hospitals robbed the family of a much needed commodity, the labor of the mother, which was a totally "ill-placed Generosity," for by taking the wife away, the husband could slacken his own industry, having been relieved of her support. By delivering the woman at home, "as the Wife is not taken from the Husband, the same call remains upon him to exert his Industry for her Support and Convenience." In contrast to the misdirected charity of the hospitals, the aid offered by the charity would be genuine, for while it reconciled "Man to a Life of Labour, without removing the Necessity of it," its effects "would redound equally to the advantage of himself and the Public."[28]

In addition to the added incentive to the husband to labor if his wife was delivered at home, the Lying-in Charity also noted the advantage of the woman's speedier return to productive labor. In the hospitals, lying-in women were usually kept in bed for two weeks after delivery, while a woman delivered at home, "at the End of Ten Days or a Fortnight . . . is able to manage her usual Business, here is the Advantage of so much Industry to the Public, and likewise a greater Service done to her Family."[29]

Finally, the delivery of women in their own homes would have an important and lasting influence on their families. Not only was the presence of a "kind and affectionate family" one of the great comforts of lying-in women,[30] but the uninterrupted presence of the wife in the home was absolutely essential to familial stability. It was she who was the guardian of family morals, whose watchful eye kept her husband working and her daughters chaste. Her lying-in, if at home, could be a splendid occasion for the exercise of practical morality. Her children, instead of forgetting the obedience they owed and "being left to themselves for several weeks,

[27] The average length of stay of fifty women delivered by the General Lying-in Hospital in 1767–1768 was 19.5 days: see *Admissions Book* of the General Lying-in Hospital. The papers of the General Lying-in Hospital are located at the Greater London Record Office.

[28] *A Plain Account of the Advantages of the Lying-in Charity for Delivering Poor Married Women at Their Own Habitations* (London: 1767), p. 7.

[29] Ibid., p. 8.

[30] North, *Sermon*, pp. 17–18.

without the authority and direction of their parents . . . shall here be practiced in an essential duty, to comfort and assist those parents in distress. . . . Surely, there is an ingenious economy in this charity, that whilst
infants are trained to virtue, their virtues are turned to good account."[31]
Furthermore, if the wife was at home, she could exercise her moral authority, for "by Keeping the Wife at Home, you restrain the Husband's
Extravagances, perhaps his Debaucheries; you attach him more strongly
to his Wife and Children; in a Word, you preserve that Order, Harmony
and Industry, which the Presence of the Wife is found to keep up in the
Families of the Poor."[32]

The attack on the lying-in hospitals was thus an attempt to realize the
goal of safer childbirth in order to swell the nation's population, without
risking the dangers of overgenerous relief. Hanway, whose name was
missing from the subscription lists of both hospitals, expressed both his
approval of their goals and his disapproval of their methods. Though
"hospitals for lying-in women in some instances may offer great relief,"
Hanway had serious qualms about them. "But we must be cautious that
our compassion does not outrun our judgment, and induce us to correct
in the wrong place." He went on to note that though he did not condemn
those people who gave to the hospitals out of a regard for "the welfare of
mankind," he recommended "to their consideration how their munificence may be applied *most advantageously* in promoting the most solid
and permanent *police*; and that no check be wanting that can administer
to the moral and religious duties of the People."[33] Again, as with the
Foundling, Hanway admonished restraint while urging action. Hanway
felt that he had found the perfect agency for promoting both the needs of
mankind and the needs of police in the Lying-in Charity, to which he did
contribute.

It is not surprising that the supporters of the Lying-in Charity should
have been, like Hanway, overwhelmingly of the commercial classes.
While almost 18 percent of the British Lying-in Hospital's subscribers
were upper class, less than 2 percent of the Lying-in Charity's were.
Though unusually supportive and active (two-thirds of the annual sub-

---

[31] Ibid., pp. 14–15.

[32] *Plain Account of the . . . Lying-in Charity*, p. 8.

[33] Jonas Hanway, *The Defects of Police, the Cause of Immorality* (London: J. Dodsley,
1775), pp. xx–xxi. "By the subscription of a generous Public, [lying-in] Hospitals have been
erected and are supported. . . . Without in the least depreciating them, or detracting from
their utility, it may yet be truly said, that there are some superior advantages attending the
present plan [for home delivery]": George Horne, *Sermon Preached before the Governors
of the Benevolent Institution* (Oxford: D. Prince & J. Cooke, 1788), "Charity Recommended on its true Motive," p. 14.

scribers in 1767 were still present and active in 1770),[34] they seem to have been cautious people, desiring to remain annual contributors. By giving their support on a yearly basis, they could keep a check on the operations of the charity, whereas if they had donated only a large sum initially, they would have lost some of this control. While many members of the charity were, like Hanway, undoubtedly of a deeply religious though tolerant bent (as witnessed by the substantial number of subscribers who also belonged to the Society for Promoting Religious Knowledge among the Poor—an organization that, unlike its older Anglican counterpart, the SPCK, distributed the works of middle-of-the-road theologians of all the Protestant denominations) it is unlikely that they were motivated by "rapturous flights or wild chimeras." Their frame of mind might best be described as "rational and pious."[35] Their religion was sensible and their business interests were well entrenched. Many of them held offices in their guilds, acted as secretaries and lawyers to the large City companies or served on the boards of the City's growing number of insurance companies. In politics, they seem to have been moderate and conservative; many were opposed to the 1769 Wilkes movement.[36] Like Hanway, then, they appear to have been people who felt the obligations of Christian charity, but thought that prudence and public utility should dictate the direction of their contributions. In the Lying-in Charity they found an ideal vehicle for the most secure fulfillment of this obligation.

The Beginnings of the Marine Society

While the Foundling and lying-in hospitals continued to expand through the 1750s, other schemes were being suggested to care for orphaned and poor children, and to make this neglected section of the populace more useful in the service of the nation. These new proposals aimed at the preservation and maximum utilization of the labor of these children while avoiding the problems that had plagued the Foundling. In the main, they did this by proposing to care only for older children, who were less difficult and expensive to raise than infants. But, there were other reasons why these new charities concentrated only on the care of older children. Many philanthropists believed that a way had to be found to aid the chil-

[34] Fifty-four out of 303 subscribers to the British were upper class, in the Lying-in only 10 out of 381 subscribers were. Of the 959 subscribers to the Foundling Hospital in 1767, 139 were upper class.

[35] Words used to describe Job Orton, whose writings were a favorite giveaway of the Society for Promoting Religious Knowledge among the Poor. At least forty-one of the subscribers listed in the 1767 rolls of the Lying-in Charity also subscribed to the SPRKP.

[36] At least twenty-eight signed what George Rudé has called the Petition of the Loyal Addressers of March 1769, an anti-Wilkes declaration. See Rudé, "The Anti-Wilkite Merchants of 1769," *Guildhall Miscellany*, no. 7 (September 1965), p. 2.

dren of the laboring poor without entirely removing their care from their parents' shoulders. Hanway, for example, maintained that instead of depending on the aid of the charitable, "Men who are born free should endeavor to preserve their children by industry."[37] Institutions like the Foundling, therefore, which took babies at birth and thus relieved parents of all further responsibility, encouraged, it was said, the poor to abandon their progeny and lead lives of idle abandon. However, if the children of the poor were not aided at all, they would either die young or grow up to be useless to themselves and the nation, living out their lives in grueling poverty and idleness, or what was perhaps even worse, turning to lives of violence and active criminality. The proper aid to the children of the poor would avoid both these dangers. For, though misplaced charity was severely criticized, especially that sort which allowed parents to lessen their labor, it was widely accepted to be the obligation of the upper classes to aid in this endeavor when the best efforts of the parents failed. Charity was to be a mediator between the rich and poor; benevolence ought to distribute wealth in the manner that best served the interests of the state. One important function of charity, therefore, was to restore a proper balance and equilibrium to the life of the nation by caring for the nation's offspring.

In addition, the proper charitable care of the children of the poor would have desirable effects on the nation's military strength. Rightly directed aid would channel the natural ferocity of the poor toward the achievement of England's military goals rather than allowing it to erupt into internal warfare and mayhem.[38] And, as we have already noted, the resumption of war in 1756 intensified the need to husband the nation's population resources and rehabilitate London's poor children so they would be fit for national, especially naval, service. Even before the outbreak of fighting, the current methods of naval recruitment, which relied heavily on impressment, had come under severe criticism:

> it is a Reproach to the whole Nation, to see Families numerous in Children, starving and mourning, the Husband and Father, by whose Labour they liv'd, being dragged from the Loom, or from the Trowel, to the Fleet and forc'd to quit the industrious Care of providing for his Family to fight at Sea, where, perhaps, he never was in his life.[39]

[37] Hanway, *Letters to the Guardians of the Infant Poor* (London: A. Millar & T. Cadell, 1767), p. 12.

[38] Ibid., p. 13.

[39] Seaman, *An Infallible Project for the More Effectual . . . Manning of the Navy* (London: sold by M. Cooper, 1745), p. 23. For difficulties of naval recruitment, see Daniel Baugh, *British Naval Administration in the Age of Walpole* (Princeton: Princeton University Press, 1965), chap. 4.

As we have already noted, many held that unless sailors and soldiers could be recruited from hitherto untapped sources, the nation would be badly depopulated at the end of the war. The inevitable result of such depopulation would be a rise in the price of labor, which in turn would raise the finished price of manufactured goods to such a height "as to render them unsaleable at foreign markets." With such a decline in trade would come a decline in power, and England would fall "prey to any enterprising prince, that is in a condition to transport a few thousand men to invade us."[40] But where could alternative sources of sailors be found? Either men had to be impressed who were also needed on the land or in the merchant service, or other sources had to be discovered. Henry Fielding, mustering troops in the 1750s, despaired of the rising generation: "Are these wretched Infants [nourished on and conceived in Gin] (if such can be supposed capable of arriving at the age of maturity) to become our future sailors, and our future grenadiers?"[41] Clearly steps would have to be taken both to increase the number of men found and to improve their quality. Emergency measures such as mass impressments and rewards to informers for revealing the whereabouts of truant sailors were enacted. Similarly, severe laws against luring workmen out of England were strictly enforced: on July 9, 1755, "Martin Warren, a Dane, was convicted before Bolton Mainwaring, Esq. for seducing seven persons, artificers in the glass manufacture, to depart this kingdom. The penalty for every person seduced, or attempted to be seduced is £500 plus twelve months imprisonment."[42] Hanway commented that if the difficulties of naval recruitment "could happily be removed, the *naval power* of *Britain* might awe the world."[43]

The method hit upon to man the fleet more efficiently while rescuing boys from a life of crime and idleness was the establishment of "a new Hospital, for the Entertainment of all the Youth within a certain Age, who should voluntarily enter themselves in it." These boys were "thence to be disposed of in the Fleet as the Navy or Admiralty Board should find convenient."[44] Following the spirit of this early recommendation, the Marine Society was founded in 1756, and, though not a hospital, it served as a placement agency for young boys (and men, in its early days) providing clothes and Bibles, as well as medical attention. This charity, while designed to promote naval preparedness, would also rehabilitate the street youth, and introduce a sense of gratitude into the hardened young hearts.

[40] Ibid., intro., n.p.; see also [Hanway], *Candid Historical Account*, p. 11.
[41] Henry Fielding, *An Enquiry Into the Causes of the Late Increase of Robbers* [1751], in *The Works of Henry Fielding* (London: J. Johnson, 1806), p. 365.
[42] *Gentleman's Magazine* (July 1755), p. 329.
[43] Hanway, *Letters to the Guardians*, p. 10.
[44] Seaman, *An Infallible Project*, p. 12.

Hanway claimed that new clothing was the first step in the acquisition of respectability, and the gift of clothes, as well as producing "an agreeable sensation" in the boy, would also give him the "*pleasure* of being *remembered* by the mercy of his fellow-subjects."[45] Thus, Hanway and most of the other founders of the Marine envisioned the charity as serving a twofold function: aiding in recruitment while serving the street youth of London. The twin objects of the charity, Hanway remarked, were "to purge the streets of London" and to "relieve the miseries of the hungry and naked, and *him that hath no helper but God.*" Boys who were sent from the country had to get specific recommendations and approval before they were aided by the society. However, since the society was deeply involved and "instrumental in manning our fleets and succouring the hungry and naked belonging to many other places beside London,"[46] branch offices were eventually set up in the provinces.

The Marine Society was mainly a London charity. The boys it aided were predominantly Londoners, and its donors were largely City bankers and merchants. In 1757, for example, of 396 listed donors, only 27 were upper class. The charity was widely subscribed to by the guilds and companies of London. The East India Company donated £200 as an initial subscription, and the Russia Company £100. Eleven of the City guilds contributed £100 each.[47] London's merchants stood much to gain by aiding and ensuring the proper manning of naval and merchant vessels. As early as July 1755 they had "subscribed the sum of £300,000 in case a war should be declared, to fit out a fleet of privateers, on a private expedition."[48] This private fleet would have been useless, and the merchants' investment lost, if insufficient numbers of men and boys could be found to man it. However, despite the practical interest the merchants had in the success of the society, the desire for gain was not their only, or even perhaps their predominant, motive. In the minds of most merchants, there seemed to be no reason for conflict between the interests of the boys, the interests of the nation, and their own enrichment. Hanway commented that "there is a certain generosity which no mercenary consideration can inspire, that must be the ruling principle of such a Society." He did not fail to point out, however, that the needs of war, "our peculiar

---

[45] Jonas Hanway, *An Account of the Marine Society* (London: n.p., 1759), p. 47.

[46] Hanway, *Letters to the Guardians*, p. 61.

[47] The contributing guilds were the Apothecaries, Clothworkers, Carpenters, Drapers, Fishmongers, Grocers, Stationers, Skinners, Salters, Merchant Taylors, and Vintners. See *To the Marine Society, in Praise of the Great and Good Work They Have Done* (London: n.p., 1759), which contains a list of subscribers to the charity from June 1756 to December 1757.

[48] *Gentleman's Magazine* (December 1755), p. 569.

circumstances . . . and particular situation," made the formation of the Marine especially important and timely.[49]

Like Hanway, many of the early contributors to the Marine combined Christian piety with a strong sense of the profitable. A case in point was Benjamin Boddington, a director of the South Sea Company and the Million Bank, the master of his guild, the Clothworkers, and an early subscriber to the Marine Society. In his lifetime he devoted time and money to charitable interests ranging from the Lying-in Charity to the Society for Sunday Schools. All in all he gave to at least five different charities and served on the governing committees of at least two of them. His posthumous bequests, like those of many of his class and era, were meager. Though he left small sums to the London Hospital, St. Thomas's, the Lying-in Charity, and the British Lying-in Hospital, as well as to a number of religious organizations (£50 to the fund for widows and orphans of dissenting ministers and £50 to the committee for civil affairs among dissenters), he left the vast bulk of his estate, worth £200,000, to his eldest son, Thomas. Yet, in a codicil to his will, drawn in the year of his death (1791), we get a deeper glimpse into the man. He bequeathed to a business colleague "£100, or in Lieu of any amount I may lend him or Bond or not if more than that sum as his affairs are settled, for tho' I expect to lose about £400 by his failure, *yet his misfortune does not render him less worthy of the character of an honest man.*"[50] At a time when many of the dissenting sects were excommunicating members who had the ill fortune to go bankrupt, Boddington, a dissenter himself, while not minimizing his business losses, could nevertheless record his esteem for an unfortunate acquaintance. Boddington is but one example of the sort of "interested" philanthropist of the 1750s and 1760s to whom the Marine Society was designed to appeal. So was Jacob Bosanquet, a Hamburg merchant whose family was involved in international trade and finance, who was an old friend of Hanway's and one of the original subscribers to the Marine Society. When Bosanquet became a governor of the Levant Company and of the East India Company, he used these positions to secure funds and places for Marine boys. Thus, his interest and involvement in the affairs of the Marine was vital, though he left the society no posthumous bequest at all.[51] Another English member of the Hamburg merchant community, friend and colleague of Hanway on numerous charitable ventures, John Thornton, though an early and constant subscriber,

---

[49] Jonas Hanway, *A Letter from a Member of the Marine Society Shewing the Generosity and Utility of Their Design* (London: C. Say, 1757), p. 26.

[50] The wills cited can be found in the Public Record Office, Chancery Lane, under their probate numbers: Benjamin Boddington, PROB 11/1208/416; emphasis added.

[51] See Jacob Bosanquet's will, PROB 11/929/209; and Grace L. Lee, *The Story of the Bosanquets* (Canterbury: Phillimore, 1966).

refused to allow himself to be elected to the governing committee of the Marine because he disapproved of the undecorous conduct at Marine Society dinners.[52] The subscribers then were men of principle and men of business, men who approved of the commercial spirit and the importance of the human soul. It is because the Marine was able to appeal to such a multiplicity of motives, because it was "calculated at once to call forth the *ardour* of the *warrior*, the *prudence* of the *merchant*, the *policy* of the *statesman* and the *zeal* of the *saint*," that it was such a resounding success.[53] It is surely no slur on the generosity or well-meaningness of the Marine's subscribers to note that one of the most powerful arguments for its support was fiscal. Hanway estimated that it cost the government about £10 to impress a man into the navy. The Marine Society could do the same for only £5, and in addition supply the sailor with clothes and religious tracts. Thus, Hanway could boast, "Where is the hospital which, in so short a time has *saved so many lives* as this *Society?*"—and, he could add, at so small a cost.[54]

The society's main aims were to provide men for the navy, to clear London's streets of young idlers and beggars, to find young boys employment as naval servants and sailors, and to infuse into them a sense of religion and patriotism. In this way, police and humanity would both be served. Policy would be aided by sending the boys to sea at a young age, before they had contracted that fear and dislike of naval duty that led Samuel Johnson to say that life in gaol was preferable to life on board a ship.[55] The boys who were aided and started off in an active, possibly prosperous life, would have been rescued from "the *gallows*, or from a noxious infection; saved . . . from *penury* and *disease*; from *misery* and *untimely death*."[56] The aid of the society would transform potential thieves and beggars into instruments for the glory of the nation and of their own salvation.

In the attempt to rehabilitate these young hooligans, the society exhibited both humanity and a real sensitivity to the youths themselves. It wished to use gentle suasion rather than compulsion to recruit and reform the boys sent to its offices. Thus, the governing committee advised the guardians of young boys to consider the "genius and disposition" of their charges rather than simply forcing them to enlist. The society also taught

[52] *Dictionary of National Biography*, 19:781.

[53] Hanway, *Letters to the Guardians*, p. 23. See also Hanway, *Account of the Marine Society*, where he first introduces this notion: "But this Society is guarded at all points; it assists the warrior and the merchant; it acts the part of the zealous citizen, the tender parent of the poor, and the true friend of the public" (pp. 23–24).

[54] Ibid., p. 24.

[55] Hanway, *Account of the Marine Society*, p. 11.

[56] Hanway, *Letters to the Guardians*, p. 24.

the boys to play the fife as part of their training as sailors. Fife playing, while not a necessary accomplishment of the good sailor, was a valuable and harmless recreation. Hanway and his friends realized that "amusement is necessary to life, and keeps a seaman in some degree from the desire of roving, therefore to withhold any gratification of this kind from him, which can be *consistently* granted, and *conveniently* supplied, would be as little *politic* as *humane*."[57]

THE ASYLUM FOR ORPHANED GIRLS

Shortly after the foundation of the Marine Society, three important tracts appeared that urged the immediate creation of an asylum and school for deserted or orphaned girls and for penitent prostitutes. These were John Fielding's *Plan for a Preservatory and Reformatory for the Benefit of Deserted Girls and Penitent Prostitutes*, Joseph Massie's *Plan for the Establishment of Charity Schools for Exposed and Deserted Women and Girls . . . and Penitent Prostitutes*, and Saunders Welch's *Proposal to Remove the Nuisance of Common Prostitutes*. It was soon decided that the care of girls and fallen women had to be kept strictly separate; care of girls was to be modeled on, and become a counterpart to, the Marine Society, striving to protect its girls from falling into a life of vice and crime, while preparing them for useful service.

Sir John Fielding, one of the original members of the Marine Society and a London magistrate, was an important force in the foundation of the Asylum for the Reception of Orphaned Girls at Lambeth (the Lambeth Asylum), begun in 1759. At its inception, however, the Lambeth Asylum had to work hard to convince philanthropists of its importance, for it lacked the vital support of Jonas Hanway and many of his associates. Why this should have been so is mysterious indeed. It is Hanway's only unexplained lapse from charitable participation in a major philanthropic venture. Some historians have speculated that Hanway refused to sponsor this charity after his conflicts with Sir John Fielding on the governing board of the Marine.[58] Hanway's only comment on the Lambeth Asylum is ambiguous. Writing just a few years after its establishment, he noted that, "Observing how successful the Marine Society had been in providing for so many vagabond boys . . . it was natural for any man to turn his thoughts to girls of the same stamp; but this did not appear to me to be equally practicable. I once consulted our friend the Bishop of Worcester . . . but his lordship stated many difficulties." By 1761, however, Hanway had changed his mind about the value of the charity, com-

[57] Hanway, *Account of the Marine Society*, pp. 73, 51.
[58] See, for example, J. S. Taylor, *Jonas Hanway: Founder of the Marine Society* (London: Scolar Press, 1985), pp. 97–98.

menting that he conceived it "to be an excellent model for a well-regulated house, for the female poor, in their state of childhood." His only remaining criticism, vague as it was, is all we have to explain his subsequent absence from its lists: after commending the Lambeth Asylum, he remarked that it was a model charity "as far as it goes."[59]

For whatever reason Hanway absented himself, he was clearly missed. The Lambeth Asylum had a much less distinguished and philanthropically active directorship, in its early years at any rate, than those charities that Hanway supported.[60] Still, when the Lambeth Asylum opened its doors to needy girls, it did so confident in the belief that without some practical assistance and guidance girls were, by nature or by circumstance, likely to fall victim to vice and become the unwitting agents of national destruction.

That women were eminently, almost entirely, creatures of feeling was an ancient maxim.[61] In well brought-up and chaste women, female softness was a valued attribute; female companionship relieved men of "that rivalship of genius and those contrarieties of opinion, which too often impair, not to say poison, the enjoyments of male society." However, in women of the lower classes these same playful graces often led to moral downfall. Thinking too much of clothing, amusements, or their appearance, such women were likely to succumb to the temptations of sin. The love of dress, commendable in women of the upper and middle classes, could lead poor women directly and unequivocally to the loss of virtue and character.[62] The passionate and emotive nature of women often led

[59] Jonas Hanway, *Letters Upon . . . the Repentance of Prostitutes* (London: John Rivington, 1761), p. 6. Equally odd is the entire omission of this charity from B. Kirkman Gray, *History of English Philanthropy* (London: King, 1905); David Owen, *English Philanthropy* (Cambridge, Mass.: Belknap Press, 1964); and Betsy Rodgers, *Cloak of Charity* (London: Methuen, 1949). There is a brief mention of the Lambeth Asylum in Phillis Cunnington and Catherine Lucas, *Charity Costumes of Children, Scholars, Almsfolk, Pensioners* (London: A. & C. Blake, 1978).

[60] The Magdalen membership from 1758 to 1766 was composed of 26 percent female subscribers and 10 percent aristocrats; the Marine had only 4 percent female and 6 percent aristocratic subscribers for its first year, 1756–1757. In contrast, the Lambeth Asylum list of early subscribers (first fifteen weeks) was 53 percent female and 23 percent aristocratic. Even five years later (1763), its lists were 46.7 percent female and 18.4 percent aristocratic. See *The Plan of the Magdalen House for the Reception of Penitent Prostitutes* (London: by order of the governors, 1758); *Rules and Regulations of the Magdalen Charity* (London: W. Faden, 1769); *To the Marine Society* (1757); and *An Account of the Asylum or House of Refuge on the Surrey Side of Westminster Bridge, for the Reception of Orphaned Girls* (London: n.p., 1763).

[61] See, for example, [Jonas Hanway], *Journal of Eight Days' Journey from Portsmouth to Kingston upon Thames* (London: H. Woodfall, 1756), p. 75; and John Brown, *Sermon . . . before the Governors of the Asylum for Female Orphans* (London: L. Davis and C. Reymer, 1765), "On the Female Character and Education," p. 8.

[62] James Fordyce, *The Character and Conduct of the Female Sex and the Advantages to be Derived by Young Men from the Company of Virtuous Women* (London: T. Cadell,

them astray by making them yearn to be "better than they were." Only a proper, sound education could protect such girls from themselves and from the snares of the city.[63] Education, however, was not the only thing needed to preserve girl orphans. For the difficult practical situation of young girls left on their own in London was not ignored. Often the relatives of such girls, if any existed, could offer no support or protection, and it was acknowledged that many girls fell victim to vice through force of circumstance, not choice. Fielding, for example, asked "What must become of the Daughters" of working widows, "where Poverty and Illiterateness conspire to expose them to every Temptation?" Thinking of the extreme youth of such girls, he was moved to concede that "they become Prostitutes from Necessity, even before their Passions can have any Share of their Guilt."[64] For, work for girls was rare, and then badly paid. "Scant are the means of subsistence allowed to the female sex . . . and those so much engrossed by our sex [men]; so small the profits . . . and so difficult often the power of obtaining employment." Furthermore, many employers were loath to hire girls who had grown up on the city's streets, preferring instead the rustic innocence of newly arrived country girls.[65]

The Lambeth Asylum hoped that through the provision of religious and vocational training, female frivolousness would be lessened, and the difficulties of their practical circumstances reduced. Unlike the too-fond parent, the governors of the Lambeth Asylum announced their determination to pay special attention to the practical aspects of the girls' education. Their mode of upbringing would stress a simplicity of dress and a careful acquisition of all the skills needed in the superior domestic. The levelheaded practicality of the proposed scheme was particularly insisted upon in all attempts to raise money for the charity. Thomas Franklin, in a special sermon for the benefit of the Lambeth Asylum, extolled the charity by remarking that its value was three-fold: first, that it removed "so general a calamity" as the adolescent unwillingness to labor; second, that it "instructs them in every thing they *ought* to know"; and, finally, something "peculiar to this charity," that it instructs them "in nothing which they ought *not* [to know]."[66] In a later sermon, Porteus pointed out that

---

1776), pp. 86–87. On the deleterious effects of fancy clothing for poor women, see Hanway, *Defects of Police*, p. xxiii.

[63] Welch, *A Proposal*, p. 4.

[64] John Fielding, *A Plan for a Preservatory and Reformatory for the Benefit of Deserted Girls and Penitent Prostitutes* (London: B. Francklin, 1758), p. 7. See also Dodd, *A Sermon before the President, Vice President, Treasurer, and Governors of the Magdalen House*, 2nd ed. (London: W. Faden, 1759), pp. 14–15.

[65] William Dodd, *A Sermon Preached at the Anniverary Meeting of . . . the Magdalen Charity* (London: W. Faden, 1762), p. 18; J. J. Hecht, *The Domestic Servant Class in Eighteenth-Century England* (London: Routledge & Kegan Paul, 1956), pp. 11–12.

[66] Thomas Franklin, *A Sermon at the Anniversary Meeting of the Governors of the Female Asylum* (London: W. Bunce, 1768), p. 11. Such an institution was also advocated for

when one considered "how much not only the peace and good order of families, but the security of their properties and even the safety of their lives depends on the diligence and honesty . . . of their domestics," the work of the Lambeth Asylum could be truly valued.[67] The superior practical and moral education provided to the girls would produce women who would also make better spouses and mothers; thus, indirectly, the institution would promote marriage and procreation. "Early informed in virtue . . . they shall practice with credit the matron duties, as good wives and mothers of a numerous issue."

The second goal of the Lambeth Asylum grew from its role as an asylum. One of its important functions was to provide a safe refuge for girls who might otherwise have fallen or been sold into prostitution. If a girl was left friendless and defenseless at an early age, bereft of the benefits of a righteous and religious education, and totally "unprepared to withstand the siege of libidinous fury, to evade the wily approach of insidious passions," it was inevitable that she would be "mastered by the first temptation," and in losing her chastity, lose her character.[68] The loss of female chastity was the first momentous step "in a gradual progression in guilt" that ended only in "that entire dissolution and profligacy of manners, which are the reproach of human nature."[69] Unless this first step was prevented, unless orphaned girls could receive care and proper training until they could find employment, their vicious lives would cause profligacy, celibacy, and disease, the "desolation of our country, the utter extirpation of mankind." Against this outcome, the Lambeth Asylum would be a "little sanctuary of female honour . . . floating upon an overflowing and drowned world," and by preventing prostitution would "become effectual to the preservation of the whole female nation."[70] This female purity would also have wider social consequences: "your cities [would] thrive . . . your men may be strong to labour, *that there be no decay*, no robbing upon the roads . . . no rioting, *no complaining in your streets*."[71]

In order to understand the importance of this aspect of the Lambeth Asylum's work, as well as the reasons for the foundation and support of the Magdalen charity, which we will shortly discuss in more detail, we

---

its potential to bring up the female orphans of Irish Catholics as Protestants and "render them useful and loyal subjects and strengthen the protestant cause": Welch, *Proposal*, p. 36, footnote.

[67] Beilby Porteus, *Sermon at the Anniversary Meeting of the Governors of the Female Asylum* (London: Harriot Bunce, 1773), pp. 19–20. See also William Hazeland, *Sermon for the Female Asylum at Lambeth* (London: J. Beecroft, 1760), p. 11.

[68] Hazeland, *Sermon*, pp. 11–12.

[69] Porteus, *Sermon*, p. 13.

[70] Hazeland, *Sermon*, pp. 8, 10–11.

[71] Patrick Delany, *Sermon . . . before the Governors of the Magdalen Hospital* (London: W. Johnston, 1763), p. 13.

must briefly examine contemporary understandings of the nature and social consequences of sexual depravity. Sexual license was considered both
dangerous and the very paradigm of all licentious behavior. This larger
field of license included not only prostitution and promiscuity, but the
publication of lewd books, the spread of popular, though improper,
amusements like masked balls and pleasure parks, the reputedly high in-
cidence of adultery, and the breakdown of the institution of marriage.
Since private sexual conduct was held to have a profound effect on the
state of the nation, public immorality was not merely something to be
decried; public virtue was an important civil issue.[72] Thus, Lord Har-
wicke, in condemning Curll's *Venus in a Cloyster*, noted that "any act
[that] was prejudicial to morals was also a breach of the peace." While
the upper classes might be allowed a "limited license," a sort of decorous
private dalliance, there was no question of this for the working poor.[73]
Once they succumbed to sin they ceased to work, and thus ceased to be
the valuable upholders of the nation, the producers of wealth and the
defenders of the realm. But if working men were debased by license,
working women were utterly transformed. Hanway noted that such
women "seem to acquire every vice upon earth" by their fall.[74] Therefore,
though sexual depravity was to be universally deplored, it was inevitable,
given its more serious effects on women, that the prevention and control
of female vice would receive the most attention and correction.

The Lambeth Asylum was one such measure, begun in the belief that it
was easier to save girls from sin than to rehabilitate them once they had
fallen; that "when a city is on fire, you will more easily stop the confla-
gration by cutting off its communication with the parts that are yet entire,
than by striving to extinguish and save the buildings already in flames."[75]

THE MAGDALEN AND PENITENT PROSTITUTES

While the Lambeth Asylum was thus praised as being the easiest and most
prudential of efforts to diminish immorality, the care and rehabilitation

[72] See Hazeland, *Sermon*, p. 6. Christopher Rawlinson, in *Inquiry into the Management of the Poor* (London: printed for Benjamin White, 1767), p. 64, argued "that the inspection into the public manners should be the care of parliament; and that not casually as it may happen to be moved for by any public spirited member; a standing committee should be appointed for that great and important service, and might be called the committee for public morals."

[73] Martin Seymour-Smith, *Fallen Women* (London: Nelson, 1969), p. 105. For the sexual double standard, see Henry Fielding, *Enquiry into the Increase of Robbers*, pp. 352, 349, 357. See also *Considerations on the Causes of the Present Stagnation of Matrimony* (London: T. Spilsbury, 1772), p. 64; and Hanway, *Reflections*, p. 295.

[74] Hanway, *Reflections*, p. 293.

[75] Hazeland, *Sermon*, pp. 8–9.

of those already fallen was also advocated on both political and religious grounds. "Where there is the least prospect of reclaiming to virtue a fallen character, it should certainly be attempted," noted a cleric in a sermon to the Lambeth Asylum.[76] The effort to found an institution for penitent prostitutes was undertaken simultaneously with the creation of an asylum for the yet-chaste orphaned girl. The three tracts that we mentioned in connection with the establishment of the Lambeth Asylum also advocated such a refuge for the prostitute who truly desired to mend her ways. The Magdalen charity was given an extra boost by the interest and involvement of Hanway and many of his friends, which resulted in greater publicity than the Lambeth Asylum received, as well as a larger subscription list and annual income.[77] And yet both the Lambeth Asylum and the Magdalen, founded in 1758, owed their establishment to the recognition that young girls often faced insurmountable difficulties, and that good fortune as much as rectitude separated the innocent from the fallen. Many of the Magdalen inmates were the same age as their chaste sisters in the Lambeth Asylum. William Dodd, the Magdalen's preacher, noted that "very many of the unhappy objects in the *house* are under fourteen years of age, and a great part debauched and introduced into this wretched life, before that age."[78] There was clearly growing sympathy for and understanding of the plight of such women. Not surprisingly, the plans for their rehabilitation were quite different from Defoe's earlier suggestion that the whipping post, the workhouse, and transportation be employed to punish prostitutes, in order to "cut off the rotten Branches in this Season [to] prevent the Corruption of more in the next."[79] Even by Coram's time, there seemed to have been a turning away from "a morbid morality . . . by which an unhappy female who fell a victim to the seductions and false promises of designing men, was left to hopeless contumely, and irretrievable disgrace." Coram had lamented this harsh attitude toward the fallen

[76] Ibid., p. 9. In 1758 the Society for the Encouragement of Arts offered its gold medal "as an honorary Reward for *a Plan*, which shall be judged best calculated for the effectual Establishment of a *Charity House* or *Charity Houses*, to receive and employ such common Prostitutes as are desirous to forsake their evil Courses." Quoted in D.G.C. Allen, "The Society for Encouragement of Arts" (diss., University of London, 1979), p. 129.

[77] From its inception to 1760, the Magdalen received £9,270 in subscriptions, benefactions, and donations: see *The Rules, Orders, and Regulations of the Magdalen House* (London: n.p., 1760). While 9 of the 21 directors of the Magdalen in 1759 donated to more than one charity, only 4 of the 1763 Lambeth Asylum committee did. Of the 21 Magdalen governing board members, all but 4 gave to other charities, with the average number of charities being 4.1. In contrast, 5 of the 11 Lambeth Asylum governors of 1763 subscribed to no other charities, and the 6 that did contribute averaged only 2.4 donations.

[78] Dodd, *Sermon* (1759), p. 13.

[79] Daniel Defoe, *Some Considerations upon Street-Walkers* (London: A. Moore, n.d.), p. 8.

woman, and criticized as unjust and unchristian her subsequent exclusion from most of the comforts of human society. For one slip, he remarked, "she was branded forever as a woman habitually lewd."[80] However, it is unlikely that, by itself, the force of this humane sympathy could have been translated into the establishment of the Magdalen charity. It had taken Coram seventeen years of toil to get the Foundling organized. However much sympathy existed for the plight of the friendless girl, newly seduced, all agreed that once she became a prostitute, she was anathema to the community, a fountain-head of crime and vice, and an outstanding threat to the peace of society.[81]

If sexual vice was the paradigm of all vice, the prostitute embodied, as it were, the fears that society had about rampant sexual depravity. She combined in her person two categories for whom chastity was especially important—the poor and the woman. As one of the laboring classes, she should have been reconciled to her station, and the fruits of hard work and honest matrimony. As a woman she should have preserved her sole and only virtue, her chastity. The prostitute, thus, was unnatural and entirely disfunctional; she did not undertake those roles that Defoe and many others saw as the proper functions for women:

> The great Use of Women in a Community, is to supply it with Members that may be serviceable, and keep up a Succession. They are also useful in another Degree, to wit, in the Labour they may take for themselves, or the Assistance which they may afford their Husbands or Parents. It will be readily allowed, that a Street-walking Whore can never answer either of these Ends; Riot and Diseases prevent one, and the Idleness which directs her to this Course of Life incapacitates her from the other. How very useless then is such a Subject.[82]

The prostitute fulfilled none of her natural obligations to the nation; she was a consuming, though not a producing, agent. The effect of her mode of living was to drain away productivity, to make her own and her clients' potential labor power and time into occasions for waste of both substance and opportunity. Furthermore, she was responsible for the spread of venereal disease to the innocent, to "our children, our servants, our dependents of whatever sort." Therefore, both humanity and police dictated

---

[80] Coram, quoted in John Brownlow, *Memoranda or Chronicles of the Foundling Hospital* (London: Sampson Low & Co., 1847), p. 14. For a spirited denunciation of this view, see *Advice to Unmarried Women to Recover and Reclaim the Fallen and to Prevent the Fall of Others into the Snares and Consequences of Seduction* (London: J. F. & C. Rivington, 1761), p. 13: "Necessity is sometimes assigned as the cause of [prostitution] which is but another name for idleness and vice."

[81] See, for example, Brown, *Sermon for . . . for Female Orphans*, p. 22.

[82] Defoe, *Street-Walkers*, p. 6. See also Hanway, *Reflections*, pp. 315–16; Hazeland, *Sermon*, p. 4.

that something be done about this class of women "if we wish to prevent unspeakable distress . . . which too often the virtuous and guiltless have found, from the dire contagion of this promiscuous defilement."[83]

The situation of war, the need to maximize the nation's productive and reproductive resources, combined with a growing recognition of the importance of colonial populations was a crucial factor in the establishment of the Magdalen. Hanway's praise for the founders of this charity makes this clear: "The time in which you began this good work, is also a circumstance that strikes me, and presages good to the undertaking. . . . As war necessarily occasions devastation, we are called on to think of the properest means of saving as many lives as possible." Hanway added that this work may well draw down the blessings of heaven on an embattled England.[84] Undoubtedly, the anticipated acquisition of a great part of the North American continent also made the rehabilitation program of the Magdalen seem more plausible as well as more utilitarian. Surely here was the golden opportunity to restore lost character by emigration and thus combine, in one stroke, through reform and resettlement, the salvation of the prostitute and the strengthening of England's colonial empire.[85]

Unlike earlier attempts to handle the problem of prostitution, the Magdalen was established on new principles. Older institutions like the Bridewell and the workhouses had not made it possible or desirable for such women to quit the game. Women were merely incarcerated for a time, to return to the streets spiritually unchanged and still unequipped to earn an honest living. What was needed to bring about genuine and permanent change, the proponents of the Magdalen argued, was more than a holding institution; what was needed was an agency for moral and vocational regeneration. It was on this premise and with these goals in mind that the Magdalen began.

What is interesting about this attempt is that the founders of the institution believed such regeneration to be a practical possibility. The idea that fallen women could remake their characters and remold their lives, albeit with some philanthropic assistance, was a new one.[86] Certainly the

---

[83] Robert Markham, *Sermon . . . Preached before the Governors of the Magdalen Hospital* (London: n.p., 1776), "Encouragement Promised to Reformation," p. 7. See also Dodd, *Sermon* (1759), p. 25.

[84] Jonas Hanway, *Thoughts on the Plan for a Magdalen House for Repentant Prostitutes*, 2nd ed. (London: Sold by J. & R. Dodsley, 1759), pp. 24–25.

[85] Dodd, *Sermon* (1759), pp. x–xi.

[86] Hanway, as usual, was at the forefront. In *Letters Upon . . . the Repentance of Prostitutes*, p. 8, he disagreed with "the opinion that it is impossible to reclaim a female prostitute; not considering that the degrees of sin in this article are almost as numerous as the sinners: and though they are all criminal, they are very far from being all irreclaimable.

public saw nothing odd in Clarissa Harlowe dying of grief after her unwilling and unwitting seduction. Even the supporters of the Magdalen
painted sentimental pictures of the penitent prostitute, finally reunited
with her family, dying a speedy and beautiful death, praising the Magdalen with her last breath.[87] However, while for most the wages of sin
were always and necessarily a slow and painful death, the Magdalen
spokesmen could hope for a brighter future for their charges. Given the
right treatment, they thought it would be possible to make these useless
women into good citizens, to restore them to their proper roles as laborers, wives, and mothers. Such women, Hanway remarked, would make
perfect spouses for "sailors just landed, and who have neither the time
nor inclination for a very long courtship." By such rehabilitation and matrimony, "many persons, from *prostitutes*, have been rendered very good
subjects."[88] Such rehabilitation could only be accomplished among the
very young, for it was widely believed that the effects of sin were cumulative, that women grew hardened in the life of vice, and that it was the
years of degradation that coarsened and defiled women's characters. If a
woman could be helped when she was young, however, before she had
spent too many years selling herself, she might yet be saved. Thus, it was
hoped that if young girls could be taken into a sheltered environment,
and trained in an honorable trade and in the fear of the Lord, much might
be accomplished. Still, Hanway cautioned the overoptimistic against
imagining "that an attempt of this sort will entirely turn the current of
sensuality into the pure streams of *temperance* and *chastity*," but nevertheless concluded that

> it is *undoubted truth*, that there are many *young women* who *repent* from their
> hearts, and would show their *repentance*, if they knew where to eat a morsel of
> *honest bread*, and to find shelter from the misery they have brought on their
> own heads.—If this be so, let us proceed: if we can save such from an *early
> grave*, it will be worth our time, our money and our toil.[89]

Mankind in general are guilty of many other offenses . . . which seem as difficult to cure, as
this of female prostitutes."

[87] Dodd, it was said, got his job on the basis of a melodramatic novel about prosititutes.
In 1760 two accounts purporting to be true stories of the life, repentance, and death of
Magdalen inmates were printed. See *The Histories of Some of the Penitents in the Magdalen
House* (London: John Rivington & J. Dodsley, 1760), and William Dodd, *The Sisters* (Lon-
don: Printed for T. Welles, 1754). For more on the life and death of this colorful figure, see
Gerald Howson, *The Macaroni Parson* (London: Hutchinson, 1973).

[88] Hanway, *Reflections*, 2:9. Hanway also noted, in *Thoughts on the Magdalen House*,
that the charity will "save a number of subjects to the state . . . prevent . . . great confusion
among the lower classes of the people," and increase the number of marriages made and
souls saved. See also *Rules, Orders, and Regulations of the Magdalen House* (1759), p. 3.

[89] Ibid., pp. 59–60.

Not only did the Magdalen's founders believe reform to be possible, they also thought they had discovered why previous efforts to control the problem of prostitution had failed. These previous attempts had been based on the mistaken notion that only the public shame that followed upon a woman's fall kept more women from embracing the life of prostitution. Young women who had been arrested for disturbing the peace or vagrancy (for there were no laws against prostitution itself) had been sent to Bridewell, where they met with and were treated as common felons, abused by both keepers and male prisoners. Such treatment only served to harden a woman's determination to seek her own immediate advantage, regardless of the costs to society, herself, or her immortal soul. Both Hanway and Fielding urged that new methods be tried, for the old methods only exacerbated the situation.

> Treat a woman, young in age, and not old in sin, as a *felon*, her sense of shame will be extinguished: she will be tempted to look on herself as an *outcast* of human nature: she will continue to sin without control: her heart will grow petrified: she will grow indifferent to all events, caring not how soon, or in what manner, she leaves a world, where she finds so little mercy, and such unrelenting severity against her.[90]

Such treatment was unfair, unfruitful, and impolitic. By casting the fallen woman from society, the community lost the possibility of exercising any persuasive influence upon her. By making her an outcast and closing off all avenues that might lead to social reintegration, the only path left her was into further and more vicious criminality. Rather, such women had to be withdrawn to a place of quiet, and led back by the benevolent into an active membership in the community. And, forgetting his earlier endorsement of the Marine Society on these same grounds, Hanway remarked that the Magdalen "will do more good, *in proportion to the expence*, than any other charity; for it must be considered, that the objects are in the prime of life, capable of *working*, and when once this charity is established, we may hope to maintain the house."[91]

In order to insure the success of their program, the governors decided that the Magdalens would have to be the "cream" of fallen women; their purpose would be to act as a wedge of light in a life of darkness, to be examples of what might be done by honest penitence and charitable concern. Therefore, admission to the hospital was not obtained easily. Each applicant for admission had to face an examination by a board of governors who questioned and scrutinized her in an attempt to discover how deep and genuine her contrition was. This was an important process—it

---

[90] Hanway, *Defects of Police*, p. 54. See also John Fielding, *Proposal*, p. 76.
[91] Jonas Hanway, *A Plan for Establishing a Charity House or Charity Houses, for the Reception of Repenting Prostitutes* (London: n.p., 1758), p. xv.

was essential to distinguish those women who were truly penitent from those who only wanted a temporary vacation from all labor. It was feared that if this distinction was not carefully made, the hospital would turn into a sort of almshouse for lazy or aged prostitutes, and by thus rewarding vice, would cause the problem of prostitution to increase rather than diminish. Saunders Welch, reflecting on the harm that "a certain asylum" might have on the problem of prostitution, raised the possibility that "the loosely-inclined [will] be induced to list themselves in the troops of prostitutes, under this reflection that let what will happen, there is a certain retreat for them."[92]

If a woman satisfied the governors of her heartfelt desire to mend her ways, she still had to establish that she was under thirty years of age, had not long been in the trade, and was not pregnant. Since places in the house were limited, the youngest and least experienced women were given preference. Upon admission, the women were given whatever medical treatment was needed and a new set of somber gray clothing that identified them as Magdalens. From then on they were addressed only by their given names, and strictly forbidden to discuss details of their former lives. They were further forbidden to see or communicate with anyone from the outside world without the approval and presence of the chaplain or matron. Women were to be housed in wards occupied by women of the same social standing and education. Each woman had her own bed, which could be closed off by a set of drapes. It was hoped that seclusion and frequent isolation would give the women adequate time to repent and fill their spirits with Christian humility. Religious and moral tracts were supplied for this purpose, and women attended two religious services daily to further speed their regeneration. Conversation between the Magdalens was discouraged; cursing or insolence were grounds for dismissal. Silence, it was believed, would settle the soul and bind the lonely woman closer to God. This period of isolation would restore the purity of the woman's nature and make it safe for her to reenter the community. Temporary withdrawal was necessary for the woman's sake and for the safety of society. "Mankind," noted Hanway, "are afraid of the *infection*, and require the patient to pass through some kind of *purgation* before she is admitted within their walls."[93]

Since the governors wished to do more than merely provide a temporary haven for the weary prostitute, steps were taken on her admission to

---

[92] Welch, *Proposal*, p. 6. See Stanley Nash, "Prostitution and Charity: The Magdalen Hospital, a Case Study," *Journal of Social History* (Summer 1984), for more on the workings of this institution. See also the suggestion by William Dodd, in *An Account of the Rise, Progress, and Present State of the Magdalen Charity* (London: printed for W. Faden and sold by J. Whiston & B. White, 1766), p. i, that though prostitution was inevitable, prostitutes should individually be able to "retire."

[93] Hanway, *Reflections*, p. 289.

help her reenter ordinary life. The first thing that was done, whenever possible, was to contact her family or friends and inform them of her change of heart and desire to be reunited with them. There were many women, however, who had no family or friends, or whose connections had entirely disowned them and would not accept their return. These women needed training to enable them to support themselves when they left the hospital. This training program, besides being useful to the women in the future, was seen as having several important and immediate effects. Employment would keep the women from idleness, which everyone believed to be the cause of much sexual sin.[94] Working with their hands put the women into a more receptive frame of mind for religious instruction and helped to support the hospital. The Magdalen's preacher claimed, as had Hanway of both the Magdalen and the Marine, as a sort of irresistible advantage of the charity, "that greater good may be done, at a less expence, in this undertaking, than in almost any other charitable scheme; since it is to be supposed, that when the whole is duly regulated, the women will nearly maintain themselves."[95] A variety of needle crafts as well as laundry were recommended as suitable work for the women. Hanway was especially desirous of teaching them to make Turkey carpets, and thus, in the best mercantile fashion, both finding employment for the needy and keeping bullion at home.[96] After the women received some craft training, the governors attempted to place them in situations of service or trade where they would not be exposed to undue temptation. Perhaps too optimistically, they believed there would be many benevolent masters who would welcome the opportunity of employing these reformed and humbled women.

Thus, it was hoped that the Magdalen would aid these needy women and help to meet the nation's needs as well. Not only would the reduction in the number of prostitutes raise the general tone of society and force unwilling males into marriage, but the rehabilitated prostitute would positively contribute to the welfare of the state. To critics of the Magdalen, who called it romantic and ridiculous, Hanway asserted that "these politicians should remember, that was there nothing more in view than political prudence, with regard to the increase of the species, and the good order of the state, there is the utmost reason to check the progress of this species of iniquity." The aim of the Magdalen was simply

> to preserve from present and afflictive death, the bodies of many young and perishing fellow creatures; . . . to take from our streets, the shame of our community, the instruments of foulest pollution, and most poisonous contagion:

[94] Hanway, *Defects of Police*, p. 190. See also Hanway, *Thoughts on a Plan*, p. 58.
[95] Dodd, *Sermon* (1759), pp. v–vi.
[96] *Rules, Orders, and Regulations of the Magdalen House* (1759), pp. 17–20.

... to introduce to health and industry, to happiness and to heaven, many, who could otherwise, neither ever have been employed, nor ever restored.[97]

The rehabilitated prostitute would contribute to England's wealth through her labor, and by marriage would increase the number of England's inhabitants, "a circumstance by no means so inconsiderable . . . in a commercial nation like ours; whose strength and prosperity depend on the number of its inhabitants."[98]

LONDON CHARITY, 1750–1770

Through the 1760s, charities of rescue and rehabilitation continued to be established and to receive public support. However, the relationship between the charities and parish officials, as well as between themselves, continued to be difficult. Furthermore, those charities that were of a more flexible and less institutional form, that processed people in greater numbers and more cheaply, without the large initial investment that the building of a hospital or asylum involved, increasingly attracted more support than the older and more expensive societies. If a charity could care for people on an outpatient basis, as in the case of the Lying-in Charity, or could do away with the need to commit itself to many years of nurture, as in the case of the Marine Society, the chances that the very operations of the charity would encourage a harmful dependency were lessened. The longer and more expensive the course of aid offered, the less likely it was to retain public popularity and charitable financing.

Let us look first, however, at the charities' relations with each other and with their local officials. We have seen both in the Marine and in the Lambeth Asylum some of the squabbling that could go on between charities. That this was not uncommon is illustrated by a remark made in the *Gentleman's Magazine* of May 1758: "The open competitions between different hospitals and the animosity with which the patrons oppose one another, may prejudice weak minds against them all: . . . The spirit of charity can only be continued by a reconciliation of these ridiculous feuds." Not only did the various charities compete for the hearts and purses of donors, but in the performance of their benevolence, charities sometimes refused to cooperate with each other or to establish links between their operations. For example, in December 1770, when the General Lying-in Hospital had to find a place for an orphaned infant whom they had delivered, they turned to the Foundling Hospital for assistance.

[97] Hanway, *Thoughts on a Plan*, p. 26; Dodd, *Sermon* (1759), p. 19.
[98] Dodd, *Sermon* (1762), p. 25.

The Foundling replied that the child would have to take his chances with the rest, and no special assistance could be offered.[99]

On the other hand, we see in certain instances at least a growing ability of parish and city officials to work with charitable societies. These sorts of links were formed very early with the Marine, and even after Fielding left the society the connection remained strong. The London Workhouse sent the Marine a boy in October 1770 along with £2. Three years later the City of London donated £500 to the charity, for unspecified reasons. Yet, while the Marine and the authorities worked quite well together, the case was quite different in the relations between the General Lying-in Hospital and its parish. Though the hospital decided to seek some sum as security to indemnify the parish for each single woman they delivered, Lambeth parish officers attended the quarterly meeting of the charity and asked the governors to request a parliamentary grant to reimburse the parish for all the bastards born into it. Some time later, the same officials insisted on having access to the hospital's admission books because, they said, women who were not entitled to parish assistance were wrongly claiming relief, falsely insisting that their babies had been delivered at the hospital. Thus, in some cases where care was not long-term or residential or where it did not lead to legal settlement, public and private agencies were able to cooperate; where this was not the case, however, a fair degree of friction continued.[100]

Despite the General Lying-in Hospital's difficulties with Lambeth parish officials, the charity that fared worst in the 1760s was the Foundling Hospital. We have seen how, under the impetus of parliamentary pressure, the Foundling overexpanded in the late 1750s. Perhaps it was the effort of attempting more than they could possibly hope to accomplish that resulted in the loss of confidence the Foundling suffered thereafter. For during the four years when the institution admitted babies indiscriminately, taking in almost fifteen thousand infants, more than two-thirds of these children died in infancy. The high cost of running such a charity, both in terms of money needed for long-term maintenance and in terms of this enormous mortality rate, must have made the hospital appear as a losing concern to the charitable public. This conclusion was perhaps not really fair or well-founded, and the subsequent contraction of funds and therefore of services was perhaps unwarranted. Everyone

[99] *Gentleman's Magazine* (May 1758), p. 215; General Lying-in Hospital, *Weekly Minute Book* (1769–1777), December 18, 1770.

[100] Marine Society, *Subscription Book #1*, MSY/V/1. The Marine Society Papers can be found at the National Maritime Museum. The General Lying-in's decision to require security (May 2, 1769), parish officers ask governors to petition Parliament (December 5, 1769), and their desire to examine the hospital's books (May 19, 1772), *Weekly Minute Book* (1769–1777).

seemed satisfied with what the hospital had accomplished in its first years of operation. During its first decade, the Foundling had admitted a total of 821 infants, of whom 376 had died under the age of two, a mortality rate of 46 percent. When the hospital resumed limited admissions in 1760, it admitted a total of only 387 children in the following decade, and lost 126 of these in infancy, a mortality rate of 33 percent. Thus, it was clearly the temporary policy of overadmission, rather than any innate defect in the conception or management of the institution, that was responsible for the especially high mortality rate. In terms of its popular appeal, however, the harm was done, and the Foundling was never again in the eighteenth century to achieve the level of aid or enthusiasm that it had enjoyed in its early years.[101]

Of all the charities started between 1740 and 1760, the one to do best financially, the most popular, highly praised, and least criticized, was the Marine Society. In addition to performing a vital service, it, unlike the Foundling, could expand or contract its operations as the situation demanded. For, what it offered was mainly placement aid—it would take boys off the street and find them suitable employment at sea. Other than the new suit of clothing, medical care, and religious tracts that it provided, its expenses per boy ended as soon as he was placed. In times of war it had no difficulty in attracting subscribers; in its initial years, during the Seven Years' War, it had a subscription list of 397, and in 1798, again in wartime, it had an enormous list of 1,148 contributors. In times of peace, though the numbers of its supporters contracted, the remainder represented much of the power and wealth of London. The subscription lists of the Marine Society for the year 1774, for example, though having few upper-class and even fewer women's names, included just those sorts of donors who could be expected to bring to a society a thoroughgoing knowledge of finance, administration, and the everyday workings of charitable institutions. Thus, for example, of its forty-man governing committee, 70 percent (twenty-eight) were subscribers to other charities, almost two-thirds of whom gave to three or more other organizations.[102]

---

[101] In the seventeen year period from 1739 to 1756 the hospital had received a total of £45,807.14.9 in subscriptions and benefactions (or about £2,700 per annum), which made up 42.6 percent of its total income. In the fourteen years between 1757 and 1771, the hospital received a total of only £8,247.2.7 from these sources (or about £590 per annum), which made up 13.3 percent of its income. The Foundling received 69 legacies worth £13,990 for the decade 1739–1748, 122 legacies worth £21,895 in the following decade, only 68 legacies totaling £8,530 for the period 1759–1768, and 28 legacies amounting to £3,650 for the 1770s: see McClure, *Coram's Children*, pp. 265–66.

[102] More than one-third of these governors subscribed to five or more other charities: see *A List of the Governors of the Marine Society* with Samuel Glasse, *A Sermon Preached before . . . the Marine Society* (London: Dodsley, 1778). See also the advertisement in the

In contrast to the popularity of the Marine, its female counterpart, the Lambeth Asylum, attracted only moderate initial support, both in terms of knowledgeable subscribers and large donors. Forty-three percent of its 1763 subscribers were women, and though the queen and the archbishop of Canterbury were early members, these were not the types of people that seemed to contribute to the successful maintenance of a charitable foundation. Perhaps it was the large number of female subscribers (who tended on the whole to give fairly small amounts) and the nonappearance of many of the great men of wealth that accounts for the relative smallness of their early receipts, under £2,000 per annum for its first ten years. Doubtless its lack of success in attracting donors and donations on the same scale as the Marine can be attributed to the fact that, in times of war, girls played a less visible and less important part in attaining national military goals than boys, and so the Lambeth Asylum did not exhibit the same clear advantages and quick visible returns for the charitable investor. The Lambeth Asylum, like the Foundling but unlike the Marine, also had premises that had to be maintained, and had as well an inevitably slower turnover rate, since the girls had to be trained before being apprenticed. This long stay in the institution meant that the charity could not rapidly decrease the care it offered when times and money demanded it. Instead, by once admitting a girl, the governors committed themselves to caring for her for several years and to seeing to it that she was released only when conditions were suitable. Thus, during the 1760s the departure rate from the Lambeth Asylum was quite low. Perhaps the governors felt uneasy about releasing the girls into the world when economic conditions were unsettled and unfavorable. In the 1760s the price of bread was rising, there was a general trade depression, bad weather, and crop failures, and the governors obviously feared to send their girls out. In addition to the long period of necessary care, and therefore expense, that the Lambeth Asylum program called for, the governors were disappointed in their hopes of offsetting these expenses by making the institution self-supporting. Though the sums derived from the girls' knitting and needlework varied from year to year, and though the girls earned relatively more than did most of the charitably employed, their earnings, at best, amounted to only about 9 percent of the Lambeth Asylum's total annual receipts.[103]

Times (London), March 29, 1782, describing their annual anniversary dinner, complete with the full text of its commemorative ode.

[103] The range of income that the girls made for the Lambeth Asylum went from £279.7.10, or 9.2 percent of revenue of £3,031.15.8 for 1775–1776, to £226.15.9, or 4.4 percent of a total income of £5,119.8.8: see *An Account of the Proceedings . . . of the Guardians of the Asylum* with George Horne, *A Sermon Preached . . . the Anniversary Meeting of the Asylum for Orphan Girls* (London: Harriot Bunce, 1774); *An Account* with

Thus, fiscal aid for the institution would not come from this direction. This was a difficulty that all charities that cared for women and girls ran into—institutional aid to women could never be as cheap and efficient as comparable aid to men; women needed more sheltering and training, and earned less. Hence, it invariably cost more to offer them relief. Thus, through the 1760s at least, societies caring for women and girls appeared to be less profitable investments than other sorts of charities.

Though the Magdalen attracted much more initial support than the Lambeth Asylum, many of its subsequent difficulties were similar. We have seen how an important element of the early popularity of this institution centered on the fearful devastation that was attributed to the prostitute, and the necessity for its alleviation. Perhaps the charity's enormous success in collecting more than £5,000 in subscriptions and donations during its first eight months can be explained by the hypothesis that the care of fallen and lascivious women engaged the public imagination. Not only did the Magdalen manage to attract more money than the Lambeth Asylum because of its more spectacular program, but also many of its supporters, like Hanway, were intimately involved in widespread charitable activities and well-skilled in fundraising and administration of collected money. The initial enthusiasm for the work of the institution was sustained for the charity's first decade. This can be seen by the large number of active subscribers from 1759 whose names reappeared on the 1768 list, by the increasingly large number of women admitted to the house during this period, and by the charity's continued financial soundness. However, even while the institution flourished, the same problems we have noted in the Lambeth Asylum were also present here. The early expectations of the governors about the amount of financial assistance that the work of the women would provide proved unfounded. Although the women managed to earn £282, or 5 percent of the charity's income, for 1761, this was most likely due to the novelty of the endeavor and the public's willingness to buy such work, whatever its quality, for its curiosity value—the product of the hands of "fallen women." In subsequent years this source of income shrank as the novelty wore off, amounting to 3 percent in 1763, 2 percent in 1766, and fluctuating around 1 percent thereafter. Like the Lambeth Asylum, the Magdalen could not expand and contract its services at will and could not balance its expenditures by the size of its receipts. Thus, during the 1760s it admitted large numbers of women annually, and managed to place relatively few. In addition to the difficulties that the Magdalen and the Lambeth Asylum shared, that is, the nonprofitability of women's work, the long-term nature of their

Robert Markham, *A Sermon Preached . . . in the Chapel of the Asylum for Female Orphans* (London: W. Oliver, 1778).

care, and the continuing expense of their relief, the governors of the Magdalen faced another problem during the 1760s—the need to dismiss or set free a large number (43 percent) of the women they had admitted, either for unsuitable behavior or because of the discovery that these women were not really as interested in repentance and rehabilitation as in a sanctuary from the pressures of the outside world. In the late 1760s, in response to this high dismissal rate, the Magdalen started cutting down the number of women admitted annually, undoubtedly screening more thoroughly, and successfully reduced the dismissal rate dramatically. However, by the late 1760s the early optimism of the first decade came to be tempered, and the hopes of rehabilitation and resettlement, which had attracted so much initial support, began to appear less realizable.[104]

The British and the City of London lying-in hospitals also flourished during the 1760s, offering more aid than ever before. Both institutions, as we have already noted, delivered more babies in this decade than they had in the 1750s. However, by the end of the 1760s, though the number of deliveries at the British Lying-in Hospital had increased, the rate of this increase had slowed down, and the number of its subscribers had actually fallen (going from 303 in 1757 to 204 in 1770). Thus, though the lying-in hospitals were not to feel the full effects of the shift in the direction of charitable giving, and would not suffer the same cutback in services as other institutional charities like the Foundling until later in the century, it was clear by the late sixties that the great heyday of the hospitals was past. Support had shifted from these more cumbersome charities to cheaper, more efficient outpatient services like the Lying-in Charity. On the whole, these newer charities initially tended to be supported by different sorts of people than had supported the hospitals. There were far fewer aristocrats and gentry and many more merchants and tradesmen in the lists of the Lying-in Charity. These sorts of donors, more cautious and involved in the workings of the charity, favored the type of aid that, while freest of the dangers of overgenerosity or overdependency, was able to

---

[104] Of the 377 subscribers to the Magdalen charity in 1759, 126, or an amazing 33 percent, gave some proof (committee membership, annual subscription, stewardship, etc.) not only of continued contribution, but of active interest. By March 1767, the Magdalen had admitted 961 women; 281 were admitted within the first two and a half years of operation, of whom 32 (11 percent) were dismissed for bad conduct; 402 were admitted in the next four years, of whom 72 (18 percent) were similarly dismissed; and 278 were admitted in the following two years, with another 72 dismissals (26 percent). By the mid 1770s the dismissal rate fell to about 10 percent of admissions and stayed at that relatively low rate throughout the century. Less than ten years after its foundation, the Magdalen had attracted more than £24,000 to its service. See *Rules, Orders, and Regulations of the Magdalen* (1759); General Accounts of the Magdalen Charity along with Richard Harrison, *Sermon Preached before the Governors of the Magdalen Charity* (London: J. Hughes, 1768); *General State of the Magdalen Hospital* with Samuel Glasse, *Sermon* (1777).

deliver the largest number of babies at the least cost per birth. This the Lying-in Charity was demonstrably able to accomplish. While the hospitals doubled the number of their annual deliveries in the 1760s, the Lying-in Charity increased the number of its deliveries twelvefold—from a yearly average of only 100 in the years 1757 to 1760, to a yearly average of 1,200 between 1760 and 1769. The Lying-in Charity's efficiency undoubtedly explains its growing popularity. In the three years from 1767 to 1770 its subscription lists doubled, managing not only to attract many new donors, but to retain most of its earlier subscribers as active, annual supporters.[105]

In contrast, the Lock Hospital tottered through the 1750s and 1760s. While numbers cared for increased, the Lock faced continuing problems of directorial support. Thirteen board meetings in these decades had to be canceled because of insufficient attendance. In 1758, 1761, and 1762 subscriptions were much in arrears and tradesmen's bills unpaid. In May 1752 the governors had hired a collector in an attempt to bring in more of the promised donations; by January 1754 the governors were bringing an action against this very collector for retaining donated funds. The matron and the cook of the hospital were dismissed in May 1763 for not giving the patients their full food rations. By April 1765 the hospital owed its tradesmen more than £1,100. Its survival during these decades seems to have been due to inadvertence and good fortune more than to planning and foresight.[106]

Thus, we see in many of the charities that started between 1740 and 1760 that once the initial outburst of optimism and enthusiasm had calmed down, the charities that did best both in terms of subscribers and funds were the ones that appealed to a "commercial sense," that promised the quickest returns and the greatest operating efficiency. In addition, the sorts of charities that seemed increasingly to generate most support were those that were not seen to reduce or impair self-reliance and what was called "independence." Perhaps the great success of the Seven Years' War diminished those anxieties about population size that had encouraged much of the charitable enthusiasm of the 1740s and 1750s. Thereafter, other concerns appear to have been uppermost in the minds of the chari-

[105] See *A Plain Account of the Advantages of the Lying-in Charity for Delivering Poor Married Women at their own Habitations* (1767); and *An Account of the Lying-in Charity . . . Instituted in 1757 with the state of the Charity to January 1770* (London: 1770). While the subscription lists of the British Lying-in Hospital for 1770 had 81 upper-class subscribers (or 28 percent of a total list of 294), the Lying-in Charity's 1770 subscription list contained only 29 upper-class names (or 5 percent of a total of 603 subscribers).

[106] Information on the Lock Hospital can be found in Lock Hospital *General Court Book # 1* (July 4, 1746, to May 29, 1762), and *General Court Book # 2* (October 1762 to January 1773). The Lock Hospital Papers are in the library of the Royal College of Surgeons, Lincoln's Inn Fields, London.

table, especially efficiency and self-support. That these two criteria were successfully met in the operations of certain charities seemed to the increasingly cautious donors of the 1770s sure proof that these charities were founded on proper principles and most deserved public support.[107] In chapter 5 we will look more closely at the practical and theoretical shifts that writers on relief, as well as charitable donors, seemed to make in the 1770s, and examine in more detail the growing repugnance among the charitably inclined to support any institution that might conceivably encourage dependency.

[107] Thus, for example, the Surrey Dispensary lauded its activities in these terms: "The immense sums expended on building and supporting great houses are more usefully employed in relieving a number of objects from the distresses of sickness. . . . A very great number of patients are accommodated at a small expense and those of the most useful part of the poor: for relief is administered not to the profligate and lazy only, but more especially to the industrious artisan": see *A Plan of the Surrey Dispensary* (London: James Philips, 1777), pp. 8–9.

CHAPTER FIVE

Poverty and the Attack on Dependency

WE HAVE SEEN how the support of large-scale institutional relief was already declining by the 1770s, while charities that treated their patients on an outpatient basis, that could easily adapt the numbers they aided to the revenue they received, or that were not saddled with long-term relief commitments, gained and grew in support. Thus, although to the historian of eighteenth-century charity the 1770s and 1780s appear, in many ways, to have been a transitional period in charitable theory and practice, while the charitable community seemed dissatisfied with the older forms of giving and had as yet developed no new programs, the one innovation of these years was the remarkable mushrooming of outpatient clinics or dispensaries. Between 1769 and 1805 at least twenty-one dispensaries were established in London alone, fifteen in the 1770s and 1780s.[1] In chapter 3 we indicated the practical and monetary considerations behind such a change in the direction of charitable activity. In this chapter we will look at changes that occurred in the general theory of how the poor should be relieved, or the "climate of ideas" that surrounded the giving of charity, not only in order to understand the transitional nature of these philanthropic ventures, but also to introduce the themes that were to become central to the restructured and reformulated charity of the century's last decade.

In chapter 1 we considered the religious and moral notions underlying the complex practice of charity in the first half of eighteenth-century London. In chapter 2 we have seen how in this flurry of theorizing about the proper function of charity the provision and encouragement of industry and industriousness were seen as prime concerns. In chapter 4 we indicated why, at midcentury, this concern ceased to hold center stage in the minds of the charitably active, and how attempts to increase population size and promote virtue usurped the role that the provision of employ-

---

[1] Sampson Low, *The Charities of London* (London: S. Low, 1850). Like so much else in this general area of inquiry, there is no substantive historical account dealing with the meaning or creation of these outpatient clinics. It is quite clear, however, that most of the older hospitals encountered grave financial difficulties in these years: see, for example, the advertisement in the *Gazetteer* of March 14, 1787, by the Middlesex Hospital, noting "the distresses of those excellent institutions, the Westminster and St. George's Hospitals. . . . [and] the considerable and unexpected decrease of Legacies, Benefactions and Subscriptions" to the Middlesex itself.

ment had held. With the end of the Seven Years' War, one might have expected a renewal of interest in make-work schemes of all sorts, and the appearance of charities devoted to this end. Certainly, there is every indication that unemployment once again became a serious problem. Not only were the poor rates steadily increasing, but there were outbreaks of food rioting and machine breaking in the later 1760s, as jobs became more scarce and food prices went up. The price of both bread and milk rose, and meat was expensive and scarce. The financial crisis of 1772 resulted in the collapse of several of London's important banks, and the monetary stability of all of Great Britain was threatened. Overseas trade to North America and the Continent was declining, and there is some indication that even the resumption of war in 1776 did not alleviate this problem.[2] Yet, in writings about proposed charities and schemes of poor relief during the postwar years, there were few suggestions for the charitable provision of employment. One important reason for this absence may have involved changes that were occurring in opinions about the nature of labor, and the best methods of insuring that men labored as long and as hard as they were able.

PHILANTHROPY AND THE PSYCHOLOGY OF LABOR

Explaining why something did not happen is much more difficult than describing why it did. Still, the absence of proposals for the provision of employment is a significant, though negative, feature of this period. The explanation for the nonresumption of such schemes offered here rests on changes in thought and opinion. I do not mean to suggest that new economic and philosophical ideas were causally responsible for new attitudes toward charity or for the growth or absence of new charitable endeavors. The relationship between theory, opinion, and practice is seldom so straightforward and often is not apparent at all. However, in the third quarter of the eighteenth century, these three factors were brought together in two important ways. First, the theorizing that took place during these decades was based on observations and speculations about the ordinary lives of ordinary men. Thinkers concerned themselves in the main with practical rather than metaphysical problems. They were interested in how and why men labored, the effects of agriculture and commerce on the wealth and manners of nations, and the role of public and private action in increasing the nation's wealth and power. Like contemporary philanthropists, they were intensely interested in maximizing labor and encouraging industriousness. Both philosophers and philanthropists were

[2] T. S. Ashton, *Economic Fluctuations, 1700–1800* (Oxford: Clarendon Press, 1959), conclusion. See also A. H. John, "War and the English Economy."

increasingly aware of the centrality of economic issues in discussions of the nation's needs and future policy. In addition, many of the leading philanthropists of the last quarter of the century had not only thoroughly read, but were profoundly influenced by, these earlier thinkers. Men like Bernard, Colquhoun, and Wilberforce had all been challenged and excited by their readings of such writings. That is not to say that these leaders of the charitable community entirely accepted the teachings of the theorists; indeed, we will see how the views of the political economists were transformed by utilitarian and evangelical opinion, how the philanthropy of the late 1780s and 1790s can be seen as a rejection or severe modification of some of the basic premises of the economists. But, whether they accepted or rejected the new theories, innovative philanthropists attempted to come to terms with the insights offered by the philosophers.

Philosophers, however, were not alone in their growing concern with economic and commercial topics. There was also a striking, simultaneous involvement of clerics in such theorizing. While Britain's leading intellectual clergymen had made outstanding contributions to philosophic speculations and systems in the first half of the eighteenth century, in its second half, clerical interest spilled over into, and pushed forward, the new science of economics. In fact it was the Reverend Josiah Tucker, dean of Gloucester, who first proposed that commerce be studied in such a manner. Refuting the charge that he had "made the whole of Religion to consist in the Promotion and Extension of Commerce; or in other Words, *of making Trade my Religion*," he argued that it was impossible for an "all-wise, first and benevolent Being" to have created a world in which self-interest, commercial interest, and religion were not providentially identical. Tucker's work, with its view that "the Ends both of Religion and Government" were best answered by a "System of Universal Commerce" was a paean to the instinct to truck, barter, and exchange.[3] William Paley, archdeacon of Carlisle, also made notable contributions to a scientific understanding of economics and was credited by contemporaries with anticipating the Benthamite notion of utility.[4] Religious thinkers, like

[3] Josiah Tucker, *Four Tracts together with Two Sermons* (Gloucester: J. Rivington, 1774), pp. xiii, xiv, 11, 12; Adam Smith, *The Wealth of Nations* [1776], Edwin Cannan, ed., 2 vols. (London: Methuen, 1961), 1:17. The clothier William Temple agreed, observing that "those who have closely attended to human nature and to the progress of human affairs, know that commerce naturally leads to justice, temperance, industry and frugality": *A Vindication of Commerce* [1758], in J. R. McCulloch, *A Select and Valuable Collection of Tracts* (New York: A. M. Kelley, 1966), p. 545.

[4] See the *Dictionary of National Biography*, 15:100–107, for this anticipation. Paley noted in his *Moral and Political Philosophy* [1785], in *The Works* (Philadelphia: Crissy & Markley, 1857), p. 39, that "it is the utility of any moral rule alone, which constitutes the obligation of it." This sentiment was found even earlier in John Fielding, *An Account of the*

contemporary philosophers and philanthropists, shared to a great extent in the creation of new psychologies of labor impelled by the centrality of commerce. In their conclusions, however, the clerics retained a distinctive and important voice. We shall hear from them again and again throughout this chapter and in the next.

Although philanthropists of the 1790s and onward amended the thinking of their forebears in a host of ways, on the question of the psychology of labor they can be seen as the direct heirs and adherents of one of three theories popular between 1750 and 1780. The first and oldest of these held that men labored because they must. Labor, an unpleasant activity, was not voluntarily sought out; men worked because they were forced to do so by the demands of hunger and cold. This argument was virtually the only argument ever given, when one was given at all, in the earlier literature of charity to explain the motivation of the working poor. For the sake of convenience we will call the supporters and advocates of this argument the "minimalists."

"Nothing but necessity can enforce industry. We must take human nature as it is."[5] This was the position taken either implicitly or explicitly by a great number of political arithmeticians and early exponents of the charitable provision of employment. They saw the poor as living from hand to mouth, spending whatever they earned. This improvidence of the poor was not seen to be an unmitigated evil, but in fact to be one of the chief and few incitements to further labor. It is this view of the psychology of the working poor that explains, at least in part, some of the opposition to high wages. By interfering with the prods of necessity, by allowing a laborer to subsist for a week on the work of four days, high wages made it less likely that the productive capacities of the laboring class would be fully utilized. Therefore, many believed that wages should be kept low, not that the poor starve, but that England be able both to undersell her foreign rivals in the marketplaces of the world and be more productive. Thus, the improvidence of the working poor, combined with low wages, would result in a generally enriched economy. Hanway, for one, was an ardent minimalist, noting that he "question[ed] much if we should be near so rich as we are, if the common people did not live so much from hand to mouth."[6]

Origin and Effects of a Police (London: A. Millar, 1758), where he claimed that the support a charity received would depend upon "the Public's Opinion of its utility" (p. 48).

[5] Temple, *A Vindication*, p. 512. See also Secker, *Fourteen Sermons* (London: J. & F. Rivington, 1771), pp. 270–71.

[6] Hanway, *Letters to the Guardians of the Infant Poor* (London: A. Millar & T. Cadell, 1767), p. 13. Temple argued that "the only way to keep a populace temperate is to deprive them of the means of debauchery by paying them low wages; and to increase their numbers by propagation" (*Vindication*, p. 516).

If the poor were to be paid low wages and continue to live from day to day, and if indeed this was for the benefit of the nation, it became the duty and obligation of the rich to care for the poor when such care was needed. Thus, Temple proposed a scheme in which a fund would be raised through a system of public taxation, from which the poor could be paid "a certain sum per head . . . in times of sickness, dearth, want of work, or any other distress." Though most philanthropists of the first half of the century, like Temple, may have had a very low opinion of the rationality and foresight of the working poor, they felt themselves obliged to make up for this deficiency, since they and the nation profited by it. Since the poor "never provide against the times of calamity . . . which they all might do,"[7] it was the job of the state and of charitable individuals and institutions to establish and maintain hospitals, stocks of raw materials, and workhouses, so that when ordinary employment failed, the laborer could find some honorable work to tide him over, and when illness or other distress interfered with his labor, he could expect the charitable to care and provide for him. This type of paternalistic minimalism seemed to wane as the century went into its third quarter. Undoubtedly one of the reasons for its declining popularity was the enormous growth of the poor rates, from £700,000 in 1748 to £1,500,000 by 1775.[8]

Though this particular form of the minimalist argument became less frequent in the writings dealing with the care of the poor in the last twenty-five years of the century, another form of the argument remained very popular. Unlike their paternalist predecessors, these later minimalists maintained that though the poor might only be motivated to labor through the pressure of necessity, the necessity need not be immediate. The fear of future want, they claimed, was also a powerful stimulus to labor. Lord Kames noted that

> Fear of want is the only effectual motive to industry with the labouring poor: remove that fear, and they cease to be industrious. The ruling passion of those who live by bodily labour, is to save a pittance for their children, and for supporting themselves in their old age: stimulated by desire for accomplishing these ends, they are frugal and industrious; and the prospect of success is to them a continual feast.[9]

---

[7] Temple, *Vindication*, pp. 513–14. Although the sentiment had become uncommon, as late as 1789 the vicar of Dallington, Joseph J. Rye, acknowledged the inability of the poor to save enough to pay for medicine or care during illness: see *Sermon for the Northamptonshire Infirmary* (London: W. Chalken, 1789).

[8] L. O. Pike, *The History of Crime in England*, 2 vols. (London: Smith Eden, 1876), 2:236.

[9] Henry Home, Lord Kames, *Sketches of the History of Man*, 4 vols. (Edinburgh: W. Strahan, 1778), 3:72.

In this view the poor still had to be driven to work, but the passion of fear, rather than immediate necessity, could be the stimulus. In many ways, this latter view was far more sophisticated than the earlier minimalist one. For, if the poor worked only as long as they needed to fill their bellies and clothe their backs, the total amount of work to be expected from each individual laborer was severely restricted. Since output per head was so limited, the earlier minimalists felt it necessary to increase population size in order to increase production. However, if the poor could be made provident and made to feel anxious about their future welfare and the welfare of their families, their output would be greatly increased in the attempt to allay this anxiety. The newer minimalists also believed that it was important that the laborer marry and have children for whom he would have to work to support, but the purpose of these additions would be as much to increase his anxiety about their future welfare as to provide additional productive units: "It has been generally observed, that the sober married man, who has a family, works two, three or four hours in the day more than him that has none, and is generally in a more spirited and masterly manner. . . . The reason is plain, it is the consequence of the love he bears to his wife and children, and the sense he has of his duty."[10] The practical effects of this revision was a critique of all relief programs that, by holding out guaranteed or regular aid to the laborer in times of distress, reduced his desire to provide for such emergencies out of prudential savings. Thus, revised minimalism strongly urged the withdrawal of guaranteed aid or employment to the poor, and held that by destroying the need to lay up a store for hard times, the aid given actually increased the numbers of poor and idle. Opposing automatic poor relief, Lord Kames warned the British of the fate that they, like the Lyonnaise, might expect: "The poorhouse at Lyons contained originally but forty beds, of which twenty only were occupied. The eight hundred beds it contains at present are not sufficient for those who demand admittance."[11]

With the recognition that the poor were not inevitably children, and thus inevitably improvident, came the view that the poor were only acting in a childish manner, that is, not exercising mature prudence, because such behavior was encouraged and rewarded by regular and dependable private and public charity. If they were not so encouraged they would have to grow up and become more responsibly accountable for their own

[10] [Jonas Hanway], *A Candid Historical Account of a Hospital . . . for Exposed and Deserted Children*, 2nd ed. (London: G. Woodfall, 1760), p. 46.

[11] Ibid., p. 73. There were those, however, who, though agreeing in principle with the supersession of the workhouse mode of relief, were loathe, on humanitarian grounds, to curtail or revoke this type of aid. For an example of this see the *Monthly Review* (October 1779), p. 311, for an unfavorable review of such proposals in Arthur Young's *Political Arithmetic* [1774] (New York: A. M. Kelley, 1967).

welfare. Through such a program of enforced maturation some few individuals might suffer from the abolition of workhouses: "If by neglect or oversight any happen to die of want, the example will tend more to reformation, than the most pathetic discourse from the pulpit," noted Lord Kames.[12] On the whole, such an action would be very beneficial to the nation.

At the same time as this revised minimalist argument was gaining popularity among social theorists, another quite different theory was being formulated. Like the "necessity" argument, this new theory held that labor, or the steady, repetitive exertion at the same task, was a forced activity, inherently unpleasant and unnatural to man. However, the centrality of such labor to the nation made it important to find an efficient method to extract the greatest amount of productive capacity from the individual worker. David Hume, a founding member of the school of political economy, noted that "everything in the world is purchased by labour, and our passions are the only causes of our labour."[13] Unlike the minimalists, who believed that only the fear of want drove men to work, the political economists hoped to accomplish this same end by calling forth the universal passion for self-betterment. It was the great insight of Hume and his followers that self-interest, unlike fear, was a entirely limitless passion; that, if it appealed to his interests, the free laborer would work as much as he was able, for his own boundless wants would be more merciless and effective taskmasters than any external compulsion.[14] For political economists, only the prospect of enjoyment, of material or social betterment, or an appeal to self-interest, could ensure that kind of continual and maximum industry that commercial and industrial society required. The author of *Considerations on the Policy, Commerce, and Circumstances of this Kingdom* remarked that

> To toil incessantly in want, is too hard a condition for a human creature to endure. Men will not be laborious, but on the prospect of reaping some enjoyment therefrom; nay, it would be the most detestable tyranny to require it on other terms. The want of due encouragement must naturally make men sink into despondency or plunge into desperation.[15]

The use of necessity to drive men to labor would be unjust as well as unprofitable. It would result in work of an inferior quality than that produced by the well-paid wage laborer. "In the one case, you must be sat-

---

[12] Kames, *Sketches*, 3:102–3.

[13] Quoted in W. L. Taylor, *Francis Hutcheson and David Hume as Predecessors of Adam Smith* (Durham, N.C.: Duke University Press, 1965), p. 67.

[14] Sir James Steuart, *An Inquiry into the Principles of Political Economy* [1767], Andrew S. Skinner, ed., 2 vols. (Chicago: University of Chicago Press, 1966), 1:51.

[15] Thomas Mortimer, *Lectures on the Elements of Commerce, Politics, and Finance* [1772] (London: A. Strahan for T. L. Longman, 1801), pp. 90–91.

isfied with the common drudgery of an enervated slave, in the other you may expect new efforts of ingenuity, extraordinary exertions of abilities, and every good effect of a mind at peace, and a body in the vigour of health."[16] Unlike the minimalists, the economists therefore urged high wages as the best incentive to increase skill and further the division of labor. Tucker thought that increased wages would be more than compensated for by the increase in subsequent quality and size of output.[17]

The political economists used the extent to which the passion of self-betterment had historically been allowed concrete expression as the organizing principle in their new historical sociology. This sociology was among other things a critique of the use of fear to motivate men. The use of fear to extract labor was seen to characterize primitive societies; in this new sociology it was the lessening of coercion and the growth of individual freedom that indicated historical progress from one epoch to another. "Nay [slavery] is known, *experimentally* known, to be incompatible with an extensive progress."[18] Freedom for the political economists meant the enjoyment of the fruits of property; hence, slavery was natural only to the most backward stages of human development, when the freedom of many individuals was totally nonexistent. In the second stage of social development, men were not exactly slaves, for they could by stealth enjoy some of the fruits of their labors. But they were still not free, for those that could accumulate "some little stock . . . would naturally conceal it with great care from [their] master, to whom it would otherwise have belonged."[19] The right to enjoy the fruits of labor depended more on the caprice of good fortune, or the incompetence of masters, than on the protection of the law. This second stage, in fact, was characterized by a servile dependency, a state just short of, and almost as demeaning as, slavery. Adam Smith described this state as bereft of commerce or industry, without which the wealthy "have no possible means of spending their property, having no domestic luxury, but by giving it in presents to the poor, and by this means they attain such influence over them as to make them, in a manner, their slaves." In characterizing as virtual slavery what earlier thinkers had called Christian hospitality, Smith viewed hospitality not as a "free" gift, but as the purchase of the loyalty and dependency of the recipient in exchange for the donor's "mess of lentils."[20]

[16] Quoted in Mortimer, *Elements of Commerce*, p. 85.

[17] Tucker, *Four Tracts* pp. 16–33.

[18] Tucker, *A Sermon for the Charity Schools* (London: J. & W. Oliver, 1766), p. 19. The political economists were not alone in this critique of slavery. Both the lively antislavery movement and the Wilkite movement stressed both antidependency and the need for liberty.

[19] Smith, *Wealth of Nations*, 1:426.

[20] Adam Smith, *Lectures on Justice, Police, Revenue, and Arms* [1763] (New York: A. Kelley, 1964), p. 16. As late as January 6, 1736, "George Goodwill" noted in the *Daily*

This state of dependency, however, did not entirely end with the introduction of arts and commerce into society. Although in a commercial society it was possible to be a free laborer, there were still groups of men who did not depend on the sale of the products of their labor to procure their necessities. These groups, called nonproductive laborers by Smith because they received wages though they did not create new products, were still in a state of servile dependency. The personal or menial servant was the least free, and the most slavish of all laborers. Not only was his maintenance solely derived from the bounty, and dependent on the good will, of his master, but his future employment depended not on any objective talent or skill of his own, but on his master's continued good opinion of him. He was as close to being in the condition of slavery as it was possible for a free man to be: "so long as [a man] . . . is subjected to the power of another, who useth him as he thinks proper, that man only enjoys a mere animal existence. Humble and dependent, like his brother spaniel, he licks the hand that strikes him."[21] We shall see later how the political economists hoped that by shrinking this nonproductive and slavish sector of the economy and the liberation and transformation of the laborer into a productive citizen would result in the general improvement of the morals and manners of society.

Thus, the political economists, like their minimalist contemporaries, came to criticize the provision of employment through public relief or private charity. For them, the acceptance of alms bound the recipient to the donor in a degrading and unmanly fashion, bringing him into a condition of near slavery. Similarly, the workhouse was characterized as demeaning, and as denying to the working poor some of their natural and civil liberties.[22] The Law of Settlement, which gave the poor the right to claim relief only in the parish in which they had a legal "settlement," also came under attack for its infringement of men's natural right to move about. The provision of relief to the poor in old age, remarked Arthur Young, could not be a "sufficient compensation for the slavery of their youth." While many supporters of guaranteed relief to the poor still existed, it seemed clear that confidence in the value of the provision of employment, or relief in the workhouse, was gone, replaced by a hesitant

---

Post that "Hospitality, which is but a Branch of Charity, has always been placed in the foremost Rank of national Virtues." For more on the meaning and practice of hospitality, see Felicity Heal, "The Idea of Hospitality in Early Modern England," *Past and Present*, no. 102 (February 1984).

[21] Quoted in "Review of Anderson's *Observations on National Industry*," *Monthly Review* (March 1778), pp. 181–82.

[22] Thomas Mendham, *A Dialogue between a Gentleman, a Pauper, and His Friend . . . intended as an Answer to "Observations on the Poor Laws"* (Norwich: J. Crouse, 1775), p. 35. See also Henry Zouch, *Remarks upon the Late Resolutions of the House of Commons* [1776] (London: T. Cadell, 1787), pp. 31–32.

defense of existing institutions as, despite their numerous and acknowledged faults, the established methods of aid.

> The law of humanity, and the law of the land, may both be abused; both fre-
> quently are abused; . . . But it doth not follow from hence, that all principles of
> charity should be extirpated from our breasts, the Poor Laws erased from our
> Statute-Book, and distressed Innocence suffered to perish for fear Vice should
> fraudulently contrive to steal encouragement that is not intended for it.[23]

This kind of halfhearted apology seemed increasingly unable to meet the
strong economic as well as theoretical objections made against such aid.
Certainly most members of the charitable community would have agreed
that *their* funds could be better spent elsewhere. Even if workhouses were
to be publicly supported, they were uneconomical and unpromising undertakings for organizations that depended on public subscriptions for
the greatest part of their revenues. The notion that the charitable provision of employment could be made to pay for itself, or even run at a slight
loss, seems to have been entirely abandoned.

As well as the injustice, inefficiency, and general ill effects that the provision of employment would have, the political economists put forward
yet another argument against this sort of relief. In brief, they argued that
a fund of limited size existed that could be employed for the maintenance
of labor. The stock of a country could be divided into two parts; the first
essentially went to pay the productive laborer, and the second was the
revenue of the manufacturer or landowner. Insofar as funds for the voluntary or compulsory care of the poor came out of that portion destined
for the support of productive labor, the nation was impoverished.[24]
Rather than use funds to gainfully employ people who would produce
wealth, this money went to the nonproductive. On the other hand, if
charity were to come from that portion of the public stock intended for
revenue, and therefore if the money given to charity was provided by sacrifices in the consumption of the rich, the nation would not suffer. But
benevolence, like prodigality, did not usually come from revenue—people
did not cut back on their personal expenses so that they could give alms
or pay the poor rates—but from capital. The charitable man, therefore,
was like the prodigal

> who perverts the revenues of some pious foundation to profane purposes, he
> pays the wages of idleness with those funds which the frugality of his fore-

---

[23] Young, *Political Arithmetic*, p. 332. See also Adam Smith for his critique of the Laws
of Settlement in *Wealth of Nations*, 1: chap. 10; Lewis Bagot, bishop of Norwich, *A Sermon
Preached in the Cathedral Church of St. Paul . . . for the Charity Schools* (London: Ann
Rivington, 1788), p. 6.

[24] See Smith, *Wealth of Nations*, 1:353.

fathers had, as it were, consecrated to the maintenance of industry. By diminishing the funds destined for the employment of productive labour, he necessarily diminishes, so far as it depends upon him, the quantity of that labour which adds a value to the subject upon which it is bestowed, and consequently the value of the annual produce of the land and labour of the whole country, the real wealth and revenue of its inhabitants.

It might be argued, however, that it was proper that charitable provision of employment be financed from the funds for the employment of productive labor, since the activities of workhouse inmates were productive. The political economists disagreed. For them, the employment of capital at less than its peak efficiency had the same economic result as prodigality. In "Every injudicious and unsuccessful project . . . though the capital is consumed by productive hands only, yet, as by the injudicious manner in which they are employed, they do not reproduce the full value of their consumption, there must always be some diminution of what would otherwise have been the productive funds of the society."[25] The workhouse was a truly undesirable solution to the problem of unemployment. It demoralized and corrupted men while squandering and misdirecting the funds that acted as the lifeblood of the nation. Thus, both the minimalists and the political economists roundly condemned regular or guaranteed relief for the poor either by charity or the Poor Law. Men had to learn, Smith said, that "it is not from benevolence, as the dogs, but from self-love that man expects anything. The brewer and the baker serve us not from benevolence, but from self-love. No man but a beggar depends on benevolence, and even they would die in a week were their entire dependence on it."[26]

Since the acceptance of alms robbed men of their human dignity and robbed the nation of funds that might have been better employed, such a transfer was doubly pernicious. Only by their integration into the labor market and their refusal to accept alms could the poor become autonomous, self-regarding, and self-providing adults. It is but an indication of the strength with which the provision of employment was rejected that the only charitable employment project discussed during these years that obtained substantial support was a call to the benevolent to distribute parcels of land to the rural poor and aid in the purchase of a cow or pig.[27] This scheme would have applied, of course, only to the agricultural poor.

[25] Ibid., 1:360, 362.

[26] Smith, *Lectures*, p. 169. See also his reformulation of this point in *Wealth of Nations*, 1:18.

[27] See R. Potter, *Observations on the Poor Laws and on Houses of Industry* (London: J. Wilkie, 1775), pp. 70–71; Mortimer, *Elements*, p. 195; Arthur Young, *Agriculture in Lincolnshire* (1779), quoted in *Arthur Young on Economics and Industry*, Elizabeth Pinney Hunt, ed. (Philadelphia: Bryn Mawr, 1926), pp. 31–32, 79.

There were, as far as I have been able to determine, no new proposals to aid or supplement employment for the urban poor.

POPULATION AND THE MARKET

As we have noted in chapter 2, the midcentury witnessed a great out-pouring of books and articles on the state of the nation's population. Despite the diversity of views expressed, the interest in the proper size and true state of the population was founded on several assumptions that continued in force through the 1770s and 1780s. All agreed that a large population was a cause of a healthy and growing economy and a consequence of proper internal policy. Hume noted that the size of the population of a state "implies important consequences and commonly determines the preference of their whole police, their manners, and the constitution of their government." All agreed that a large population, busily engaged in labor, was an important and desirable end of national regulation. In the 1750s, however, the majority of writers had believed that the population was declining, that the growth of cities and the introduction of luxury and manufactures had deranged the national growth processes and endangered the future of the state. Cities were not only unhealthy, and thus hindered population expansion by plagues and illnesses, but were generally the scenes of dissipation and extravagance.[28]

Although most demographers of the 1750s held that England was becoming more sparsely populated, this opinion was by no means universally held. Hume, for example, arguing from the vast improvements made in commerce and industry, said it was self-evident that these must have caused population growth.[29] Both Richard Forster and George Burrington argued that such an increase had taken place, and both used more evidence and less deduction than Hume had to prove their point. Forster said that although appearances alone suggested a population increase, he had gone further in search of the truth. Not trusting mere conjecture or armchair reasoning, he had adopted "the English way of philosophizing . . . not to sit down in one's study and form a hypothesis, and then strive to wrest all nature to it; but to look abroad into the world, and see how nature works; and then build upon certain matter of fact." This study had convinced him that population was indeed increasing "in a very rapid

---

[28] David Hume, *Writings on Economics*, Eugene Rotwein, ed. (Edinburgh: Thomas Nelson & Sons, 1955), pp. 11–12. See also "Letter from Dr. Brackenridge to G. L. Scott" [1755], in *The Population Controversy*, D. V. Glass, ed. (Farnborough: Gregg International Publications, 1973), p. 268; Thomas Short, *New Observations, Natural, Moral, Civil, Political, and Medical, on City, Town, and Country Bills of Mortality* (London: Longmans, 1750), pp. 121, 123.

[29] Hume, *Writings on Economics*, p. 146.

manner." Forster did not rest content with asserting that numbers had grown, but proceeded to question the value of a large population: "The first [mistake] is that all ways to increase a people would be for the public welfare . . . numbers of people without employment are a burden and disease to the body politic; and where there is full employment there the people multiply of course." Like the minimalist argument about the value of necessity to enforce labor, this view also stretched back into the seventeenth century. The novelty of Forster's restatement consists in its vehemence and in its implications. While the earlier advocates of the primacy of employment over population had recommended the expansion of trade and manufacture in order to encourage population growth, writers like Forster were increasingly doubtful about the possibilities of such an expansion.[30]

The next wave of works discussing population came in the 1770s and early 1780s (though Sir James Steuart's book was first published in 1767). The majority of these writers, whatever their other views, still agreed that a large and growing population was desirable. While the "truest opulence of a nation" was acknowledged to be the numbers of its people, depopulation was taken as a sure sign of national decay. "The increase of numbers in a state shews youth, and vigour; when numbers do not diminish, we have an idea of manhood, and of age when they decline."[31] However, past this point of agreement, divergences in opinion occurred. These differences were the result of different views of the actual size and state of the population and of different notions of the significance and economic implications of such populousness.

There were still writers in the 1770s, like Price and Kames, who believed that England's population size was shrinking disastrously.[32] But these fears were being increasingly challenged. By the 1770s many writers believed that population was increasing, or that its size was not as signif-

[30] Richard Forster, "Letter to Thomas Birch," (1757), in Glass, *Population Controversy*, pp. 461, 463.

[31] Vicesimus Knox, *Essays Moral and Literary*, 2 vols. (London: E. & C. Dilly, 1779), 1:272. See also William Wales, *An Inquiry into the Present State of Population in England and Wales* (London: J. Bigg, 1781), p. 74; Steuart, *Inquiry*, 1:76.

[32] It is important to stress the overlapping nature of the debate on population. It was not as though in one day, or one year, people changed their minds en masse. Thus, in Cookson's *Thoughts on Polygamy* (Winchester: J. Wilkes, 1782), we read this version of the earlier thesis: The encouragement of marriage "ought to be particularly attended to in this land of freedom, where POPULATION must in some measure supply the want of territory, and, in conjunction with freedom, give vigour to trade and commerce, the *basis* of our national greatness" (pp. 445–46). See also Kames, *Sketches*, 3:126; Richard Price, *An Essay on the Population of England* (London: T. Cadell, 1780), p. 62; Hanway, *Defects of Police*, p. 56; Mortimer, *Elements*, pp. 41–45; Francis Moore, *Considerations on the Exorbitant Price of Provision* (London: T. Cadell, 1773), p. 21.

icant a factor as had formerly been thought. These attacks on theories of declining population led to the reformulation of attitudes about the value of encouraging any increase in population.

Arthur Young was one of the earliest and most vociferous opponents of the pessimistic view of population. Young went through the factors that the pessimists had thought to be the causes of depopulation and illustrated, one by one, how each had in fact resulted in an increase in population. Cities, insofar as they were centers of commerce and manufacture, Young contended, increased population by increasing the demand for labor. Agricultural change had not caused a decrease in the total number of rural residents. Neither war nor emigration could hurt population size if the demand for labor remained high. "Take a quantity from the market," whether beef, wheat, or men, reasoned Young, and "certainly you add to the value of what remains, and how can you encourage the reproduction of it more powerfully than by adding to its value?"[33]

From worrying about population decline, and how population might best be supported and encouraged, population growth was increasingly seen as a symptom, rather than an important cause, of a prosperous economy. Thus, "the most decisive *mark* of the prosperity of any country is the increase of the number of its inhabitants." Population was seen as responding to, rather than responsible for, external economic circumstances like the amount of food available or the current demand for labor. Reproduction could therefore be left to the operations of the market. "In this manner the demand for men, like that for any other commodity, necessarily regulates the production of men; quickens it when it goes too slowly, and stops it when it advances too fast. It is this demand which regulates and determines the state of propagation in all the different countries of the world."[34]

A state always had the population that its economy demanded. If an economy was in good health, people would be produced as needed. "Thus the generative faculty resembles a spring loaded with a weight, which always exerts itself in proportion to the diminution of resistance."[35] Though the long-range effects of this mechanical production of population were believed to result in an equilibrium between the number of laborers needed and the number of laborers available, in the short run, gluts in the production of laborers might occur. For this reason there was no need to encourage population growth; rather, there was a need to discourage "mere procreation." Sir James Steuart questioned the value even

---

[33] Young, *Political Arithmetic*, pp. 61–65. See also *Arthur Young on Economics and Industry*, pp. 70–71, 363–64.

[34] Smith, *Wealth of Nations*, 1:54, 62, emphasis added. See also Steuart, *Inquiry*, 1:32.

[35] Steuart, *Inquiry*, 1:32.

of those who could maintain themselves. For the first time, we see the emergence of the concept of a "useless population."

> Now I consider multiplication as no otherwise useful to a state than so far as the additional number become so to those who are already existing, whom I consider as the body-politic of society. When it therefore happens that an additional number produced do no more than feed themselves, then I perceive no advantage gained by their production.[36]

Until the 1770s the prevalent view was that a population was redundant and undesirable only if it was unemployed, and that it was the obligation of the state, or of private individuals, to provide employment. In all circumstances, a growing population was to be desired and actively encouraged. From the 1770s onward we begin to see the emergence of the view that additional population growth had to be justified on some solid economic grounds. The argument for the value of population increase on the grounds of its usefulness in national defense was also being questioned, and with the new psychology of labor and its corollary, the elevation of personal independence, children ceased having the same crucial role either in the creation of wealth. Though population increase was still seen as part and parcel of a booming economy, its increase ceased to be a desired goal in itself. Thus, though the question of charitable involvement in the field of population growth was much more unresolved than the value of the charitable provision of employment, in these years we can see the beginnings of doubts about the advisability of such aid. The specter of a redundant population, though not yet feared, began to be seen as a shadowy outline, and it was therefore urged that population "ought to be left to its own course."[37]

THE PRODUCTION OF VIRTUE

In their analysis of the moral state of the nation, the minimalists and the political economists sharply disagreed about the causes and cures of undesirable public behavior. The minimalists, both of the earlier and latter varieties, believed that the self-interestedness that was the chief characteristic of commercial society had produced social breakdown by leading to a loss of social cohesiveness and a degeneracy in the sense of common purpose. "In every opulent city that has long flourished in extensive commerce," noted Lord Kames, "every man studies his own interest. . . . And thus in the progress of manners, men end as they begin; selfishness is no less eminent in the last and most polished state of society, than in the first

[36] Ibid., pp. 32, 87.
[37] Young, *Political Arithmetic*, p. 69.

and most savage state." The minimalists believed that the pursuit of magnificence made "men less sensible of true glory and less desirous of true honour" and led to the eradication of all civic virtue; the very freedom that commercial society made possible led only to an increase of licentiousness and crime. In such a society, men were restrained from heinous crimes by the dread of punishment, the love of justice having fled.[38] And, as Hanway commented on the frequency of robbery in Britain, this dread was a very imperfect restraint. Even more significant than the damage done to the general state of public morale was the harm that the workings of a free and commercial state had on the morals of the lower classes. The "great wages and certainty of employment" that were common in expanding economies "render the inhabitants of cities insolent and debauched." Licentiousness in the common people was the prime defect of a free society, where they "may wallow in disorder and profligacy without control, if they but refrain from gross crimes, punishable by law."[39]

The effects of luxury on the individual were seen to be equally pernicious: "Luxury besides renders the mind so effeminate, as to be subdued by every distress." This enfeeblement of its citizenry would have very dangerous consequences for the strength and security of the nation. A rich and peaceful state, absorbed wholly in the business of making money, would be an easy and tempting prize for any invader. The bulk of the people, "by having their minds constantly employed on the arts of luxury . . . grow effeminate and dastardly."[40] The dreaded prospect of injury to property would cause such an emasculated citizenry to surrender without a fight to the enemy, and thus the state would be "reduced to flattering [his] enemy, because he hath not the courage to brave them." The critics of luxury contrasted the modern state with ancient states, and in the important qualities of social virtue, personal probity, and military valor, found the former wanting. The refinements that commerce introduced were seen as only external embellishments. "The highest degree of generous virtue, and the truest politeness of the mind, may be found among nations to whom these arts are almost totally unknown."[41]

[38] Kames, *Sketches*, 1:346–47. Wallace, *A Dissertation on the Numbers of Mankind in Ancient and Modern Times* (Edinburgh: Archibald Constable & Co., 1753), p. 337. See also Hanway, *Observations on the Causes of the Dissoluteness which Reigns among the Lower Classes of the People* (London: J. & F. Rivington, 1772), p. 74; Kames, *Sketches*, 1:401.

[39] Temple, *Vindication*, p. 535; Hanway, *Observations*, p. 74; Kames, *Sketches*, 3:28–29.

[40] Ibid., 2:145–46. Though Smith holds that the nation's martial spirit declines with the growth of commerce, he feels that the division of labor, which creates greater national wealth, would also, in the form of a standing professional army, create a powerful military force: see *Lectures*, pp. 257–58.

[41] Kames, *Sketches*, 1:410–11; James Dunbar, *Essays on the History of Mankind in Rude and Cultivated Ages* (London: W. Strahan & T. Cadell, 1781), p. 150.

This severe condemnation of commerce and luxury was sometimes tempered by a discussion of historical epochs, each with its own specific needs. There were several writers who believed that in the early stages of human development, the introduction of commerce and an economy geared to the satisfaction of nonessential wants had had a civilizing and humanizing effect on mankind. As societies leave the state of mere subsistence, their citizens "acquire a relish for society . . . a pleasure in benevolence, in generosity, and in every other kindly affection." However, this happy state inevitably gave way to a new state of barbarism, a state more disordered than its original because it was bereft of friendship or any other social passion.[42]

The minimalists therefore held that the prevalence of public licentiousness and the widespread tendency to luxurious consumption demanded a return to a more hierarchically ordered society, where each man was either master or servant,[43] where sumptuary laws were enforced, and where neither the state nor private charity interfered in cushioning the idle and improvident from the inevitable effects of their vice and laziness. On the whole, they advised civic-minded citizens to encourage and aid attempts to educate and regulate the morals of the lower classes, while practicing a studied noninterference with the meting out of just and deserved punishments to the improvidently poor.

In contrast to the gloomy picture and severe recommendations for improving the state of public morals painted by the minimalists, the political economists offered a more optimistic view of the possible improvement of national morality. Unlike the minimalists, they felt that antisocial or unsocial behavior was the result of dependency. When a man was servile, either by being employed in a menial (i.e., service) capacity or by being underpaid for his work, he would slip into despondency and drink or be driven to a life of crime. Thus, it was the absence of personal servants that made manufacturing and commercial towns so law-abiding. Intemperance was not, the political economists maintained, caused by the presence of alehouses or the absence of taxes on alcohol; it was "the vexation and distress of mind, when provisions and the necessaries of life are so dear, that they [the workers] cannot even maintain their families by incessant toil that often drives them to hopeless despondency."[44] Crime, too, both in the commission of particular offenses and in the spread of immorality, was attributed to the same debilitating dependency. James Anderson, for example, recommended the removal of "tyrannical power" to curb

[42] Kames, *Sketches*, 1:399, 400, 197. Both John Brown and Thomas Short agreed with Kames.

[43] See Hanway, *Virtue in Humble Life*, vol. 2 (London: Dodsley, 1774), p. 379.

[44] Mortimer, *Elements*, p. 89. See Smith's remarks on alcohol consumption in *Lectures*, p. 179, and *Wealth of Nations* 1:382–83.

crime: "Instead of an abject slave, make the man of whom you complain, an independent, active being, and you remove the cause of all his former meanness."[45]

The political economists hoped that the introduction of commerce, by freeing men from binding and degrading servility, would lead to the overcoming and extirpation of most criminal activity.

> The establishment of commerce and manufacture, which brings about this independency, is the best police for preventing crimes. The common people have better wages in this way than in any other, and in consequence of this a general probity of manners takes place through the whole country. Nobody will be so mad as to expose himself upon the highway when he can make better bread in an honest and industrious manner.[46]

In fact, by the 1780s some claimed the effects of this improvement were already visible. For example, John Howlett argued that the only reason people continued to bemoan the decline of public morals was the tendency in writers of every period, for reasons of their own, to exaggerate the degree of improvidence and vice among the working people. Therefore, Howlett held, the complaints of these writers must not be taken as an accurate reflection of the real condition of the people. When William Eden addressed himself to the state of the nation's manners, he asked his readers to look around and see "whether the social intercourse of men is that corrupt, impoverished and desolating kind which tends to popular distress and to the annihilation of private and public virtue." Eden's answer was a resounding "no." Others agreed. William Wales rejoiced in the age in which he lived, despite its luxury, extravagance, and dissipation. For, he said, "it by no means follows that they are carried higher now than they were formerly; or that they are of a more wicked nature, or of a more dangerous tendency." When Wales compared his age with preceding ones, he compared such things as styles in fashions, amusements, and vices, and concluded that "the circuit of these things is changed, but not enlarged."[47]

According to these writers, not only had the growth of commerce

---

[45] Anderson, quoted in *Monthly Review* (March 1778), p. 181. See also Moore, *Considerations*, pp. 78–81; and Mortimer, *Elements*, p. 85.

[46] Smith, *Lectures*, pp. 155–56. See also Taylor, *Hutcheson and Hume*, p. 114; and Kames, *Sketches*, 2:246.

[47] John Howlett, *The Insufficiency of the Causes to which the Increase of our Poor and the Poors Rate Have Commonly Been Ascribed* (London: W. Richardson, 1788), pp. 24–25; William Eden, *A Fifth Letter to the Earl of Carlisle . . . on Population* (London: B. White, 1780), pp. 43–45; Wales, *Inquiry into Population*, pp. 20, 21. Although this point of view became increasingly uncommon, it could still be found in the anonymous *Letter to a Member of the Society for the Suppression of Vice* (London: Thomas Collins, 1804), p. 25.

helped to eliminate vice, but the operations of an expanding economy would continue to foster virtue. The desire for betterment, or for increased material goods, would act as a compensation for other "defects in human nature, such as indolence, selfishness, inattention to others . . . as one poison may be an antidote to another." The political economists stridently denied that refinements led to selfishness and self-involvement. Instead, with the growth of commerce and the accumulation of wealth, men "flock into cities . . . [and] feel an increase of humanity from the very habit of conversing together."[48] Thus, the increased social intercourse that commerce made possible would not only lead to an increase of benevolent feelings, but to a calming of party hatreds and parochial sentiments. Some of the political economists even claimed that the civilization brought about by commerce would not lead, as the minimalists had claimed, to a decline in courage or in the determination to defend one's country. Instead, Hume supposed, England had no reason to fear for her martial spirit, for "the arts have no such effect in enervating either the mind or body. On the contrary, industry, their inseparable attendant, adds new force to both."[49]

Thus, the political economists believed that if men could only be freed from the degrading effects of dependency, and commerce and manufacture could be sufficiently encouraged, the vices of the nation would decline of their own accord. The modern commercial state, insofar as it would be able to replace servility with economic interdependence and an active pursuit of rational self-interest, would achieve a maximum of wealth, strength, and security. Institutions or laws that shackled men to each other by noncommercial bonds, such things as the Poor Law or voluntary charities, were therefore seen to be retrogressive, a return to premodern forms of dependence.

Unlike the Spartan encomiums of the minimalists or the natural progressivism of the political economists, clergymen offered older remedies for the growth of license and poverty. Agreeing with contemporaries on the need for action, they preached reconciliation and the strengthening of personal loyalties, the reforging of links of obligation and respect within the framework of market values and a market society. And charity was the perfect agent for such an endeavor. Waving aside cavils about the harmful effects of misdirected almsgiving, they instead stressed the positive features of such giving. Thus, the dean of Canterbury, Brownlow

---

[48] Hume, "On the Refinement of the Arts," in *Essential Works of David Hume*, Ralph Cohen, ed. (New York: Bantam Books, 1965), pp. 513, 507. See also Kames, *Sketches*, 1:345; John Howlett, *An Examination of Dr. Price's Essay on the Population of England and Wales* (Maidstone: J. Blake, 1781), p. 8; and Howlett, *Insufficiency of Causes*, p. 54.

[49] Temple, *Vindication*, pp. xxi, 540, 545; Hume, "Refinement of the Arts," pp. 506, 509; and Short, *New Observations*, pp. 129–30. See also Young, *Political Arithmetic*.

North, noting that since it was essential that the people "may be happy in their submission to government, that they may esteem themselves blessed in a peaceable acquiescence under the necessary laws of subordination," recommended charitable giving to his audience. For, he continued,

> in the minds of the most hardened there are some seeds of virtue remaining, which, by well-seasoned acts of kindness and charity may yet be called forth, and raised to yield the fruits of attention and obedience: this, I say, may be done by well-seasoned acts of kindness and charity, when the cold enforcement of the law shall fail of that effect.[50]

Porteus lauded charity for its ability to reward virtue while discountenancing vice. Aid to the needy in their times of distress, "the tenderest compassion and most liberal relief" when compared to the cold shoulder and neglect that the idle encountered, would "probably do more towards reforming their manners than any argument or expedient that has yet been tried." Both Willis and Parkinson stressed the desirable consequences of noncompulsory giving, "what is given here is given voluntarily; not as the demand of society, but as the tribute of compassion." Such generosity would allow for the exercise of "the best feelings of the heart," not only between donors and recipients, but for all social interaction. The poor, Willis ventured, would as a consequence "at all times follow the humane steps of their benefactors, and show that kindness one to another, which . . . is shown to them."[51] An equally valuable result of charitable giving would be that the rich and poor would become truly known to each other. Being "drawn out of their obscurity into notice and protection" would humanize and civilize the poor, who, "equally surprised and pleased [at] finding themselves thus regarded . . . quickly become different creatures." To recapitulate then, in exchange for the care and concern of the rich, the poor "owe to the rich gratitude, thankfulness and respect for all the good they receive from them." Such exchanges of good offices would convince the poor to renounce that "dispiriting suspicion that they are a distinct and rejected class of beings" and would lead to rejoining "the several links of that great chain of society which has too long been broken and separated; I mean that which has united the rich and poor."[52]

---

[50] Brownlow North, *Sermon for the Lying-in Charity* (London: J. Robson, 1771), p. 17.

[51] Beilby Porteus, *Sermon at the Anniversay Meeting of the Governors of the Female Asylum* (London: Harriot Bunce, 1773), p. 10; T. Parkinson, *Sermon for . . . Addenbrooke's Hospital* (Cambridge: J. Archdeacon, 1787), p. 13; Thomas Willis, *Sermon for the County Hospital at Lincoln* (London: C. Lourse, 1788), "The Public as well as Private Advantages of Hospitals," p. 13.

[52] George Horne, *Sermon*, "Sunday Schools Recommended," (Oxford: Clarendon Press, 1786), p. 12; Richard Watson, *Sermon Preached before the Stewards of the Westminster*

While clergymen felt at home with the analysis of the political economists, they retained their own voice and opinions about the role of charity
and the ineffectualness of the marketplace to promote social and moral
harmony.

CHARITY AND THE ATTACK ON DEPENDENCY

The period between the mid 1770s and early 1790s seemed to be one of
unresolved and opposed views on both the theory and practice of charity
and relief. On the theoretical side, the only area of agreement was on the
impropriety of providing employment to the poor. We have seen how,
whether they belonged to the rising school of political economy or the
remodeled school of minimalist thinking, social theorists agreed that neither charity nor poor relief should stand between men and either the pressure of necessity or the pulls of their desires for self-betterment. Most
philanthropists agreed that guaranteed relief and care in an institution
like the workhouse would increase the total burden of poor relief, harm
the national economy, and ruin the laborer's character.

This critique of the ill effects of institutional care spilled over from the
area of the provision of employment to other sorts of charitable enterprises. Increasingly those charities that were of an institutional sort, the
Foundling, the lying-in hospitals, the Lambeth Asylum, and the Magdalen, had to justify themselves to the charitable public by minimizing the
effects that their structure was thought to engender. For, a long period of
confinement within a charitable institution would clearly render inoper-
ative either the pricks of necessity (since everything was provided within
the house) or the prods of desire (since there was little incentive for self-
improvement as everyone dressed alike within the institution and received
the same allowance of food).

However, there was more disagreement about the value of artificially
promoting population increase, and about the true state of the nation's
morals. While all schools of thought still held a large population to be
desirable, the value of stimulating its growth by charitable or public measures had been questioned, and not really answered. Though the political
economists and the minimalists did not try to discourage this growth,
neither did they feel a growing population was the major foundation of
an increase in national productivity. Since the earlier minimalists had
thought the poor to be naturally improvident, and the increase of population to be vital to the nation's economy, they had encouraged those
charities that aided the poor in their propagative efforts. When improvi-

Dispensary [1785] (London: T. Cadell, 1793), pp. 10–12; *Plans of the Sunday Schools and
Schools of Industry Established in Bath* (Bath: R. Cruttwell, 1789), p. ix.

dence was no longer seen as inevitable, it became important to insure that any aid would not cause dependency or a lessening of labor. In a limited way, we can see the change from the earlier to the later type of minimalism in the works of Jonas Hanway. We have seen how Hanway had attributed the wealth of England to the improvidence of its laborers. However, in a later work he seems to have changed his mind, and in counseling the charitable to give to lying-in charities rather than hospitals, his main rationale was that "our common people, at least in these cities, are bred up too much in an opinion, that their preservation depends more on the *virtue* and munificence of others, than upon their own virtue, industry and *foresight*."[53]

The sharpest disagreements between the political economists and the minimalists involved the question of what effect the growth of commerce had on the state of public virtue. While the minimalists saw licentiousness everywhere, and felt that the poor had become more insolent and unruly than ever, the political economists felt that commerce was spreading culture and refinement, as well as encouraging the development of foresight and the exercise of rational self-interest. When it came to practical issues, however, both political economists and minimalists agreed about the moral evils of dependency and the desirability of promoting providential reckoning among the poor. Therefore, those institutions that increased the need to provide for oneself, that did not make their charges dependent, but encouraged a sense of self-sufficient adulthood, should be supported.

Thus, in the period 1770–1790 we can see three notions emerging that were to challenge, to varying degrees, the validity of the charities established earlier in the century: a strong feeling against institutional care, an uncertainty about the value of encouraging population growth, and a determination to eradicate debilitating dependency.

Not surprisingly, the Foundling Hospital was hardest hit. We have seen how, even in the 1760s, public support for this charity had started to decline. By 1773 this decline had become so serious that the governing committee of the hospital noted that they were "inquiring if expences could be lessened, for they said, 'Subscriptions had fallen to a very low ebb, and the Hospital was living on a capital none too large.' "[54] We have three types of indications that the charity was undergoing a severe crisis of confidence. First, the number of subscribers to the charity declined from 828 in 1781 to 466 in 1799. There are reasons to believe that real subscriber involvement must have fallen even more than these numbers

[53] Willis, *Sermon*, p. 53; Hanway, *The Defects of Police, the Causes of Immorality* (London: J. Dodsley, 1775), p. xxi.

[54] R. H. Nichols and F. A. Wray, *History of the Foundling Hospital* (London: Oxford University Press, 1935), p. 89.

indicate. We must remember that in 1773 the Foundling Hospital had closed the last of its provincial houses. If we examine the 1781 list, we see that 42 percent of the subscribers, all of whom were life governors, had probably joined the hospital because of their residential proximity to one of these provincial houses. Thus, the 1781 subscription list, when shorn of these provincial members, is little larger than the original charter of 1739. And when the social composition of the subscribers in 1745 is compared with that in 1781, an interesting fact emerges. While I have been able to identify at least ninety merchants and monied men in the earlier list, the later list, though seemingly much larger, contains only seventy-four such subscribers.[55] The absence of City and merchant members must have been in part responsible for the maladministration of the charity in the 1780s and 1790s. When "suggestions of gross mismanagement were made in April 1795, the Finance Committee appear to have taken the blame freely to themselves!" When the cost of maintaining the provincial house at Ackworth was compared with the cost of running the London establishment, the governors of the latter were found sadly wanting.[56]

By the late 1790s the charity faced great difficulties. The 1799 list of subscribers was almost half that of 1781, and more than half the subscribers in the later list had already been mentioned as lifetime subscribers in the earlier one. Thus, less than half of the 1799 subscribers had joined the charity in the eighteen year interval. The other 244 might well have lost all interest, decided the charity was harmful, or died.[57]

However gloomy the future looked for the hospital in the 1790s, there were also signs that it was determined to reestablish itself. Sometime between the mid 1790s and the early nineteenth century, the governors voted to lease some of their valuable real estate and so bring in larger revenues. In addition, the hardheaded approach of Thomas Bernard, who was appointed secretary to the charity in 1795, and the determination of the governors to restrict and restrain their charity, which we shall shortly discuss, may have encouraged a revived interest in it among the business community. An indication of this is the increased percentage of merchants and monied men involved in the Foundling by 1799. (Though the

[55] Many of the founders and early governors of the Foundling, men like Hanway and his circle, were either very old or dead by the 1780s. Of the 43 men whom I know served a term as a governor of the Foundling in the 1740s or 1750s, at least 17 were dead and another 7 were over the age of sixty by 1780. While 23 from the 1745 list gave to more than one charity, 49 from the 1781 list were such donors. Thirty-three of these had become important in the charitable world before 1770 and were often old and retired by the 1780s.

[56] Nichols and Wray, *History of the Foundling*, p. 89.

[57] There were 821 subscribers to the Foundling Hospital listed in 1781. By 1799 support had fallen to 466 subscribers, of whom only 222 had not appeared on the 1781 list: see *An Account of the Hospital for the Maintenance and Education of Exposed and Deserted Young Children* (1781), (1799).

number of such contributors in 1799 was sixty-one and less than the seventy-four such donors we have noted in 1781, we must remember that the charity as a whole had decreased by much, much more.) Much of the upswing in popularity that the hospital was to encounter must be credited to the attempts of the governors to retrench and put the charity on a firmer, if narrower, foundation. This retrenchment led to an even further restriction of services: in 1786 it was decided, for example, to accept only ten children per year into the hospital. By 1790 a further decision was made to insure that applications for admission were more stringently screened, and that "care was to be taken that children received should be proper objects of the Charity, viz., foundlings or exposed and deserted children who there is the greatest reason to think would not be taken care of and supported unless it was for the humane interposition of the charity."[58] The governors of the hospital had originally maintained that as many exposed and deserted children as the hospital could support should be admitted. They now saw their responsibility to lie only with the care of those children whose sponsors could offer proof that they would otherwise perish. It must have been exceedingly difficult to offer such proof. However, by these new regulations the hospital tried to dispel widely held fears that its existence was encouraging the working poor to idleness by giving them an easy refuge and escape from their legitimate responsibilities. With admission to the hospital virtually impossible, the poor would be set on their own feet, to care for and provide for their offspring by the fruits of their own labor.

The Lambeth Asylum too seemed to encounter a crisis of confidence in the 1770s, but one it emerged from more successfully than the Foundling.[59] This crisis can be measured in the falling numbers of subscribers in the 1770s as well as in the subsequent steps the Lambeth Asylum took to retrench. The charity weathered the crisis because, unlike the Foundling, it was apparently successful at finding places for its girls, so that their actual stay in the institution became shorter and shorter, and they, in turn, became self-sufficient sooner. Thus, though between 1773 and 1777 the charity admitted 50 percent more girls than they had the previous four years, the asylum was able to increase its placement of girls by an even larger amount. By the end of the 1770s, while increasing the number of girls taken in, the Lambeth Asylum was able to place out, on average, three-quarters of the number admitted annually. This trend was to con-

---

[58] Nichols and Wray, *History of the Foundling Hospital*, p. 89.

[59] The Lambeth Asylum ran an advertisement in the *Morning Herald* of January 9, 1783, informing the public that they had paid the debts incurred by the late treasurer, despite having to sell a considerable part of their stock. That this successfully reassured its subscribers is illustrated by the comment in the *Times* of April 26, 1787, that the affairs of the asylum had been rescued from ruin "a few years since."

tinue. In the thirty-five years from 1777, while the admission rate dropped slightly to an average of thirty girls per annum (as compared with thirty-four in the year 1772–1773, or thirty-two per annum in the period 1773–1777), the number placed out rose to twenty-eight girls on an average per annum—a turnover of almost 100 percent per year. While the ultimate success of the asylum in sending out so many of its girls could be, and no doubt was, applauded from the viewpoint of efficiency and the encouragement of early self-reliance, one fears that perhaps this was accomplished as much by a more casual attitude toward the employers the girls went to, or to the growth of industries that were glad to employ young children at minimal wages.[60]

Unlike the Foundling, too, the Lambeth Asylum assured the public that it did more than merely rear children. By its careful and practical training of orphaned and deserted girls, it attempted to deal with the pressing problem of public and especially of female immorality. This concern of the asylum must have been manifest by the presence on the 1797 committee of a police magistrate (Jonathan Stonard), two City politicians (Alderman Williams and Common Councillor Daniel Coxe), and a clergyman, the Reverend Dr. Vyse, notable for his strong views on public immorality. Thus, by a program designed to make their girls hardworking and independent, by processing them quickly through the institution and thus not destroying their need or desire to support themselves by long-term confinement, the asylum was able to reassure the public that their work was in line with the new approach to poor relief.[61]

The Magdalen also seemed to encounter a crisis in the decade between 1776 and 1786. The total number of Magdalen subscribers dropped from 701 in 1776 to 565 in 1786, and the revenues reflected this by declining 17 percent, from an average annual income of £3,369 from 1765 to 1775 to £2,764 from 1776 to 1786. Its committee membership also shows an unusually high turnover rate and a dearth of experienced directors. During this period its ability to attract new subscribers also fell to a low point.[62]

[60] See *An Account of the Institution and Proceedings of the Guardians of the Asylum for Orphan Girls*, with a list of the Guardians (London: Logographic Press, 1789).

[61] The charity was able to convince the subscribing public that it was a financially responsible institution. On January 9, 1783, it placed an advertisement in the *Morning Herald* informing the public that it had paid the debts of its late treasurer, despite having to sell a considerable part of its stock to do so. The success of this program is reflected in the record number of new subscribers (286) that the charity attracted in the 1780s: see *An Account*.

[62] Of the 21 governors of the Magdalen in 1766, 9 had served on the board in 1759. Of the 32 directors of the charity in 1776, 6 had also served a decade before. Some returning stability can be seen by 1786, with 9 of the 32 directors having served for at least ten years, and with two new directors being the sons of a founding member. In 1798 the enlarged directing committee of 35 had 8 members with more than a decade of service, and another

TABLE 5.1
The Magdalen House

Year	Number of Subscribers	New Subscribers (Percent of Total)
1766	446	62
1776	701	44
1786	565	26
1798	615	60

Like the Lambeth Asylum, the Magdalen managed to survive this crisis of confidence by reducing the number of women it admitted and raising the number it sent out. While in its first twenty years of operation the charity had taken in an average of ninety-six women per annum and placed fifty-five per annum in positions of service, manufacture, or with their families, the decade from the mid 1770s to the mid 1780s saw a lower admission rate (on an average, eighty-seven women per year) and a far higher outflow rate (seventy-two per year). While the smaller number of women admitted may have represented the "cream of the crop" (and the smaller number of dismissals of undesirable women in this decade seems to support this inference), it is unlikely that the possibilities for their employment or reconciliation could have increased sufficiently to account for these large increases. Instead, it may be supposed that the administrators of the charity, feeling the financial pinch and perhaps suspecting that some of the women were freeloading, decided to relax their rules and standards, investigate potential jobs less closely, and let girls back into the world more easily.[63]

Even charities free from the charges of overly long confinement or the encouragement of dependency seemed to show some signs of uncertain public support. In the case of the Lying-in Charity, this hesitancy may have been the result of the growing questions raised about the desirability of stimulating population growth. While the charity continued to grow, both in numbers and in revenue, it seems to have hit its peak by the late

---

offspring of a founder. The decline in support is also reflected in the charity's five yearly annual incomes. These figures are the result of subtracting the unspent residue from each year's total funds while expenses remained fairly constant throughout, for 1770–1775 there was an average of approximately £3,693; for 1776–1780, £2,179; for 1780–1785, £3,462: see *Rules, Orders, and Regulations of the Magdalen Hospital . . . with a List of the Governors* (London: n.p., 1787).

[63] Ibid. See also *Bye Laws and Regulations of the Magdalen Hospital* (London: 1791); *Bye Laws and Regulations of the Magdalen Hospital* (London: 1802); *A List of the Governors of the Magdalen Hospital* (London: 1798); and *A List of the Governors of the Magdalen Hospital* (London: 1803).

sixties and early seventies, and to have slowed down for the next decade, both in support received and services offered. While the charity's subscribers doubled in the years between 1767 and 1770, it was more than twenty years before the number of its subscribers doubled again. In addition, while its subscription lists were gradually enlarging during this period, its annual revenue seems hardly to have increased, going from £1,485 for the year 1769–1770, to £1,500 for the year 1790–1791. Furthermore, the number of women it delivered fell, from an average of 4,942 per annum in 1771–1776, to 4,346 per annum in 1781–1786.[64]

The charity with the most curious record during these decades was the Lock Hospital. As we have already noted, by the mid 1760s, the administration of the institution had just barely survived several major crises of funding and confidence. More were to come in the next twenty years. Although income and numbers cared for increased through the mid 1780s, the end of the war in America created a crisis at the Lock. Commenting on the more than 530 patients treated in the hospital between 1783 and 1784, the governors noted that of "the numerous Objects received into the Hospital," many of them "arrived from abroad after the close of the last War." Preceding this massive increase in numbers cared for and pressure on hospital resources, a bitter and almost fatal conflict arose between the governors and the hospital's doctor, William Bromfield. Although the minutes are very unclear about the exact nature of this confrontation, the facts are these. In May 1780 Dr. Bromfield was accused of having used hospital drugs for his private patients. Somehow, and the account grows especially murky here, Bromfield vindicated his behavior, and then presented a report to the governors less than a year later accusing them of mismanagement or misconduct and of allowing the charity to slip into financial ruin. In response, the governing committee issued its own report, affirming the health and vitality of the hospital ("a very fortunate circumstance" they noted, "considering that the Revenue of most other Charities have been affected by the Distresses of the Times") and suggesting that any problems that had arisen were caused by the pernicious influence of an unnamed individual, perhaps Dr. Bromfield himself. Bromfield subsequently resigned and sent letters to all his friends urging them not to renew their subscriptions.[65] This breach was only par-

---

[64] See *An Account of the Lying-in Charity . . . with the State of the Charity to January 1770* (London: 1770); *An Account of the Lying-in Charity . . . with the State of the Charity to January 1791* (London: 1791). In 1767 the charity had 337 subscribers, 613 in 1770, and 1,103 in 1791.

[65] The select committee of the Lock, in order to fight this pernicious influence, put advertisements in the newspapers advising subscribers and supporters of the hospital to disregard the cards sent out by Bromfield and to continue their contributions to "this most useful and humane Charity": *Times*, March 18, 1782, p. 1.

tially healed after Bromfield's intercession on the hospital's behalf in the mid 1780s. By that time the hospital was once again in the throes of severe monetary problems brought on as a consequence of a malignant fever in the wards and the need to clean and refurnish the entire institution, as well as a decline in chapel income because of the refusal of their minister to give regular sermons. This led to "a considerable deficiency in its Income," which by 1798 had become so serious that the hospital, "now nearly fourteen Hundred Pounds in Debt," could care for only about half the number of patients that it had served ten years before.[66]

Thus, the charities started in the 1740s and 1750s, under the impetus of war and in the belief that charity had a vital part to play in encouraging a large population and in promoting a purer national morality, came to be questioned and criticized in the 1770s. While few social theorists or philanthropists were yet willing to condemn these charities entirely, there seemed to be a general lack of confidence and a loss of enthusiasm about the purposes and methods of the existing charities. Increasingly they came under attack as being mere agencies of support, a charge they had to clear themselves of if they hoped to survive. For, unlike the philanthropists of the midcentury who saw their activities as being positive aids to the nation's welfare, the new theorists forced the charitably minded to question relief that discouraged its recipients from being self-supporting. Thus, the great value that had been attributed to charity's contribution to the fulfillment of the nation's best interests came to be questioned, and it was suggested that other agencies—whether the operations of the market, of enlightened self-interest, or of necessity—might more effectively and cheaply solve the "problem" of the poor and their care. It was not until the 1790s, however, that the charitable community once again seemed to find, and become filled with, a sense of purpose, and to reformulate an important role for itself in relation to the national police.

[66] The Lock Hospital *General Court Book # 3* (April 1773 to March 1789), esp. pp. 108–14; and *General Court Book # 4* (April 1789 to March 1816), p. 88. The Lock Hospital Papers are found at the library of the College of Surgeons, Lincoln's Inn Fields, London.

CHAPTER SIX

The Charities of Self-Help

IN THIS CHAPTER we will consider how and why the ideas formulated by the political economists came to be used, expanded, or rejected by philanthropists of the 1790s. What we wish first to consider, therefore, is the interaction of views and circumstances that set the stage for the revitalized charitable effort of this period.

DECADES OF TRIAL: LONDON IN THE 1780S AND 1790S

The 1780s were a decade filled with alarm and incident. In its first year the Gordon Riots occurred, impressing itself most vividly on the minds of contemporary observers. Commenting on the riots many years later, John Aiken noted that "the British metropolis . . . was the scene of riots more dangerous to its safety and disgraceful to its police, than it has witnessed in modern times."[1] Four hundred and fifty people were killed or wounded, many of London's jails were burned to the ground, the Bank of England was attacked, and mobs roamed the streets of the capital for ten days.

The early years of the decade were also spent in the midst of a costly and damaging war.[2] It is clear that the loss of the American colonies dealt

---

[1] John Aikin, *Annals of the Reign of King George III*, 2 vols. (London: Longmans, Hurst, Rees, Orme and Brown, 1820), 1:260. Note also the title of the work that Jonas Hanway wrote immediately after the riots: *The Citizen's Monitor, Shewing of a Salutary Police, with Observations on the Late Tumults, the Merits of the Soldiery and the London Volunteer Police Guard* (London: n.p., 1780). While it is popularly accepted that the Gordon Riots were most important in arresting the widespread movement for parliamentary reform, a correspondent to the *Gentleman's Magazine* noted only three years after the riots the need for a national moral reformation as "a preparative to a Parliamentary reformation" (August 1783, p. 666). In January 1784 another correspondent to the *Gentleman's Magazine* argued that unless moral regeneration took place soon, "The people, being still brought up in ignorance and wickedness . . . [will] by some more successful attempts than those memorable ones in June 1780 . . . at last overturn the constitution and bring all into anarchy and confusion" (p. 20). This supports the new interpretation put forward by Nicholas Rogers in an unpublished article, "Crowd and People in the Gordon Riots," that the riots were used by radical reformers as an example of what would occur in a corrupt and immoral regime.

[2] This sense is present as early as 1777 in the frontispiece to the *Gentleman's Magazine* (January 1777): "Meantimes, while this exhausted state / Stands tottering on the brink of fate, / . . . Or, if this empire soon must end, / May foreign states more wise attend, / And learn those shallows to avoid / Which Britain's fame and wealth destroy'd!"

a dire blow to the spirit of self-confidence and assurance that had been so important a motivating factor in the work of many of the leading philanthropists of the midcentury. The loss of the colonies forced England to reexamine and reformulate its views and policies about its newly diminished imperial role. A striking example of this reevaluation can be seen in a speech by Pitt during the debates on the Peace: "I was taught Sir, by one whose memory I shall ever revere, that at the close of a war, far different indeed from this, she [England] had dictated the terms of peace to submissive nations. That . . . was the memorable era of England's glory. But that era is past. . . . The visions of her power and pre-eminence are passed away."[3] In addition to the psychological damage that the loss of the first empire entailed, other serious consequences of the war were noted by contemporaries: the parlous state of the East India Company, the doubling of the national debt, and the renewed troubles in Ireland.[4]

With the peace came a growing concern about the problems of crime and poverty, which were intimately associated in the public mind. It was also in this decade that a serious reevaluation of the workings of the Poor Law, as well as the efficiency of public charities and hospitals, was undertaken. The magnitude of the anxiety about growing criminality can be appreciated when one notes that the *Times* reported that the criminal underclasses of London in the 1780s were "computed to compose one-sixth part of its inhabitants."[5] Perhaps because contemporaries believed that these problems were more visible and serious than ever, an increase in the level of criminal prosecutions and executions took place, both in London and throughout England.[6] But contemporaries were not only concerned about the best method of punishing the criminal and aiding the poor— they wished to deal with the root causes of crime and poverty. And in seeking to understand the nature of both problems, they turned away from political economy, which had promised the automatic disappearance of such problems,[7] and turned to other sorts of explanations.

[3] Quoted in Reginald Coupland, *The American Revolution and the British Empire* (London: Longmans, Green & Co, 1930), p. 45.

[4] See letter signed Theophrastus, "The Political State of Britain in 1763 and 1783 Compared," *Gentleman's Magazine* (October 1785), p. 790.

[5] See J. R. Poynter, *Society and Pauperism: English Ideas on Poor Relief, 1794–1834* (London: Routledge & Kegan Paul, 1969), chap. 2; *Times*, November 15, 1786, p. 3, and August 1, 1786, p. 2. See also Henry Home, Lord Kames, *Sketches of the History of Man*, 3 vols. (Edinburgh: W. Straham, 1778), 2:305–6; Alderman S. T. Janssen quoted in M. Dorothy George, *London Life in the Eighteenth Century* (New York: Capricorn, 1965), p. 391, n. 1; J. M. Beattie, *Crime and the Courts* (Princeton: Princeton University Press, 1986), pp. 582–92.

[6] It was said that "the spirit of the times [required] severity" (quoted in Beattie, *Crime and the Courts*, p. 583). For the inadequacy and growing costs of the hulks and the problem of overcrowded prisons, which eventually led to the start of a penal colony at Botany Bay, see ibid., pp. 593–95.

[7] The Rev. William Magee argued in his *Sermon before the Association for Discounte-*

We have already noted the skepticism of clerics to the likelihood of an automatic improvement in public morals as foreseen by the political economists. Instead, the clergy grounded their hopes for such betterment on a national regeneration through Christian education and charitable practice. These views continued to be expanded and elaborated, becoming in fact the predominant theme of Anglican sermons for the next thirty years. Though the message was similar to that widely preached in the 1760s and 1770s, the tone had subtly but significantly changed. Though charity could still serve to reconcile men and classes to each other, a clear need for prior religious reform was stressed before any benevolence could be successful. Henry Beeke, a Berkshire minister, pointed this out in a sermon to the governors of the Devon and Exeter Hospital. Though the sermon was given to raise funds for the hospital, Beeke noted that "even compassion, though the most amiable emotion of the breast . . . would not lead to that [socially desirable] general and deliberate beneficence which is founded in religious principle."[8] However, it was not until a group of nonclerical Anglican activists adopted and promulgated this viewpoint, making it the center of their moral politics, that we see the beginnings of a massive groundswell of support for such a new attack on poverty and crime.

This attempt to reform society through a redemptive police, which was to be one of the most potent and important social movements of the last two decades of the eighteenth century, lasting well into the nineteenth, has been described by historians as the Evangelical Revival. Since this phrase is ambiguous, by evangelicalism I mean that variety of Anglicanism that both acknowledged the utter depravity of man and the ubiquity of palpable evil and misery, and the necessity for individual moral reform and conversion before social improvement could take place. For the evangelicals, the unredeemed world was essentially evil. Misery was not

---

nancing Vice (Dublin: W. Watson & Son, 1796), p. 15, that it was exactly the kind of economic growth that the political economists had lauded that introduced "the unfailing corrupters of national morals" to English life. See also Rev. Joseph Berington, An Essay on the Depravity of the Nation (Birmingham: Myles Swinney, 1788), pp. 15–16.

[8] Henry Beeke, Sermon Preached for the . . . Devon and Exeter Hospital (Oxford: James Fletcher, 1790), p. 8. See also Vicesimus Knox's blistering attack on "humanity without religion . . . benevolence without beneficence" in his Sermon for the Opening of the Chapel of the Philanthropic Society (London: Philanthropic, 1807). Evangelical clergymen continued this attack on "mere charity" through the century. For example, Bishop Porteus argued that "unless our virtue is built on this foundation, unless it be grounded on true evangelical principles, it may be very good pagan morality, but it is not Christian godliness": Beilby Porteus, Sermons on Several Subjects, in The Works of Beilby Porteus, 16th ed., 6 vols. (London: T. Cadell, 1823), "Purity of Manners no Less Necessary to a Christian Character than Benevolence," 3:136–37. Porteus (1731–1808), bishop of Chester and later of London, was an evangelical sympathizer and a "pluralistic but energetic, improving prelate," according to Richard Soloway, Prelates and People (London: Routledge and Kegan Paul, 1969), p. 35.

merely the result of improper social or economic arrangements, as the political economists had claimed, but was a constituent element in the very nature of things. "Our creator has made *moral and natural evil* the instrument of his operations in this world; and the means of awakening the energy, and invigorating the virtues of those rational creatures, which he has imbued with sufficient wisdom and strength to be virtuous, and *as far as their nature admitted*, happy."[9]

Although it was possible to aid in the salvation and improvement of individuals, society-at-large was doomed to suffer the effects of evil in the form of misery. While individuals could be rescued from the morass of sin and suffering, the belief in real and permanent societal betterment was illusory. One could no more eliminate evil than one could eliminate bad weather—both were inconvenient, but both served a higher purpose.

However, while they acknowledged the omnipresence of evil and the need for moral regeneration before material improvement could take place, it would be wrong to think that evangelicalism had the effect of making people throw up their hands and abandon philanthropic activities in despair. On the contrary, the evangelical doctrine of sanctification, of living a life of social usefulness in imitation of the life of Christ, spurred its adherents on to increased action. John Aiken, in his *Letters from a Father to his Son*, admirably illustrates both the importance and limitations that such a campaign against misery must have:

> it is not in the power of merely political institutions to do more for the advantage of the lower classes, than secure them from oppression, and prevent their interests from being sacrificed to the avarice and ambition of the higher. . . . Evils no doubt, moral and natural, will remain as long as the world remains, but the certainty of the perpetual existence of vice, is no more an argument against attempting to correct it, than the same certainty with respect to disease, is a reason against exercising the art of medicine.[10]

Evangelicalism called men to lives of usefulness, dedicated to the true improvement of mankind, that is, to the diminution of vice.

---

[9] *Reports of the Society for Bettering the Condition and Increasing the Comforts of the Poor* (SBCP), 5 vols. (London: printed for the society by Savage & Earingwood), 2:35–36.

[10] John Aiken, *Letters from a Father to his Son*, quoted in *Monthly Review* (May 1794), p. 6. Henry Thornton's granddaughter noted that her grandfather gave three-fourths of his total expenditures to charity between 1790 and 1793: see letter to the *Guardian*, June 19, 1907, quoted in G. R. Balleine, *A History of the Evangelical Party of the Church of England* (London: Longman, 1909), p. 149. For the charity of the Clapham Sect in general, see Ernest M. Howse, *Saints in Politics* (London: Allen & Unwin, 1960), p. 126. However, Thornton's charitable policy, according to his friend Zachary Macauley, was to "weigh the best mode of imparting relief so as to raise no false hopes, and to produce no future unhappiness, and so to join, if possible, the interests of eternity to those of time": quoted in Robin Furneaux, *William Wilberforce* (London: Hamilton, 1974), p. 116.

Although it is quite clear that the main lineaments of evangelical thought were not radically new in the 1780s, the "prehistory" of this body of ideas in the eighteenth century has yet to be written. Many of Jonas Hanway's friends and associates were the fathers and the uncles of latter-day evangelicals, sharing with their progeny a common theological and social outlook. They had had less social impact, however, possibly because Hanway and his friends had spent so many years abroad, and so they were less polished, more business oriented, and less urbane and sophisticated than their sons and heirs. Henry Thornton, a Bank of England director and pillar of the select "Clapham Sect," remembered his father, John, as having been "rough, vehement and eager,"and criticized him "for his indifference to education, for his incorrectness of speech, for alloting too little time to secret prayer, and for being a Jack of all trades."[11] Unlike their fathers, the philanthropists of the century's end were gentlemen and were dedicated to the rehabilitation and reorganization of both polite and low society.[12]

A brief comparison of the major charitable donors of the thirty year period beginning in 1790 with those of the midcentury might be illuminating. Of the 150 donors who gave to at least half (that is, four) of the most important charities of this period, an even larger percentage were men of commerce than in the earlier sample (59 percent versus 51 percent). There were fewer aristocrats and fewer gentry among this latter group, as well as fewer women. Largely male and mercantile, but more sophisticated than their fathers, they were also more politically and religiously active. The five clergymen to be found in this group were merely symbolic of the new seriousness; almost 40 percent of this group belonged to some religious organization or were well known for their personal, practical piety. The web of family, social, and business connections, which we have discussed for the important donors of the midcentury, was even tighter and more widespread in this latter period. In many ways, the Thorntons were in the center of it all, having six family members among this group of major givers.[13]

---

[11] Henry Thornton quoted in E. M. Forster's marvelous *Marianne Thornton* (London: Edward Arnold, 1969), p. 22. See also James Stephen, *Essays in Ecclesiastical Biography*, 2 vols. (London: Longman, Green & Co.), pp. 200–201; and Catherine Hall's fine thesis, "Evangelicalism and the Creation of Bourgeois Values, 1780–1820" (University of Essex, 1977).

[12] In a letter to her mother, Mary Ann Thornton, Henry's wife, explains the need for new clothes by noting: "Mr. T. tells me we must do good both to the bodies and souls of men and to gain an influence over the minds of our equals is perhaps most necessary, which cannot be done if we are not equally free from austerity and ostentation": Forster, *Marianne Thornton*, p. 27.

[13] The percentage of aristocrats and gentry was half of what it had been in the earlier sample, the percentage of females only a quarter of what it had been. Whereas less than 14

However, it was not only that the evangelicals of this second generation were better situated to convince their contemporaries, but that their fellow Londoners were more willing to hear, had in fact already decided, that a major moral reformation was necessary. As early as 1783, two years before the "conversion" of William Wilberforce, who became the most prominent evangelical, two correspondents to the witty and worldly *Gentleman's Magazine* diagnosed the problems of England to be a result of "the want of a religious principle." This want, they asserted, would cause "the judgment of Heaven . . . [to] be executed upon us, for our neglect of the Gospel, our vices and infidelity." Even charity, if not "grounded on true evangelical principles . . . may be very good pagan morality . . . but it is not Christian godliness." "The only radical cure," another correspondent asserted a year later, for the malaise that plagued British society, was a grand "REFORMATION OF MANNERS." And so civic-minded citizens once more called for "the most effectual means for the prevention of crimes . . . an amendment of the *police*."[14]

At the decade's end, the French Revolution began, resulting in the overthrow of the French monarchy and war. It is clear that events in France served to deepen an already widespread anxiety about Britain's future. The war intensified the problem of importing enough grain to feed a fast-growing population, especially in the years of extreme dearth in the mid 1790s. All this seemed to make more clear the alternatives facing British society, "Reform or Ruin."[15] The increasing dependency and immorality of the poor, their procreative energy combined with their inability to maintain either themselves or their families, seemed to threaten not only the economic but the moral health of the nation. It was in Thomas Malthus's *Essay on Population*, first published in 1798, that these fears found concrete form. Malthus's book became immediately and immensely popular, not because of the novelty of its ideas, but because it so mirrored

---

percent had belonged to a religious organization like the SPCK in the midcentury, by century's end almost two-fifths of the sample did. A smaller, though still significant, rise occurred in the percentage of donors with other family members (going from 33 percent in the earlier group to almost 37 percent) and business acquaintances (going from under 17 percent to more than 19 percent) among the sample.

[14] *Gentleman's Magazine* (August 1783), letter signed "T.N.," pp. 666–67; a letter to the *Gentleman's Magazine* (January 1784), signed "A Parish Officer," pp. 18–20; Beilby Porteus, *Sermons*, 3:136–37; *Times*, April 7, 1787.

[15] This was the title of a popular essay by John Bowdler, the evangelical expurgator of Shakespeare, the Bible, and Gibbons. It went through eight editions in one year. See also Richard Soloway, "Reform or Ruin: English Moral Thought during the First French Republic," *Review of Politics*, 25 (January 1963). Wilberforce noted the particular appropriateness of evangelical religion to revolutionary times: "Never were there times which inculcated more forcibly, than those in which we live, the wisdom of seeking happiness beyond the reach of human vicissitudes": quoted in *Public Characters*, 10 vols. (London: R. Phillips, 1800), 2:42, footnote.

public sentiment with its emphasis on the inherent evil of the human condition, and the perniciousness of the French philosophes, and its application of what appeared to be a scientific method to the study of social and demographic questions.[16]

Convinced of the need for immediate action, assured that positive change could only come about as the result of prior moral improvement, philanthropists turned to scientific or utilitarian techniques to aid them in this effort. "In the labour of charitable love to one another," noted the bishop of St. Davids, "utility should be the main consideration."[17] We will see how this systematic, scientific approach to social problems, based on universal rules of human psychology and aimed at the goal of the greatest good for the greatest number, provided a method and justification for the new charities of the century's end. Elements of evangelicalism, political economy, Malthusianism, and utilitarianism combined to make a powerful platform from which to combat poverty through charity. Both evangelicalism and Malthusianism set the tone and the agenda, political economy the limits to interference, and utilitarianism the methods by which the benevolent attempted to reknit the tattered fabric of English social life and strove to recreate social harmony through the reunification of interclass bonds and interests.[18]

THE ATTACK ON IMMORALITY: EDUCATION AND INFORMATION

"The Sabbath is shockingly prophaned and neglected, and our ears are daily surrounded by curses and blasphemy . . . Reforming societies are therefore much wanted, and might be of infinite service if established in eary parish in the kingdom."[19] The 1780s witnessed a growing national

[16] In 1815 a critic of Malthus raised the claim of Robert Wallace, author of *A Dissertation on the Numbers of Mankind in Ancient and Modern Times* (Edinburgh: Archibald Constable & Co., 1753) as the progenitor of these ideas. See the *Examiner*, October 29, 1815, p. 701. See also the extremely favorable review of Malthus's book in the *Monthly Review* (September 1798), pp. 3–7, that praises it for its refutation of the "mistaken and wicked" doctrines that led to the French Revolution.

[17] James Yorke, *Sermon . . . for the New County Infirmary in Lincolnshire* (London: W. Word, 1777), p. 18.

[18] An interesting example of this combination of evangelicalism and utilitarianism can be seen in the works of Arthur Young, the advocate of "scientific" agriculture: see Arthur Young, *An Enquiry into the State of the Public Mind Amongst the Lower Classes* (London: W. J. & J. Richardson, 1798), p. 34. See also Bishop Watson's sermon to the Society for the Suppression of Vice, as quoted in the *Gentleman's Magazine* (June 1804), p. 535.

[19] Letter to the *Gentleman's Magazine* (August 1783), p. 666. See also [T. H. Horne], *Some Hints in regard to the Better Management of the Poor* (London: T. Cadell, 1784), p. 24: "We know by experience the dangers and excesses of lawless mobs: and perhaps, these might in a great degree be prevented, if the lower order of people were, from infancy, taught implicitly to regard wholesome laws and regulations, and to respect their superiors."

movement to improve manners and correct morality, a movement of greater magnitude than, but resembling, that of the late seventeenth century. And, like that earlier campaign, this crusade led to the establishment of a number of organizations, some regulatory and some charitable.

When Adam Smith wrote of the application of the increased division of labor, he was well aware that a new educative system would have to be provided to replace the discipline and purposes of family-oriented production.[20] It was just this sort of education that Raikes and his Sunday schools attempted to provide. The Sunday school movement, begun in Gloucester in 1781, served admirably to integrate boys and girls into modern mechanical employment and make them more docile and hard-working:

> great reform has taken place among the multitudes whom they [pin and sack manufactories] employ. From being idle, ungovernable, profligate and filthy in the extreme, they say the boys and girls are become not only cleanly and decent in their appearance, but are greatly humanized in their manners—more orderly, tractable, and attentive to business, and, of course, more serviceable than they were expected to find them.[21]

Unlike the earlier charity schools, which, critics claimed, gave "to the meanest of the people an education beyond that station which Providence had assigned them," the Sunday schools had the further advantage of allowing their pupils to continue at their jobs and remain with their families, thus insuring that their expectations were not unnaturally raised. Also unlike the charity schools, which, their opponents argued, accustomed their pupils "to a more easy and comfortable manner of living than they have afterwards the probability of enjoying,"[22] the Sunday schools were more realistic, for they dispensed

> not that species of instruction which is to elevate [the poor] above the rank they are destined to hold in society, but merely a sufficient portion to give their minds a right bias; a strong sense of religion and moral honesty; a horror of vice, and a love of virtue, sobriety and industry; a disposition to be satisfied with their lot; and a proper sense of loyalty and subordination.[23]

[20] Adam Smith, *Lectures on Justice, Police, Revenue, and Arms* (New York: A. Kelley, 1964), p. 257.

[21] Robert Raikes, quoted in M. Quinlan, *Victorian Prelude* (New York: Columbia University Press, 1941), p. 47. See the interesting letter sent to the *Gentleman's Magazine* that contains a copy of Raikes's announcement of his plan, signed "A Friend to Virtue," June 1784, pp. 411–12. For the confused genesis of the Sunday school movement, see T. W. Laqueur, *Religion and Respectability* (New Haven: Yale University Press, 1976).

[22] Thomas McFarlan, *Inquiries concerning the Poor* (Edinburgh: J. Dickson, 1782), p. 240. See also Jones, *Hannah More*, pp. 146–47, on the compatibility of the Sunday school movement and the economic and social status quo.

[23] Patrick Colquhoun, *Treatise on Indigence* (London: J. Hatchard, 1806), p. 142.

This was to be accomplished by giving the children little practical training. The principal function of the schools, in addition to habituating their pupils to a life of industrial efficiency, was to teach Christian morality, "to make men serious *Christians* and peaceable *Subjects*."[24] Where religious education was combined with vocational training, the skills taught were menial.[25] Writing and numbers were often not taught—reading alone was thought to be necessary for salvation.[26]

It is perhaps because the aims of the Sunday schools were both so limited and so important, that a national society, the Society for the Support and Encouragement of Sunday Schools, was founded in London in 1785. Like the earlier charity schools, the Society for Sunday Schools was sponsored and supported by the SPCK. Unlike the earlier educational movement, the Society for Sunday Schools was very popular, having among its contributors many eminent bankers and merchants and several evangelical members of Parliament.[27] They were also fortunate in convincing some of the ablest ministers of the day to preach numerous sermons in their behalf. During one of these, Bishop Horne noted that "the necessity of taking some speedy measures toward a reformation among our com-

---

Colquhoun (1745–1820), a retired merchant and traveler, became a London police magistrate, writer, and philanthropist, and was one of the principal founders of the Meat and Soup charities of the 1790s. See also Beilby Porteus's remarks on Sunday schools in his *Letter to the Clergy of the Diocese of Chester concerning Sunday Schools* (London: T. Payne & Sons, 1786), pp. 10, 21–23.

[24] John Warren, *A Sermon Preached . . . to the Charity Schools* (London: Ann Rivington, 1792), p. 16. The charity-school movement also witnessed a revival in the 1780s with the foundation of the Society of the Patrons of the Anniversary of the Charity Schools.

[25] In the schools of industry, social rather than economic virtues were taught and rewarded: "at the Sunday schools, the objects of reward . . . should not be *brilliancy of talent*, or even *proficiency in learning*; but that kind of merit which might offer to *every scholar* the ground of competition—viz. *regularity of attendance, cleanliness of person, habitual diligence and orderly behavior*": *Reports of the SBCP*, 3:240. See also Thomas Ruggles, *History of the Poor: Their Rights, Duties, and the Laws Respecting Them* (London: W. Richardson, 1797), p. 262. Even so, some, like the correspondent to the *Times*, thought they were dangerous because they prepared their charges for "the *sword* and the *pen*," rather than "the *flail* and the *spade*" (October 1, 1794, p. 2).

[26] McFarlan, *Inquiries*, p. 250. See *Reports of the SBCP*, 2:310; and John Donaldson, *Sketches of a Plan for the Effectual and General Reformation of Life and Manners* (London: T. Cadell, Jr. & W. Davie, 1794), p. 5. See also Table 12, "The Proportion of Sunday Schools in various cities teaching reading only, reading and writing only, etc.," in Laqueur, *Religion and Respectability*, p. 103.

[27] Among its more eminent subscribers, whom Laqueur has called the "capital's Evangelical *haute bourgeoisie*," were Benjamin Boddington and son, Thomas Raikes, the bankers Robert Barclay and Thomas Coutts, four of the Thorntons, and William Wilberforce and his cousin William Morton Pitt. By 1812 six of its thirteen vice presidents were M.P.s: see Laqueur, *Religion and Respectability*, pp. 33–35. Almost 30 percent of its subscribers also gave to other charities: see *Plan for a Society for the Support and Encouragement of Sunday Schools* (1788) for membership.

monality cannot be controverted: . . . this new establishment . . . may prove, in this respect, of important utility."[28]

Horne was not alone in his use of the language of utility in describing the work of the schools. Raikes himself saw the movement as civilizing the children of the poor through the use of scientific philanthropy. He thought of both the enterprise and the method in scientific terms. He viewed himself "as a Nurseryman botanizing in human nature and the Sunday schools were his botanical garden." In this light, one can see that Raikes's admiring biographer missed the point when he concluded from Raikes's claim that his work in child education was an "experiment" that he entered with misgivings. On the contrary, by viewing it as an experiment, Raikes was affirming his belief that, like experiments in the natural sciences, this venture would result in untold benefits to mankind and in a deeper and more useful understanding of the social organism.[29]

Education of the young was only one avenue of attack on the all-pervasive problem of moral corruption. The attempt to purify and enforce the Sabbath was the adult equivalent of the suasion of the Sunday schools.[30] It is perhaps in this area that we can best observe conflict between the earlier optimism about public morals and the growing conviction that the nation was fast sinking into a morass of sin, irreligion, and licentiousness. The advocates of this pessimistic view held that something more than mere employment was needed to return people to the proper paths, head off national disaster, and restore Christian morality to a purer state, as well as to curb the worship of St. Monday. What was needed was a revitalized, "serious" Sunday.

The first official attempt to enforce the Sabbath was a law, introduced by Bishop Porteus in the House of Lords and Sir Richard Hill in the House of Commons, that would more strictly enforce the proper Lord's Day observances, as well as, interestingly enough, ban those debating societies that met on Sunday.[31] One is left with the impression from perus-

---

[28] George Horne, "Sunday Schools Recommended" (1785) quoted in *The Monthly Review* (November 1789), p. 473. See also John Acland, *A Plan to Render the Poor Independent* (Exeter: R. Thorn, 1786), p. 53; and Samuel Crumpe, *An Essay on the Best Means of Providing Employment for the People* (London: G.G.J. & J. Robeson, 1793), p. 55. The connection between the provision of such education and the prevention of crime is made particularly vivid in *A Sermon Preached before . . . the Yearly Meeting of Children Educated in the Charity Schools* by Samuel Hallifax (London: Ann Rivington, 1789), pp. 9–10. Thus, Porteus remarked that "it is the discipline of the heart, more than the instruction of the head, for which the Sunday Schools are chiefly valuable" *Letter to the Clergy*, pp. 21–22.

[29] J. Henry Harris, *Robert Raikes: The Man and His Works* (London: National Society of Sunday School Unions, 1928), p. 79.

[30] See James E. Bicheno, *An Inquiry Into the Nature of Benevolence* (London: Rowland Hunter, 1817), p. 9. Bicheno (1785–1815) also wrote on criminal jurisprudence, political economy and science.

[31] This effort was part of Sir Richard Hill's maiden speech in the Commons. For more on

ing the notices in the *Monthly Review* that the 1780s saw a sharp increase in the number of sermons and tracts advocating the stricter enforcement of the Sabbath and the laws against vice. In 1783 the *Monthly Review* was hesitantly critical and latitudinarian about the stern views of such moralists. By the end of the 1780s, however, both the *Monthly Review* and the *Gentleman's Magazine* frequently stated, as a proven fact, the licentiousness of the common people and the moral necessity for a holy Sabbath.[32] This movement to purify the nation's manners led in 1787 to the creation of William Wilberforce's Proclamation Society and in 1802 to the founding of the Society for the Suppression of Vice. Both organizations differed from the earlier societies for the reformation of manners in boasting the names of some of England's most influential men and most important charitable donors.[33]

One of the targets of this new seriousness about public manners, and one of the favorite subjects of attack of many influential members of the Proclamation Society, was public amusements. The theater came under particular attack. By the 1790s many held, with Colquhoun, that "the principles [of the poor], their language and their habits of life, are inevitably corrupted" by theater going. Not only should the theater be more tightly regulated to insure a minimum of corruption, but all public entertainments should come under the direction of the metropolitan police, to insure that "all Public Exhibitions . . . be rendered subservient to the improvement of morals, and to the means of infusing into the mind a love of the Constitution, and a reverence and respect for the Laws." Thus, Colquhoun maintained, "since recreation is necessary to civilized societies," the new science of police must "encourage, protect and control such

---

Hill and Porteus, who had already used his bishoprical authority to change London's Sabbath practices, see the *Dictionary of National Biography*, 9:857–58; 16:195–97.

[32] See the review of a sermon by Benjamin Kennicott in the *Monthly Review* (March 1783), p. 284, and a review of a pamphlet urging local officials to punish Sabbath breaking in the *Monthly Review* (November 1786), p. 383. For the growing public and press opinion that a stricter enforcement of the laws against vice and immorality was urgently needed, see Quinlan, *Prelude*, p. 55; a letter to the *Gentleman's Magazine* (Supplement 1785), pp. 1020–21; and the *Monthly Review* (March 1789), pp. 244–45.

[33] For example, of the 152 members of the Proclamation Society, I have been able to identify 135 by profession; of these, 21 percent were well-known clergymen, 15 percent were peers, and 25 percent gentry—61 percent of all identified members belonged to the higher orders of society. In addition to the weight of station, the weight of parliamentary membership was also added. Nearly 50 percent of all the members were M.P.s at one time or another. Furthermore, these men were active and influential in the charitable concerns of the day: 119 of them (78 percent) gave to at least one charitable society; 43 of them belonged to five charities or more; and the average number of charities they belonged to was at least 4.5. My thanks to Joanna Innes for information on this society. For the ssv and its constituency, see M.J.D. Roberts, "The Society for the Suppression of Vice and its Early Critics," *Historical Journal*, 26 (1983), pp. 159–76.

as tend to innocent recreation, to preserve the good humour of the Public, and to give the minds of the People a right bias."[34] Thus, not only were youth to be habituated to industrious and respectable habits by the Sunday school movement and the disciplines of the Sabbath, but also their entertainments and amusements were to be regulated and turned into wholesome recreations that were conducive to self-maintenance and hard work.

One of the most intriguing national charities of this period, combining at its inception strong elements of political economy, evangelicalism, and a vogue for science, was the Society for Bettering the Condition and Improving the Comforts of the Poor (SBCP). Begun in 1795 by Thomas Bernard, William Wilberforce, and Shute Barrington, bishop of Durham, it was designed as an umbrella organization, publicizing benevolent experimentation and the latest scientific charitable techniques. The underlying premise of the SBCP was that while the poor could maintain themselves, they needed great help in the administration and ordering of this maintenance. It was this management that was the prime responsibility of rich and well-educated philanthropists.[35]

This society, which by 1804 had attracted the attention and support of some of England's most prominent donors, dedicated itself to putting philanthropy on an exact and rational basis. The creation of a science of charity was the only possible method of successfully introducing beneficial changes into poor relief: "that principle, without which *all is conjecture and hazard*, has never yet been properly applied to the concerns of the poor."[36]

How could the higher classes scientifically aid their poorer neighbors?

[34] Patrick Colquhoun, *A Treatise on the Police of the Metropolis, Containing a Detail of the Various Crimes and Misdemeanors*, 6th ed. (London: T. Gillet for J. Mawman, 1805), pp. 347–48.

[35] *Reports of the SBCP*, 3:335. Bernard (1750–1818), the society's secretary and spokesman, was also influential in the foundation of the Royal Institute and the British Institution for the Promotion of the Fine Arts. The Society for Improving the Condition of the Poor at Clapham, like its parent, the SBCP, vowed "to employ the leisure, wealth and talents with which Providence has blessed them . . . to the good of their poorer neighbours": *Rules and Regulations of the Society for Bettering the Condition of the Poor at Clapham* (London: Henry Teape, 1805), p. 27. The society believed that the adoption of Count Rumford's methods of relieving poverty would inaugurate "a new era in the science of managing the poor" (p. 8).

[36] More than 30 percent of its 604 members belonged to at least one other charity; many to a great many other charities. For more on the SBCP see Poynter, *Society and Pauperism*, pp. 87–89; *Reports of the SBCP*, 1:8. Science was to be the byword and method of this management; the society was to make "an inquiry into all that concerns the POOR, and the promotion of their happiness, a SCIENCE" (ibid., 1:2). For the "science of Religion" see Thomas Obeirne, *Sermon . . . before the Governors of the Magdalen Hospital* (London: J. Hatchard, 1807), p. 10.

One avenue was by the provision of soups and messes in times of great distress and scarcity. This method was always rather suspect, though often widely supported in times of dearth. Bernard himself, an early proponent of the soup kitchen, expressed this uneasiness in the third report of the SBCP. Though such palliative measures "may be beneficial in uniting the various ranks of society . . . as a remedy for an immediate evil," there was the danger that "the energy of the country will be destroyed; and as it was in corrupted Rome, BREAD AND PUBLIC SPECTACLES, to be enjoyed in listless and worthless idleness, will be the clamorous and importunate demand of the great mass of the people." Thus, even when support was provided, as in the food scheme organized by the dowager countess Spencer, steps were taken to make sure that the poor remained acutely aware of the favors they had been granted, and of their temporary nature.[37]

An even better and less dangerous innovation, however, was to teach and encourage the poor to make such soups and messes for themselves. The SBCP was convinced that the poor knew nothing of sensible diet, of the proper way to use fuel economically, or of gustatory thrift in times of plenty to provide for times of need. It was to be the business of the rich and educated to help them acquire this knowledge, to minimize their spending, to induce the laborer "to alter his course of life, as to effect a considerable saving in any one article of expense, but more especially in that of diet,"[38] so that he could "thereby secure himself a fund for future independence and increasing gratifications."[39]

[37] Though many of London's most illustrious citizens subscribed to Patrick Colquhoun's soup kitchen schemes of the 1790s, most also noted that this sort of relief was very temporary and to be applied only in times of greatest need. See, for example, Richard Burn, *Historical Dissertations on the Law and Practice of Great Britain, and Particularly of Scotland, with Regard to the Poor; on the Modes of Charity; and on the Means of Promoting the Improvement of the People* (Glasgow: Young, Gallie & Co., 1819), p. 206; *Reports of the SBCP*, 3:26–28, 217–18; and Physician, *Practical Oeconomy, or a Proposal for Enabling the Poor to Provide for Themselves* (London: J. Callow, 1801).

[38] It is especially in this matter of diet that the benevolent proposed the most suggestions. It was commonly believed that the poor indulged themselves not only in too much food, but food of too high a quality: see Ruggles, *A History of the Poor*, p. 383; Frederick Eden, *The State of the Poor* [1797], 3 vols. (London: Frank Cass & Co., 1966), 1:492; Colquhoun, *Treatise on the Police*, p. 312, footnote; and the journal entry of Patty More, describing the eating habits of glass blowers at the end of the eighteenth century, quoted in M. G. Jones, *The Charity School Movement* (London: F. Cass, 1964), p. 165.

[39] Eden, *The State of the Poor*, 1:494. Dr. Richard Pew, author of *Twenty Minutes Observations on a Better Mode of Providing for the Poor* (London: L. Ben, 1783), pp. 2–4, went even further, and held that the poor were poor because of this lack of domestic economy. That the poor were the most hidebound and traditionally prejudiced, the least rational and scientific, was a bit of "popular knowledge": see Eden, *The State of the Poor*, 1:491–92. It was the task of the philanthropist to aid the laborer out of his web of ignorance. *Reports of the SBCP*, 3:162, 2:28.

An added advantage of the power such charity would give the rich was that they could use their influence to educate the willful and ignorant poor into becoming providential, self-regarding, and morally responsible adult-citizens. Charity, judiciously applied, would not promote servility, but could be made to appear as "an honourable reward for . . . good conduct, and as an encouragement to persevere in . . . industrious habits."[40] Finally, this type of charitable assistance would bind the classes closer together and insure social harmony, leading to the preservation of good order among the lower classes of "society, who, having men of principle for their charitable subscribers, trustees and directors, are less likely to be incited to insurrections and disturbances than those who having no communication with any class of men superior to themselves, are easily led to those riotous proceedings which are a scandal to good government."[41] This aspect of charity was presented as being vitally important in a world in which the classes were becoming increasingly separate and antagonistic. Thus, scientific charity would lessen poverty and have desirable effects on the state of social unity.[42]

As we have seen, the initial outlook of the SBCP was a combination of the limited interference and emphasis on independence that political economy suggested, evangelical piety with its hierarchical polity, and the rhetoric, if not the practice, of science. Although it retained these ideas throughout its published reports, from 1798 onward a new tone of pessimism and a new and restricted sphere for the charitably inclined began to emerge. In 1798 Bernard wrote that the science of philanthropy "will add to the virtue of the nation, by increasing its happiness." This confidence rested upon the belief, shared with Hume and Smith, "that the same principle [self-betterment] which has produced such beneficial effects among the thriving and active members of the other classes of society, would, if properly encouraged, generate among the poor of the same nation, that degree of industry and prudence, which we have in vain endeavoured to produce by compulsion." In 1798 Bernard felt that the poor were not poor because they were immoral; they were so because of circumstances largely not of their own making. Thus, if "the vices and faults of the poor must be deemed the vices and faults of unfavourable situation,

[40] Robert Young, *The Undertaking for the Reform of the Poor . . . in an Asylum for Industry* (London: 1792), p. 4; and *Reports of the SBCP*, 2:389.

[41] Ruggles, *History of the Poor*, p. 167.

[42] The many savings-bank schemes, annuity proposals, and Friendly Societies under the direction and management of the more enlightened classes would "convince the mass of the people that the government of the country, and the higher orders of society, are anxious for their welfare, since they have thus devised the means for protecting their little savings, and have afforded all the necessary facilities of superior skill and knowledge to render them secure and profitable": Colquhoun, *Treatise on Indigence*, pp. 135, 137. See also Eden, *The State of the Poor*, 1:350.

rather than of individual delinquency," it followed that if one were to "remove those disadvantages, you add as much to moral character as to personal comfort." Bernard, in these early reports, expressed a hope that poverty could be alleviated by giving "scope and increase to the energy of the individual, by affording to all the opportunity and hope of advancement in life. Were character, conduct, industry and attention, to receive their assured reward, candidates will not be wanting; and the example of a few will be reflected in the virtues of the many."[43] In the first two reports of the SBCP Bernard hoped to make the poor virtuous by making them happy; reports 3–5 primarily stress the need to make the poor virtuous, and happiness might follow. These later reports are filled with a heavy unease about what can be done for the poor, and more generally about the unhappiness of the human estate. Although in 1798 Bernard took an essentially Smithian position on a program for improving the plight of the poor, by 1804 he had changed his mind:

> no plan for the improvement of the condition of the poor, will be of any avail— or in any respect competent to its object—UNLESS THE FOUNDATION BE LAID IN THE MELIORATION OF THEIR MORAL OR RELIGIOUS CHARACTER. The seeds of evil must be eradicated, before the soil can be enriched to advantage, and prepared to produce the abundant and acceptable harvest. This is essential to the improvement of the condition of the poor.[44]

Increasingly, the SBCP stressed the part that charity must play in this primary task of national moral regeneration. Thus, at the end of the century, and increasingly into the next, every charitable project advocated by the society came to contain a central kernel of moral reform. Even in the soup kitchens supported by the SBCP, this note was sounded.[45] Whether under private management or publicly funded, the aims of all SBCP-recommended charities included more than mere aid to subsistence.

[43] Even in these early reports, one can see the seeds of the theme that was to overshadow this confidence, the intimation that more than ambition was needed to make the poor better and happier. For, Bernard remarked, the science of philanthropy must not be satisfied with mere appearances, but must concern itself with discovering "what has *really* augmented . . . [the] virtue and happiness of the poor": *Reports of the SBCP*, 2:11, 6–8, 14, 12. It is but a small step from this statement to the view that what really improves the poor may not be what merely seems to augment their immediate health or happiness.

[44] Ibid., 5:17–18. See also 3:101–2; *Report of the SBCP at Clapham*, pp. 26, 28.

[45] The proponents of the kitchens hoped to reward virtue through the distribution of wholesome, sensible food. For this reason the sale of soup, unlike parish relief, was not to be automatic and indiscriminate, but offered only to recommended and worthy poor. Here we see the notion of aid as a reward for virtue and true need. Lest some undeserving attempted to buy soup, "The recommendations are regularly filed, as to be easily referred to": *Reports of the SBCP*, 1:340. Both Ruggles, *History of the Poor*, p. 297, and More, in Quinlan, *Prelude*, p. 50, refused to give sick benefits to those poor who brought about their illness through immorality.

POPULATION AND POVERTY

One of the major changes in the direction of charity to occur in the last decades of the eighteenth century, which continued and increased in the nineteenth, was the sharp decrease of interest in charities that promoted population growth. Undoubtedly an important factor in the turning away from this once popular form of giving was the profound practical and theoretical effects of the loss of the American colonies. It will be remembered that much of the early support that the maternity charities received arose out of the very spirit and sense of preeminence that Pitt felt was now lost. This change in England's imperial position and the withdrawal of the colonies as places that demanded both settlers and defenders, decreased the felt need for a growing population of potential soldiers, sailors, and colonizers.

Smith's *The Wealth of Nations* also contained grave implications for the charities of population support. Thus, though to Smith and his immediate followers a growing population was a sign of a growing economy and a symptom of national prosperity, explicit in his doctrine was the notion that population size was self-regulating, tied to the demand for labor. Joseph Townsend merely paraphrased Smith when he said that "it is with the human species as with all other articles of trade without a premium; the demand will regulate the market."[46] This was not merely a descriptive statement, but normative as well; what Townsend was saying was that a free market in population, as in all other commodities, was a desirable state of affairs, for only in such a situation would the number of laborers available perfectly meet the market demand for labor. Townsend went further and called for the gradual abolition of the Poor Law (and, by implication, all infant-care charities) on the grounds that it was artificially and ruinously meddling with the natural adjustments in population size that a self-regulating marketplace would automatically ensure.[47]

The situation that allowed laborers to be considered as only a commodity,[48] the recognition that the quality, not the quantity, of labor

---

[46] Joseph Townsend, *A Dissertation on the Poor Laws* [1797] (Berkeley: University of California Press, 1971), p. 46. Townsend (1739–1816), a Calvinist early in life, was equally well known for his work in geology.

[47] Eden, too, thought that the goal of increasing population should not be supported by public funds: *The State of the Poor*, 1:338–39. Gertrude Himmelfarb, in *The Idea of Poverty in the Early Industrial Revolution* (New York: Alfred A. Knopf, 1984), presents a very different interpretation of the general tenor of Smith's views.

[48] This is stated most clearly by Edmund Burke in his *Details on Scarcity* [1795] (London: Henry G. Bohn, 1855), p. 142: "labour is, as I have already intimated, a commodity, and, as such, an article of trade. . . . The impossibility of the subsistence of a man who carries his

counted in the division of labor, which was the source of national wealth, and the spread and refinement of manufacture introduced a new element into reflections about the desired size of Britain's population. Although a few worried about machinery usurping the rights and places of laborers, this innovation was generally heralded as the means by which Britain could become wealthier and more powerful.[49] With the introduction of machinery, quality of workmanship and industriousness, rather than boosting population, became the desired goal for the laboring poor.

When a large population of laboring poor was thought to have little economic value, the existence of such a population assumed a triply sinister aspect. Since the poor had less productive value, since they consumed more than they produced, and since, by their improvidence and immorality, they often had bad effects on the manners and morals of society, there was no apparent reason to wish for their increase. It was for these reasons that Bernard commented that "it had been better for thousands of individuals to have perished in their infancy, than to have protracted an injurious and hateful existence of vice, infamy and wretchedness." Bernard's view that "there is no inducement to a benevolent mind to covet the *mere* progress of POPULATION; unless attended with well-being and virtue here, and with hopes of happiness hereafter" can explain, in part, the tremendous decline that the maternity charities and hospitals suffered.[50] These charities could only ease and facilitate birth; they offered no guarantee of the future conduct of those they delivered.[51]

Let us look briefly at the records of these charities to see what was happening. Both the British Lying-in Hospital and the Lying-in Charity maintained a steady level of aid (in terms of the number of women delivered annually) through the 1770s, though the numbers fell, as did London population growth, at the end of that decade. In the 1780s, when the

---

labour to a market is totally beside the question, in this way of viewing it. The only question is, What is it worth to the buyer?"

[49] Thomas Mortimer, *Lectures on the Elements of Commerce, Politics, and Finance* (London: A. Straham for T. L. Longman, 1801), p. 105. *Political Observations on the Population of Countries* (London: P. Elmsley, 1782), p. 3, notes that a large population is not even needed for national power and self-defense.

[50] *Reports of the SBCP*, 3:18–19.

[51] These comments of the secretary of an important charity of the day on the preservation and promotion of infant life were not unusual: "It is perhaps too hastily received, as a general principle, that the lives so saved or supported are certainly valuable to themselves and to the state: a supposition not always verified by experience. It is surely no object of philanthropy or police to nurture the mischiefs of society, or preserve the miseries of our fellow creatures. Life is in itself an equivocal thing: it may be valuable or pernicious to others; a pleasure or a burden to itself. The expense and exertions employed about a life which is productive only of sorrow and misery, is doubtless trouble and expense to procure what had better not be; and is a double drawback upon the sum of happiness; a positive cost to procure a positive ill": *First Report of the Philanthropic Society* (1789), pp. 28–29.

London birthrate showed an overall rise, only the British Lying-in Hospital showed a steady, though not unremitting, attempt to keep pace with the growing number of births. The number of deliveries performed by the Lying-in Charity fell, and remained well below its achievement of the 1770s, increasing its aid only toward the end of the 1780s. The 1790s saw a rise in both the general level of the birthrate and in the aid given by these two charities. Though the deliveries at the hospital remained high until the last years of the 1790s, the Lying-in Charity started its long decline at the height of the hungry years of the decade. As the birthrate rose through the first decade of the new century, both the hospital, and to a lesser extent the Lying-in Charity, cut back on the number of women they delivered (see Table 6.1). These were not the only lying-in charities to suffer a decline at the end of the old century and the beginning of the new. Queen Charlotte's was in a bad state of mismanagement during this period, and the Middlesex had to close its maternity ward in 1807 for lack of funds.[52]

Thus, while the birthrate for London went up, the number of deliveries performed by all the maternity charities went down. This decrease in service was not always due to a fall in revenues. In the case of the Lying-in Charity, for example, a very large number of women (5,035) were aided in a year when available funds were quite low, and when it meant putting the charity almost £100 in the red. Although the number of deliveries performed by the Lying-in Charity seemed to rise and fall with the London birthrate through the late 1770s and 1780s, by 1803 the number of women it delivered had already started to plummet. This reduction occurred despite a large increase in the charity's revenues. The British Lying-in Hospital seems to have attempted to ignore the great decline of public

TABLE 6.1
Deliveries by Maternity Charities

	British Lying-in Hospital	Lying-in Charity
1770–1780	5,639	47,290
1780–1790	5,549	44,708
1790–1800	5,971	47,352
1800–1810	2,950 (to 1808)	42,043

[52] The *Times*, December 9, 1793, p. 2, says that the Westminster New Lying-in Hospital has again become useful and that several names of great respectability have been added to the list of governors. Was this addition of governors of social standing an attempt to placate hostility to the delivery of illegitimate babies? An advertisement for the General Lying-in Hospital, Store Street, Bedford Square, in the *Times*, June 30, 1797, suggests that this charity was closed because of a massive decline in income. See also H. A. St. George Saunders, *The Middlesex Hospital, 1745–1948* (London: Max Parish, 1949), p. 16.

support, and its delivery figures do not follow the pattern set by the Lying-in Charity. In 1807, for example, when its receipts had fallen to less than half of what they had been forty years before, the number of women it delivered had decreased less sharply. In an attempt to supplement its shrunken funds, the hospital admitted paying pupils for courses in midwifery, and also took in paying patients.[53]

The Foundling, as we have seen in chapter 4, was hit by financial difficulties and lack of support even earlier than the maternity charities. By the 1790s the problem of funding had become extreme. Luckily for the future of the institution, Thomas Bernard, the philanthropist who was so influential in the organization of the SBCP, was elected treasurer of the hospital in 1795. Bernard introduced a number of economical reforms in the operations of the charity that may well have been responsible for its popular resurgence and for the increase in the number of new governors in the second decade of the new century. These economies consisted of changes in diet and changes in technique. Bernard, as we have seen, was much taken with science, and especially with the scientific inventions of Count Rumford. Rumford, an American, obtained his title by acting as Munich's most successful poorhouse manager. By the introduction of several of his own inventions, and his general plan of management, Rumford claimed to be able to care for the poor more cheaply and successfully than hitherto had been thought possible. Two of his most popular inventions were a prototype pressure cooker and a system of household ventilation, both of which Bernard installed at the Foundling. The savings effected by the reduction in diet must also have been considerable. Thus, during the lean 1790s, the children's meat consumption was cut down enormously, and the far more "healthful" and cheap rice pudding or gruel were substituted. (It was a "scientific" discovery, providentially timed, that those foods that were the most expensive, that is, beef and cheese, were the worst for the delicate stomach of the child.) The wheaten loaf was also replaced by the wheat-barley loaf, and in times of real scarcity bread was entirely omitted. By 1800 the children's diets were without solid meat, consisting either of rice pudding or dressed rice, eked out with potatoes.[54]

---

[53] In 1791 the Lying-in Charity delivered a new record of 5,035 women in one year despite the fact that their expenditure amounted to £1,559 and their income to only £1,500. In 1803, when they delivered 4,473 women, they had invested £537 in stocks and had a balance of more than £300 on hand. The British Lying-in Hospital, whose income for 1806–1807 was £1,140 (or 48 percent of the £2,400 they received in 1770), delivered 323 women in that year, or 58 percent of the 561 women delivered in 1770: *An Account of the Rise, Progress, and State of the British Lying-Hospital . . . to December 25, 1769* (London: n.p., 1770); *An Account of the British Lying-in Hospital . . . December 25, 1807* (London: n.p., 1808); *An Account of the Lying-in Charity . . . with the State of the Charity to January 1791* (London: n.p., 1791).

[54] For more on the Foundling Hospital see R. H. Nicholls and F. A. Wray, *The History*

Thus, the contraction of these once-popular charities illustrates the change in attitude toward the desirability of artificially encouraging or preserving population. More people were neither economically nor socially desirable. Many would have agreed with Townsend that those increasing fastest were the vicious and the idle, and therefore population growth meant the increase of crime and laziness. Even Howlett, who was sympathetic to the plight of the poor, thought that prudential foresight was entirely absent from the procreation of the lower classes.[55] Furthermore, machines could work harder and much more cheaply than even the cheapest laborer, and no machine had ever rioted or read Paine's pamphlets. Thus, at the end of the century the problem of poverty was seen to arise from the very numbers of the poor themselves. Burke, that splendid rhetorician, summed up this view neatly, as was his wont: "The laboring people are only poor because they are numerous. Numbers in their nature imply poverty. In a fair distribution among a vast multitude, none can have much."[56]

THE PHILANTHROPIC SOCIETY AND THE REHABILITATION OF YOUTH

New opinions about England's proper population policy, and the consequent decline in popularity of the maternity and infant charities, gave rise to other concerns and institutions. A central problem of this period, not dealt with by the Sunday schools, was the unemployed children of "the idle or criminal poor." It was thought that the most vicious and depraved criminals of the next generation would emerge from this class of youths. Therefore, the proper care of these children became the key to the solution of one of the major urban dilemmas of the day, the problem of crime.

The philanthropists of the 1740s and 1750s had perceived a similar problem and had recommended fasting, industry, solitary confinement, religious exhortation, and education. These, they hoped, when applied through the agencies of the city's charities, would raise a new generation free from the taints of vice, and do a good deal toward reforming and

---

of the Foundling Hospital (London: Oxford University Press, 1935); and Ruth McClure, Coram's Children (New Haven: Yale University Press, 1981).

[55] Townsend, Dissertation, p. 46: "The farmer breeds only from the best of all his cattle; but our laws choose rather to preserve the worst, and seem anxious lest the breed should fail." John Howlett, Examination of Mr. Pitt's Speech . . . Relative to the Condition of the Poor (London: W. Richardson, 1796), pp. 28–29. Howlett (1731–1804) was best known as a statistician and political economist.

[56] Burke, Details, p. 634. The connection between poverty and population growth had already been suggested in a sermon in 1786. Bishop Hinchcliffe noted that "poverty was largely the result of the inability of the economy to absorb 'the numbers of the poor [who] are daily increasing, while fewer means present themselves . . . for the gain of an honest subsistence' ": quoted in Soloway, Prelates and People, p. 265.

rehabilitating the older generation as well. By the 1780s and 1790s it was clear that such hopes had not been realized. The new generation seemed less laborious and more criminal, if the rising poor rates and the murder rates were, as contemporaries believed them to be, any indication. More and more people became convinced that something was fundamentally wrong. Charity, acting from mistaken and dangerous principles, was thought to be one of causes, rather than part of the cure, of these difficulties. The later philanthropists agreed with their earlier counterparts in diagnosing the problem. Punishments alone could never effect the desired results.[57] Their solutions, however, were of a different sort, for they had become convinced of the efficacy of science and the scientific method to solve such problems. "Observation and experiment compose the basis of all knowledge," Bentham said,[58] and it was on this dictum that the Philanthropic Society set to work.

The aims of the society, begun in 1788, were twofold. On the one hand, this new charity, it was hoped, would finally make some real progress in the elimination of crime and the inculcation of laborious habits. "The object in short was to unite the spirit of charity with the principles of trade, and to erect a temple to philanthropy on the foundation of virtuous industry." This would be done by taking the children of the idle or criminal classes away from their parents and giving them a proper education and vocational training. The Philanthropic Society was very careful to note that it did not attempt to break up the family and that it did not believe in large-scale institutional care. On the contrary, it was the aim of the society to employ "the sword of justice to sever those cords of paternal authority, which are used only to drag the child to ruin."[59] The authority for this breach of normal family solidarity came from the notion of the state as "a collective body . . . a common parent over all component individuals," which had an obligation to rescue its children from the bosoms of their "unnatural" and wicked, natural parents. Furthermore, the Philanthropic promised to reconstitute the family, after having removed the child from its origins, on a sounder and more stable basis: "The mode of living is in distinct houses, as separate families. A manufacturer has a house for himself and his wife, if married, and a certain number of wards; whom they are to regard as their own children. In these respects, the design is to approach as nearly as possible to common life."

[57] See Robert Young, *First and Second Reports of the Philanthropic Society*, 2 vols. (London: Couchman & Fry, 1790), 2:41–42. See also the review of a pamphlet by J. Cook, *An Address to the Public*, in the *Monthly Review* (January 1794), pp. 108–9.

[58] Quoted in Poynter, *Society and Pauperism*, p. 137. Bentham may himself have been an early director of this charity. His disciple Patrick Colquhoun was also on its board of governors.

[59] *Reports of the Philanthropic*, 1:31–32, 41–42.

Thus, the corrupt natural family would be replaced by a moral, adoptive family, but the family structure and its unique methods of socialization would be retained.

This separation of natural parents and children was seen as being beneficial to both. If the parents wished to see their child again (and they could not privately, but only accompanied by a member of the society), they would have to become more respectable. By holding the children up for ransom, the parents would be obliged to reform themselves in return for the privilege of seeing their offspring.

This aspect of their work, the enforced self-improvement of the lowest classes of London's poor, was presented as just that sort of charitable experiment necessary to set benevolence on a scientific basis. In referring to the effects of limited visiting privileges, Robert Young, secretary and early spokesman of the Philanthropic Society, said, "The experiment made was necessary to a knowledge of these dispositions in the outcasts of society, and the fact is considered as being of the first importance in a political view." This statement gives us a clue to the new and different aspirations of the Philanthropic. While all the other, older child-care charities gave prominence to the socially useful aspects of their work, the merely humanitarian appeal was always powerful and important. But with the new disdain for "mere" life, with the new economic notion that "mere" hands could not enrich the country, came the view that the only purpose of charity was to further a policy of national regeneration, and that each charity should employ the experimental method in ascertaining the most certain avenues to this end. The work of the Philanthropic Society rested on the view that the social order depended solely on mutual self-interest for cohesion, rather than seeing society as consisting of a web of duties and obligations, benevolences given and gratitude returned. Charity as duty or virtue came to be deemed futile by such philanthropists since it was "divested of any view of a return."[60] Such profitless giving was rejected by the society as "destructive to the main pillars of civil society," whereas in the workings of the Philanthropic, "the principle of mutual benefits is adopted in its fullest extent, a principle which in giving ever has views of return with interest." In keeping with this outlook, the society set up an experiment to see what the effect would be of rewarding boys for productivity; the result was that the boys' output increased by more than half.[61]

[60] Ibid., 1:32, 41–42, 44. An openhanded largesse was attacked both by Bernard, in the *Reports of the SBCP*, 3:11, footnote, and later by Bicheno, *An Inquiry*, pp. 65–66.

[61] *Reports of the Philanthropic*, 1:31–32. The experiment was conducted in the shoe-making wing. During the first three months of the experiment, before the boys were encouraged by incentives, they made £38.16 worth of shoes. During the following three months, when rewards were offered, £58.09 worth of shoes were produced: Philanthropic

Interestingly enough, the Philanthropic Society was one of the first charities of its day that had some success in making its operations pay, in part, at least, because of the adoption of the incentive scheme. While it did not make a profit—the work of the children never being sufficient to run the charity, and outside contributions always being vital to its continuance—it did better in this regard than most of its contemporaries. As we have seen, the best that the Lambeth Asylum for girls could accomplish was to net 9 percent of its yearly receipts from the work of its inmates. By contrast, by 1798, ten years after its inception, the Philanthropic was able to sell enough of the goods and services of its 180 children to make £990, or 22 percent of its receipts for that year. In 1813 they cared for 201 children, and were able to derive even more profits from their work, netting more than £2,700, or 39 percent of its receipts of £7,144. Not only were they looking after more children, but they were managing to make each child more profitable. Undoubtedly, some of the charity's phenomenal success in attracting new subscribers (going from 489 donors in 1790 to 1,871 in 1814) can be explained by its success in making itself a paying concern.[62] Nothing succeeds like success.

We have already noted, in the use of incentives, one of the reasons that the Philanthropic did so much better in this regard than other charities. Another was that, unlike the Lambeth Asylum, which trained and employed only girls, the Philanthropic had children of both sexes, and as their profits went up, so did their proportion of boys to girls. In 1792, for example, there were 93 boys and 123 girls being cared for (though strictly separated, of course). By 1798 the boys outnumbered the girls 130 to 50. The rising profit and the growing number of males cared for was not coincidental. The occupations girls were taught—spinning, weaving, sewing, and washing—were notoriously overstocked and badly paid. On the other hand, boys could be taught such well-paid skills as carpentry, bricklaying, shoemaking, and tailoring, as well as the operation of the printing press for which the Philanthropic Society was to become famous. While the work of the girls, on the whole, was applied to internal concerns— making and repairing the clothes and linens of the other children—this did not show up as a profit on the books, and did not give them much job

---

Society, *Minute Book*, 2271/2/1 (January 17, 1794, to November 27, 1795), p. 495. The papers of the Philanthropic Society are held by the County of Surrey Record Office, Kingston-upon-Thames. In August of 1797 the rewards ceased being money and became mutton with dinner; by June 1801 girls also were being encouraged by incentives to increase output.

[62] By 1815 more than 45 percent of the charity's income not derived from stocks or dividends came from the children's work. See Great Britain, Parliament, *Parliamentary Papers* (Commons), "Minutes of Evidence Taken before the Committee on the State of the Police of the Metropolis" [1817] (Shanon, Ireland: Irish Universities Press, 1968), appendix 12, p. 561.

security or pay on leaving the institution. The work of the boys, on the other hand, could be sold to the public, and provided them with skills that would allow them to achieve at least subsistence when their stay at the Reform (as the workshops of the Philanthropic were ominously named) was finished.[63]

In addition, the Philanthropic only admitted older children, usually between the ages of ten and twelve. The reasoning behind this was that

> the older boy will do at least twice at much work, and two of this age can be admitted at the same expence with one of the former [younger children]. Therefore, with the same fund, the good done to the public will be four times greater by receiving the elder than the younger. Again, the elder boy will soon be past the reach of any rescue; the younger may continue a few years longer in his course, and yet be saved.[64]

Thus, by admitting only children of the right age, and increasingly children of the right sex, the Philanthropic was able to fulfill its goal of founding charity on the principles of trade and sound policy.

The growing popularity of the charity can be seen by an examination of its committees. The members of the first committee for which we have a record, that of 1790, are, on the whole, strangers to the world of charitable giving. By 1791 we see a complete change in governing personnel. In this year the charity's general committee expanded from fourteen members to twenty-six. From this point in the charity's history, through the first two decades of the next century, the committees of the Philanthropic show a remarkable stability of membership, and an ever-increasing general charitable commitment. Two-thirds of the committeemen of the 1790s still belong to the charity in 1814. The charity's management included men of every denomination, though reflecting increasingly the influence of evangelical religion. These men, overwhelmingly merchants and monied men by occupation, were among the most involved and committed of all the charitable supporters of the day. Their continuing support insured the charity that direction and purpose, so essential to a successful operation.[65]

---

[63] There were, however, problems with teaching skills in the Philanthropic, especially to girls. Girls were more expensive and and more bothersome than boys to maintain. On October 25, 1793, the governors ordered a fence built between the Female Reform and a nearby skittles field; on March 3, 1795, they had to buy blinds for the girls' windows; and on April 8, 1796, the governors complained that "the difficulty of disposing of these Girls [in the Reform] is considerable": see Minutes of the Philanthropic Society, *Minute Book*, 2271/2/1, March 1, 1793, to March 1, 1796; 2271/1/2 for next three year period.

[64] *Reports of the Philanthropic*, 1:6.

[65] Only two of the fourteen committeemen of 1790 belonged to any of the other charities we have examined, and even they only belonged to one other charity each. Only these two committeemen played any further part in the management of the charity. Over half of all

THE RISE OF THE PENITENTIARY

The education and rehabilitation of the young was only one part, albeit a large one, of the attempt to deal with London's growing immorality and disorder. Another major effort was directed toward coping with an apparent increase in and visibility of prostitutes. For, as long as sexual vice was rampant on the streets, the purposes of virtuous education would be undermined and rendered nugatory.

Prostitution was considered both a threat to public order, because of its connections with organized crime and the spread of disease, and a fundamental attack on the primacy and sanctity of marriage and the family. In the late eighteenth century, when the family was seen as the prime nursery of civic and individual virtue, any perceived threat to it was also a grave threat to national security and the security of property. While the family was always seen as having strong economic and training functions (as we have seen in chapter 3), writers of the 1790s subordinated this element of the family's role to its role as the prime inculcator of virtue, religion, and political subordination. More than any other single institution, the family was seen as the unit most suitable for reforming and rehabilitating the corrupt mass of the citizenry.[66]

In such times of revolutionary fervor, serious rioting, and grave internal dissension, the institution of marriage became especially important in restraining "that impatience of controul which unhappily characterizes too many of our young men, and which afterwards grows into turbulence and sedition."[67] Since the married state was the linchpin of all ordered social relationships, and since "the history of mankind clearly shews, that the most important revolutions of states and kingdoms have turned upon this hinge,"[68] it followed that "where private obligation is neglected, the general obligation due to the authority of Government will also be underval-

---

the committeemen from 1791 belonged to at least one other charity; more than half of them belonged to anywhere from four to fifteen other charities. The 1791 list included four men associated with Dissent (Sir Joseph Andrews, J. C. Lettsom, Thomas Boddington, and James Martin) as well as two clergymen and one evangelical. By 1814 five of the twenty-four committeemen were either evangelicals or sympathizers with the evangelical cause: see *First and Second Report of the Philanthropic Society* (1790); *An Address to the Public from the Philanthropic Society* (London: B. White & Son, 1791); and *An Account of the Nature and Views of the Philanthropic Society* (London: n.p., 1814).

[66] See, for example, John Scott's sermon, *The Fatal Consequences of Licentiousness* (Hull: J. Ferraby, 1810), p. 25, footnote.

[67] *Gentleman's Magazine* (February 1795), p. 104. See also John Coakley Lettsom, *Hints Designed to Promote Beneficence, Temperance, and Medical Science* (London: H. Fry, 1797), pp. 59–60.

[68] Robert Sandeman, *The Honour of Marriage Opposed to All Impurities* (Edinburgh: W. Coke, 1750), p. 2. See also *An Essay on the Happiness and Advantages of a Well-Ordered Family* (London: F. & C. Rivington, 1795), p. 94.

ued and neglected."[69] Marriage thus had a political role in moderating the passions that disrupted social and political harmony: "The alwise God foresaw that a promiscuous intercourse between the sexes would be productive of the most pernicious evils in society. . . . [It would] ultimately overturn all civil government and entirely destroy the peace and happiness of men."[70]

The prostitute, the antithesis of the productive mother and wife, "disseminating the poison of immorality amidst the youthful part of the community,"[71] was deleterious to the national welfare and destructive to both marriage and social harmony. However, it must not be thought that writers on moral problems laid the entire blame for what they saw as an increase of lasciviousness solely at the feet of unrestrained women; men were taken at least as often to be responsible for vice as women.[72] Many also blamed the growth of sexual immorality on the decline of virtuous employment for women, "that the honest means of female livelihood are too generally precluded them, in the large retail shops of this metropolis." Some suggested taxes on all branches of industry "as ought to afford employment to women." Others recommended a repeal of the tax on servants, while still others suggested pressing male milliners, mantua makers, and haberdashers into the navy.[73] Women also seemed blocked from entering new occupations by prevailing notions of female delicacy, which prohibited women from venturing beyond the domestic realm to seek employment. But in terms of practical efforts, neither the view that men were the agents of sexual vice nor the lack of alternative employment was given concrete expression. Instead, Colquhoun and others recommended a sterner and better-organized science of police to deal with women of the streets.[74]

For, the problem was, and remains, a terribly difficult one. Though ev-

[69] *Reflections on the too Prevailing Spirit of Dissipation and Gallantry; Shewing its Dreadful Consequence to Publick Freedom* (London: E. & C. Dilly, 1771), p. 97.

[70] Howlett, *An Examination*, pp. 10–11. See also a review of G. Neale's *Essays on Modern Manners* in the *Monthly Review* (May 1791), p. 114. On marriage to suppress the innate wickedness of passions, see Colquhoun, *Treatise on Police*, p. 349; and to promote regularity and union, both individual and social, see *Essay on Well-Ordered Family*, p. 73.

[71] *Times*, January 15, 1785, p. 3.

[72] Ibid., p. 9; see also p. 29, and William Blair, *Prostitutes Reclaimed and Penitents Protected* (London: L. B. Seeley, 1809), p. 58. Blair was surgeon to both the Lock Hospital and the London Female Penitentiary.

[73] See the *Times*, November 15, 1788, p. 2; November 10, 1785, p. 3; July 26, 1786, p. 2; July 24, 1787, p. 2; July 25, 1787, p. 3; October 25, 1787, p. 2. See also *An Extract from an Account of the Ladies Society for the Education and Employment of the Female Poor* (London: W. Bulmer & Co., 1804), pp. 12–13; Edward Barry, *Essays on Celibacy and Wedlock* (London: Smart & Couslade, 1806), pp. 62–64; and *The Philanthropist*, William Allen, ed., 7 vols. (London: 1811–1819), 5:263.

[74] See Colquhoun, *The Police of the Metro*, pp. 334–350.

eryone wished that "some immense plan should be proposed," it was unclear as to what this should be. Part of the difficulty was due to three prevailing interpretations of the nature of sexual crime. First, the old idea that prostitution could never be eradicated was reintroduced. Rejected by the philanthropists of the midcentury, this view fit into that vision of the presence of deformity and evil that we have previously noted as being prevalent at the end of the century. To prevent prostitution in London was "as impossible as to resist the torrent of the tides," but the evil could be mitigated or "rendered less noxious and dangerous to the peace and good order of society."[75] Second, gainful employment was not seen to be the primary or essential step in the rehabilitation of the prostitute by everyone.

> The thing wanted before all these is a *moral character*, without which the "lawful means" of gaining a livelihood in this civilized and polished country are mere shadows. *Moral character* will therefore alone put a woman into the possession of daily bread; and devoid of this prerequisite, she may in vain be healthy, active, ingenious, and willing to labor with her hands![76]

Third, sexual license came to be seen as infectious, as a spiritual and corporal health hazard, an almost visible mist that destroyed virtue on contact. We have seen promiscuity described as an infection by Jonas Hanway, who described sexual vice as a fever that could be cured and recommended a period of isolation until the disease ceased being contagious, and then a release from quarantine and return to the everyday world.[77] However, when the imagery of infection was used after the 1790s, the disease no longer seemed capable of cure. Either one was irrevocably tainted, or entirely pure—recovery and rehabilitation seemed increasingly less likely.

> I am convinced that that woman who has lost, not merely the delicacy, but the feelings of her sex so far, as to wander the streets, offering her person indiscriminately to every man she meets. . . . can never again become fit to be a member of the society from whence she has been expelled. She may see the evil of her ways.—she may leave them off, and may reform,—but she never can recover that delicacy of feeling, that ignorance of evil, that innocence of mind, requisite to fit her for a companion of virtuous females. It is perfectly impossible.[78]

---

[75] Colquhoun, *Treatise of Police*, p. 337.

[76] Blair, *Prostitutes Reclaimed*, p. 13.

[77] Jonas Hanway, *Reflections, Essays and Meditations on Life and Religion* (London: J. Rivington, 1761), p. 289: "yet in this *particular* the ordinary methods do not seem adequate to this evil. Mankind are afraid of the *infection*, and require the *Patient* to pass through some kind of *purgation* before she is admitted within their walls."

[78] S. T., *Address to the Guardian Society* (London: W. Marchant, 1817), p. 14. See also

Often, the language of sexual vice and disease was directly connected with the horrors of the French Revolution. "A pestilential disease, of the most malignant nature, has corrupted the morals and mental sanity of the larger portion of Europe," said the Ladies Society for Employing the Female Poor. "If more cannot be done,—at least that sex [women] . . . should be preserved pure and immaculate; so as to be rendered the instruments of health and safety to others, whom curiosity or inattention may have exposed to the contagion." Thus, girls were cautioned against the French language, lest the very presence of such words in their mouths serve to unsettle their brains.[79] The metaphor of contagion was frequently used to describe the effects that the prostitute had on society. For example, in 1805 the Lock Asylum noted that such a woman was "not dissimilar to a person infected with the plague; who, miserable himself, is daily communicating the contagion to others, that will propagate still wider the fatal malady."[80] Licentiousness was called a "malignant pest" or a "deadly *miss mata* . . . increasing in virulence in more than geometric proportion."[81] With the demise of the view that rehabilitated prostitutes could become useful settlers, wives, and mothers in the colonies, and with prostitution now seen as an ever-growing fatal infection, the most reasonable course of action seemed to be to seek out prostitutes and quarantine them from civil society, to "remove some of those springs of corruption and disorder which accelerate the progress of national subversion."[82] Colquhoun suggested that a national program be undertaken to enact and enforce laws against prostitution because "the evil is of too great a magnitude to admit of a cure through the medium of private benevolence."[83] However, many members of the philanthropic community be-

---

"Letter to the Queen," in the *Times*, September 23, 1791, p. 3; Obeirne, *Sermon*, p. 36; Berington, *Essay on Depravity*, p. 4.

[79] *Ladies Society for . . . Female Poor*, p. 506. Thus, Obeirne noted that immorality was not native to Britain; such vice "may be said to be in our moral, what the plague and pestilence are in our physical atmosphere. They are not indigenous. . . . Whenever they visit us, they are wafted to our shores from some foreign coast, some less salubrious clime": *Sermon*, p. 25.

[80] *An Account of the Institution of the London Lock Hospital* (1805), p. 4.

[81] *An Account of the London Female Penitentiary* (1809), pp. 4–5; and *The Guardian Society for the Preservation of Public Morals* (London: n.p., 1816), pp. 24–25. Note the interesting use of Malthusian language. See also Colquhoun, *Police of the Metro*, p. 342.

[82] *London Female Penitentiary*, p. 21; see also pp. 5–6. For an interesting contemporary work on this topic see *An Appeal to the Virtues and Good Sense of the Inhabitants of the City of London . . . on the Subject of Prostitutes Walking the Streets* (London: James Harrison, 1809).

[83] Colquhoun, *Treatise on Police*, pp. 633, 627. Colquhoun wished to offer the penitent an asylum, "since by suddenly abridging their present resources, however iniquitous and reprehensible they may be, without such asylums, it would certainly be the means of many of them perishing for want." Matthew Henry too wished to see the legislature take action

lieved that it was possible for voluntary charity to cope with the problem of separating the impure from the innocent, and containing the threat of sexual vice. Thus, between 1787 and 1817 at least six institutions were started to aid the Magdalen in its attempt to restrain and contain the threat of moral pollution.[84]

The Magdalen was also on the road to recovery. We have seen how support for the institution seriously declined from 1776 to 1786. From 1786 through the 1820s, however, its subscription lists gradually increased (595 subscribers in 1786, 658 in 1803, and 750 in 1820). While the period 1776–1786 seems to have seen both a shrinking of total numbers and a decline in the number of new members, the next decade witnessed a growth both of total support and new membership. In 1796 one-half of the membership had joined after the 1786 list had been published. In 1803, although the charity was still growing, most of its members (87 percent) had already subscribed in 1796. This growth and stability continued to 1820, when a large percentage (63 percent) had shown a continuity of support of at least seventeen years.[85]

Two developments also suggest that the Magdalen had cast off its earlier hopes for the economic and moral rehabilitation of its charges, and saw its new function to be that of a house of quarantine. The first was the final abandonment of any attempt to teach the women vocational skills as a useless and unprofitable exercise. Instead, the governors employed the women as laundry maids, and consequently saw the profits of the institution rise at the turn of the century. Second, while the Magdalen continued to admit fewer women than it had during its first twenty years[86] (and those women seemed increasingly to be newly-seduced and abandoned women rather than actual prostitutes), the smaller percentage

---

against vice and had dire predictions of what would happen if this was not done: Matthew Henry, *Observations on Seduction and Prostitution* (London: Effingham Wilson, 1808), p. xiv.

[84] The six institutions I have been able to identify as originating in this period that cared for fallen women are the Lock Asylum (an adjunct of the older Lock Hospital), the London Female Penitentiary, the Refuge for the Destitute at Cuper's Bridge, the Refuge for the Destitute at Hackney Road, the Guardian Society, and Robert Young's Refuge for Industry.

[85] See *The General State of the Magdalen Hospital* with John Butler, *Sermon Preached in the Chapel of the Magdalen Hospital on the Occasion of the Anniversary Meeting* (London: H. & R. Causton, 1786); *Bye Laws and Regulations of the Magdalen Hospital* (London: n.p., 1791); *General State of the Magdalen Hospital* with Charles Peter Layard, *Sermon Preached at the Chapel . . . Magdalen Hospital* (London: Messrs. Rivington, 1802); T. L. Obeirne, *Sermon . . . Magdalen Hospital*; and *A List of the Governors of the Magdalen Hospital* (London: 1803 1805, 1821).

[86] Between 1758 and 1776 the Magdalen admitted 1,725 women (or almost 96 per year); they only took in 1,463 (or 77 per year) from 1802 to 1821; see *By-Laws and Regulations of the Magdalen Hospital* (London: n.p., 1821).

of women that were released, either to employment or friends, did not reflect this stricter selection or the greater likelihood of reconciliation.[87]

On the whole, the other asylums started during this period did very well, despite some sharp criticism. One gets the impression that in the public imagination the chasm between virtue and vice became even more unbridgeable during this period than it had been earlier. Many agreed with Hale that "the moral turpitude of a daring harlot is surely not less, but greater, than many of these [thieves, robbers and felons]; for in her abominable character centers every crime within her reach."[88] It was the widespread acceptance of this opinion that made it imperative for such women to be taken off the streets. The unconfined prostitute posed a constant danger to society. Not only was she responsible for the spread of sexual immorality, but her mere presence might corrupt and infect innocent females who needed to be protected from the dangers of "gross and polluted language and great indecency of behaviour, when walking the streets. Indeed it is to be feared, that the force of vile example, in unavoidably witnessing such scenes, may have debauched many females, who might otherwise have lived a virtuous and useful life."[89] When prostitutes remain free they endanger wives and daughters and "form that necessary agency through which female SERVANTS are daily inveigled to their ruin, and our domestic safety perpetually endangered."[90]

The strengthening of such sentiments in the first decade of the new century coincided with the flourishing state of the new asylums. The London Female Penitentiary, for example, increased its subscription list from 1,762 members in 1809 to 2,304 members by 1815. The Lambeth Refuge

[87] See Stanley Nash, "Social Attitudes towards Prostitution in London from 1752 to 1829" (diss., New York University, 1980), for more on seduced women. Although the figures are not terribly clear, 77.2 percent of all women admitted 1767–1791 were sent out to jobs or reunited with friends; from 1791 to 1822, 67.8 percent were similarly placed: see *By-Laws and Regulations of the Magdalen Hospital* (1821).

[88] William Hale, *An Address to the Public Upon the Dangerous Tendencies of the London Female Penitentiary* (London: W. Nicholson, 1803), p. 39. Hale thought that the penitentiary was creating more prostitutes by holding out an asylum to them. Prostitution and crime were believed to be intimately connected: see *Report of the Guardian Society*, p. 10; and *Thoughts on the Means of Preventing Evils, Similar to Those which have Occurred in the City of Edinburgh* (Edinburgh: Oliphant, Waugh & Innes, 1812), p. 22. For one of the few voices dissenting from this judgment, see G. Hodgson, *Strictures on Mr. Hale's Reply to the Pamphlets lately Published in Defense of the London Female Penitentiary and a Letter by Mr. Blair* (London: Williams & Smith, 1805), p. 29. Hodgson was the chaplain at the penitentiary and not a disinterested bystander.

[89] Colquhoun, *Treatise on Police*, p. 342.

[90] *Guardian Society*, pp. 13–14. See also S. T., *Address*, pp. 10–11; and *Appeal to the Virtues*, p. 7. The *Times*, September 20, 1791, noted that "A lady of sound judgment and penetration . . . although she is ever so well inclined to assist the penitent, yet cannot with any degree of prudence taken such a person into her family."

for the Destitute (an institution designed for both men and women who had broken the law) multiplied the number of its subscribers fivefold from 1806 to 1816.[91] Two features of both of these new charities may explain some of their increasing support: their relative thrift, and their ability to make the work of their inmates pay. While it cost the Magdalen about £32 a year per resident, the London Female Penitentiary got by on only £23 and the Guardian Society on a mere £14.6. Second, the Magdalen never received more than 9 percent of its total revenues from the work of its women until it turned them to laundry.[92] The London Female Penitentiary, on the contrary, was able to get at least 20 percent of its much larger annual receipts from the work of its women. The Lambeth Refuge did even better, and was able to contribute 35 percent of its large revenues in 1818. However, like the Philanthropic Society, the reason for the Lambeth Refuge's especially high income was the presence and work of men, who could do more skilled work and receive higher pay. Even the Lock Asylum, which was the only institution we know of to decline in membership during this period, still managed to reap 16 percent of its total revenues from the inmates' work.[93]

Perhaps one reason why the institutions were able to generate more income was the enormous number of women, who were probably not all prostitutes, that applied for admission during these years.[94] By 1815, 1,609 women had applied over eight years for admission to the London Female Penitentiary, and only 389 had been accepted. With admission so difficult, it is easy to see why women, once admitted, would be sure to work hard so as not to be dismissed. In point of fact, neither the Lambeth Refuge nor the London Female Penitentiary seems to have sent out many women. Unlike the Lock Asylum, which had to dismiss 50 percent of its inmates for unsuitable behavior or failure of contrition, neither institution was forced to dismiss many for bad behavior. For example, in 1818

[91] See Melville Horne, *Sermon . . . London Female Penitentiary* (London: Hatchard, 1811); and *The Annual Report of the Committee of the London Female Penitentiary to the General Meeting* (London: 1809, 1815). The Lambeth Refuge went from 311 subscribers in 1806 to 1,609 in 1816: *A Short Account of the Institution called the Reform for the Destitute, Cuper's Bridge, Lambeth* (1806, 1816).

[92] I agree with Nash's view that the Magdalen, the oldest of the penitence houses, was the "softest" on its inmates in terms of work done and general standards of upkeep: see Nash, *Social Attitudes.*

[93] The London Female Penitentiary also had a system of boarding rates for those with friends who could afford to keep them, but who did not wish to have them in their homes. See Great Britain, *Parliamentary Papers*, "Select Committee on the Police," appendix 14, p. 562.

[94] In the period from 1807 to 1817, for example, 2,000 women petitioned the London Female Penitentiary for admittance, and only 565 were accepted: see the testimony of its secretary, ibid., p. 506.

the Lambeth Refuge dismissed only two women out of 113 for bad conduct, while sending out about one-quarter to work or to friends. The London Female Penitentiary also never placed out more than one-half of its number, with a correspondingly low dismissal rate. Containment and quarantine, rather than rehabilitation and return to the everyday world, seems to have been the plan.[95]

With the acknowledged difficulties in finding employment even for virtuous women, and with a sort of pessimism about what could be done to eradicate the disease of prostitution or to find a cure or antidote for infected women, the asylums and penitentiaries of this era were more like "holding" institutions than organizations with positive, practical goals for the rehabilitated prostitute. Furthermore, the growth of popular notions of the proper delicacy and helplessness of the virtuous female made the fallen woman stand out in even more vivid contrast. With an increased emphasis on the importance of female purity and the progressive refusal to admit any earthly or corporeal passions to the female soul came a harsher condemnation of those unnatural females who, by giving themselves to a career of lust, not only sentenced themselves and their victims to a life of ceaseless suffering, but betrayed the integrity of their whole sex.[96]

CHARITY AND NATIONAL REGENERATION

In this chapter we have examined how the philanthropists of the 1790s attempted to adopt utilitarian techniques to improve the social climate of the nation and reduce the threat of poverty through self-help. What is inescapable, however, is that whatever the original aim of this scientific charity, it resulted in increased efficiency only by a severe cutback in services offered, and by eliminating as undesirable or unattainable certain important goals that philanthropists had earlier sought. In the field of child

[95] The manifesto of the Guardian Society (1815) noted that its purpose was "to check the progress of female depravity whereby to preserve public morals from contamination": quoted in Nash, *Social Attitudes*, p. 273. Nothing was said about the rehabilitation of the prostitute in this document although some reference was made to the restoration of prostitutes "to society as useful members of it" in testimony before the Select Committee on Police, Great Britain, *Parliamentary Papers*, p. 465. The minutes of this committee contain all the figures cited.

[96] Earlier in the century, Jonas Hanway had argued that it was desirable for women to acquire fortitude and lay aside "puerile fears and fantastic inquietudes" (*Journal of Eight Days' Journey* [London: H. Woodfall, 1756], p. 77). But toward the century's end Bennett could write that "a *Single* woman is, particularly, defenseless. She cannot move beyond the precincts of her house without apprehension. She cannot go with ease or safety into public": John Bennett, *Letters to a Young Lady*, 2 vols. (Warrington: W. Eyres, 1789), p. 162. For more on the rising importance of female delicacy, see Henry, *Observations*, p. 22; and a letter to the *Gentleman's Magazine* (Feruary 1795), p. 103.

care, we have seen how institutions whose main purpose was only nurturant, like the Foundling Hospital, almost disappeared, while institutions like the Philanthropic Society thrived and flourished, but only by increasingly restricting admission to children of a certain sex and age group. In order to survive at all, the Foundling had to adopt severe cutbacks in the number of children admitted as well as in their diet,[97] while the lying-in charities and hospitals similarly had to reduce available aid. And in a real, material sense, the myriad self-help charities founded and supported by SBCP members tried to shift at least part of the burden of poor relief onto the shoulders of the poor themselves, espousing all the while the moral benefits of self-maintenance. Further, although the number of institutions for the prostitute increased in this period, both the kinds of training and the expectations for a productive future for these women were curtailed. No longer were fallen women seen as potentially valuable citizens, as wives and mothers of future colonists. Instead, they were seen as a pestilence to be controlled and kept in check, with no value as spouses and procreators, and the attempt to give them value as skilled laborers was abandoned.

While many of the charities established around the middle of the century suffered a decline in support, or were forced to contract their operations and limit their ambitions, charity as a whole by no means went into a general slump. If anything, more money was poured into philanthropic ventures, and more new charities were established.[98] What had changed were the goals and aspirations of these new societies. Instead of the enhancement of the nation's wealth or international position, philanthropists felt the true goal of charity to be the reunion of the classes, sundered from each other by impersonal relief and irreconciled interest. One such healing charity, the Dorking Provident Institution, claimed that through its operations

> The whole population, high and low, become intimately known to each other. The poor labourer is no longer an insulated being, for whose welfare no one seems to care. . . . His industry will now be marked and applauded; and in the hour of his need, his wants will be supplied from the pure fountain of his own exertions and his own merits; which he can receive with an unbroken spirit.[99]

[97] Even a charity as successful as the Philanthropic had to reduce clothing and diet to a bare minimum in the mid 1790s; beef and cheese consumption were cut in May 1793, only bread of the "second sort" was used as of May 1795, potatoes were substituted for bread in December of that year, and girls were put on a "rice Milk diet" in November 1796: See *Minute Book*, 2271/2/1 and 2271/2/2.

[98] See, especially, Owen, *English Philanthropy*. See also Richard Tompson, *The Charity Commission and the Age of Reform* (London: Routledge & Kegan Paul, 1979).

[99] Henry Duncan, *Annals of Banks for Savings* (London: Luke Hansard & Sons, 1818), p. 117. The role of charity to restore social connections is made again and again in the

We can see here both the evangelical notion of the classes reunited in quasi-paternalist ties and the stress of the political economists on the spiritual and material advantages of independence. The charities of the 1820s and 1830s, like the many "visiting" charities, or the Chalmers scheme to divide large towns into "hamlets," each looked after by an interested member of the "upper classes,"[100] rested on the assumption that the material transfer of aid and goods from the rich to the poor was but the most insubstantial element of charity's true purpose. Material aid was useful only to the degree that it helped and brought about moral and spiritual reform, reform that bound social classes together in a more harmonious fashion. Thus, for the fervent and involved philanthropists at the end of the eighteenth century and the beginning of the nineteenth, true charity involved the improvement of the nation's morals and manners, as this came to be seen as not only the nation's prime need, but the only sphere in which charity had not been replaced by the operations of the market.

---

literature: see, for example, George Horne, *Sermon . . . "Sunday Schools Recommended"* (Oxford: Clarendon Press, 1786), p. 12; *Plans of the Sunday Schools and Schools of Industry Established in Bath* (Bath: R. Cruttwell, 1789), p. ix.

[100] Thomas Chalmers's *The Christian and Civic Economy of Large Towns* (1821) had a profound effect on charitable practice in both London and Great Britain as a whole. See, especially, Thomas Chalmers, *Problems of Poverty: Selections from the Economic and Social Writings*, Henry Hunter, ed. (London: Nelson, 1912). For strikingly similar changes in France, see Jacques Donzelot, *The Policing of Families* (New York: Pantheon Books, 1977), p. 62.

Tradition, Policy, and Philanthropy

THE PHILANTHROPISTS of the eighteenth century saw themselves as being involved in an endeavor new in both philosophy and method from the casual almsgiving that characterized, for them, the charity of medieval England. In many ways they were unjust to their ancestors, distorting and denying the nature of their accomplishments. However, in some important respects, they were undoubtedly right. Although the charity of the century was by no means of a piece, and in fact one of the main purposes of this book has been to illustrate the differences between the philanthropy of the midcentury and that at its end, the different currents or styles of giving over the century shared a common form, associated societies, and a common desire, to aid in the accomplishment of what philanthropists believed to be the nation's goals and aspirations.

Premodern charity rested on very different foundations and employed different methods. It accepted as providentially given that there would always be people who were poor, whether through their own fault or not. It was considered to be an important aspect of Christian charity to relieve the perennially needy. Giving to the poor, in whatever form, was encouraged, even if it was not possible, or desirable, to make an accurate assessment of the worthiness of the object of the aid. The existence of poverty being eternal, and the benefits of charity great, a little wasted largesse did not seem very important. In God's eye, the intention of the giver, not the worth of the recipient, was the salient feature.

In contrast, one central notion of most postmedieval aid to the poor has been the need for discrimination. Although medieval canonists insisted on the distinction of the idle from the impotent poor, and recommended charity only to the latter, their thinking was that the majority of the needy were of this latter sort. By the end of the seventeenth century, though philanthropists still believed that the category of the impotent poor would always exist, and always need care, they felt that the impotent constituted only a small fraction of those demanding relief. Undoubtedly, the growth of commerce and industry had made it possible for many who might not have been able to support themselves previously to be reckoned as able to labor. By a proper discrimination the truly needy could be provided with support, and the able with employment.

By the end of the seventeenth century, people had come to believe that most poverty resulted from unemployment. Since lack of employment was rooted in contingent and changeable economic circumstances rather than in the eternal nature of things, this kind of poverty was merely accidental and could be overcome by social action. Thus, for most of the poor, justice came to mean the provision of employment. Charity, in contrast, now consisted of acts of grace toward the poor and needy, which, unlike acts of justice, were totally voluntary and entirely nonobligatory.

Although charity was entirely voluntary, this did not mean that it was socially insignificant. Indeed, charity was to have a vital role to play in the nation's future. Charity, many said, could do more than aid the individual donor or recipient; properly employed it could foster national prosperity and power. In order to do this, it must be able to deal with more than the old perennial problems; it must utilize its resources to come to the aid of a changing national policy. Therefore, since its operations were no longer aimed at the individual, and its ends no longer unchanging, a new sort of organization was necessary to deal more effectively with changing social demands, a new form had to be created that would embody the voluntary flexibility of the old-fashioned almsgiving with the clearheadedness and discriminating direction of the Poor Law.

In the joint-stock company model, eighteenth-century charity found this form. Encouraged by the huge success that commercial joint-stock companies were having in the world of business, the charitable organized themselves in a similar fashion and transformed personal charity into "associated philanthropy." Usually a small group of concerned citizens evolved a plan for some scheme of local improvement, solicited funds, often became incorporated, and annually elected a board of governors or directors to run the affairs of the charity. Associated charities had the advantage of allowing their subscribers to contribute only as much and for as long as they saw the charity to be acting effectively. They also made it possible for a particular charity, and charity in general, to respond to short-term changes in the national outlook and national needs. Thus, the history of the foundations and fortunes of England's charities in the eighteenth century is, in many ways, a history of changing perceptions of England's national needs.

Although associated philanthropy had been active in a limited way from the beginning of the century, one of the first major efforts of this new form was the establishment of the Foundling Hospital. This was soon followed by organizations to aid lying-in women, other orphan and child-care schemes, and aid to sufferers from sexual vice. It is no coincidence that these three seemingly unrelated types of charitable practice arose within a single twenty-year period, or that England's major imperial wars of the eighteenth century fell within these same twenty years. It was the aim of these charities to implement the important public policies of population growth, vocational training, and moral reform. The goal of all of these charities was an increase of useful laborers, a decrease in the number of merely accidental poor, and care, by-the-by, for the young and the sick. Although their aim was national in scope, the charities were usually local in support and in their choice of recipients. Often, as in the case of the Foundling, the Marine Society, or the Magdalen, the governors hoped that the institution set up in London would serve as a model and inspiration for further charitable activity in the provinces. Still, except for the disastrous period when the Foundling opened its doors to indiscriminate admission of children from all parts of the country, the spheres of activity of these charities was largely local. The aspirations of these societies, and the writings of their supporters, on the other hand, exhibited a spirit of optimism about the future of England and the possibility of curbing and conquering poverty through properly directed aid. Their founders assumed, perhaps naively, that any increase in the wealth of the nation would result in an increase of individual wealth, that if national prosperity and power were ensured, the growth of personal prosperity was assured.

While the political economists in many ways represented the last gasp of this easy optimism, they also laid the framework for a critique of the earlier charities. They, too, believed that poverty was the result of unemployment arising from the underdevelopment of commerce and manufacture. However, as the first systematic exponents of the value of technology and the division of labor in production, the political economists challenged the political arithmeticians' view that the magnitude of production was dependent on the number of working hands available. Thus, at one and the same time, they undercut the economic value of increasing numbers of laborers and elevated instead the importance of the psychological and moral uprightness of the worker. A large and growing population was no longer seen as the best method to increase output; machines could do the work of several men and far more cheaply. What was important was that the human auxiliaries of the machines be sober, punctual, and totally devoted to their work. The preservation of life, which earlier had had a strong economic value, thus became a matter of mere sentiment, of an unwillingness to cause suffering. Not surprisingly, there was, as we have noted, a rapid decline of support for institutions like the Foundling, which merely preserved life, a more gradual decline of support for several of the lying-in institutions, and a rise in those organizations devoted to the improvement of morals.

Toward the end of the century, philanthropists seriously questioned the old purposes of the established charities, and found many of them unacceptable. The goal of increasing population, an important end of midcentury charity, no longer seemed appropriate or desirable. Not only had machines reduced the need for a growing population, but the rising poor rates, the need for enormous importations of corn, and mounting popular discontent made an infinitely growing army of poor seem anathema to many observers. The great hope of the earlier philanthropists, that the charitable provision of vocational training and employment for the able poor would prove to be the panacea for poverty, was also seriously challenged. Philanthropists of the 1770s and 1780s felt that every pound that had been contributed to these sorts of public enterprises might have been more fruitfully and properly invested in the expansion of new industries. If the charitable provision of employment had any value at all for them, it was not economic but moral. Even Thomas Bernard and the SBCP, early and ardent advocates of Count Rumford's employment schemes, came to agree with those who saw publicly supported employment as inherently unprofitable to the nation, and only of limited value for its psychological influence.

Instead of providing employment or increasing population, charitable opinion turned to the improvement of public morale. In order to attain this purpose, the old discrimination between the able and impotent would not be enough. What was needed was further discrimination: charity must be given, even to the deserving, only in the manner most conducive to the improvement of manners and morals. Having rejected the provision of employment, the only forms of sustaining aid that charity could offer came in the guise of soup kitchens and the promulgation of the principles of household frugality, so the poor could weather their situation on whatever they could earn. Even this limited aid must be uncertain, it was said; the certainty of aid, whether through the auspices of charity or the parish rates, debased and degraded the laborer and removed the crucial element of voluntariness from the beneficence of the donor. Instead of a steady and automatic flow of aid, relief should be temporary, intermittent, and conditional on good behavior. No longer did the ownership of property inherently oblige and entail the duties of charity.[1] Only a system of relief that was entirely voluntary could be just, it was said, as well as truly efficient.[2]

It is for these reasons that the self-help charities received the greatest support in the magazines and literature of the day by the early nineteenth

---

[1] For example, see Howlett, *Examination of Mr. Pitt's Speech*, p. 11.

[2] Furthermore, all aid that was certain and assured was held by many to be one of the main causes of the upsurge of poverty and one of the major factors causing growing class ruptures: "Great is the mischief that has arisen from the system of compulsory charity; it destroys the connecting feelings between the several ranks of society, and their mutual dependence on each other; it has ruined the morals of the people, rendered them odious and insolent, and independent of character": John B. Sheffield, *Observations on the Impolicy, Abuse, and False Interpretation of the Poor Laws* (London: J. Hatchard, 1818), pp. 4–5.

century. The style and distribution of charitable aid had clearly changed.[3] In the 1750s, during times of need, a number of charitably minded individuals met, agreed on a course of action, and started collecting subscriptions from their friends and the public at large to implement their program of relief. Now the charitably minded were urged to rouse their needy neighbors to action, and to collect, organize, and administer funds for their relief that had been raised from the resources of the poor themselves. The two most popular examples of this sort of aid were the savings banks and friendly societies, both of which utilized the talents and interests of the wealthy to organize and encourage the subscriptions of the poor. In practice as in theory, the role of the philanthropist was transformed from being a donor of funds to becoming a donor of time and personal attention.

We have seen a new outpouring of charitable action and theory at the end of the eighteenth century and the beginning of the nineteenth. More charities came into existence and the degree of involvement of charitable contributors deepened. Charity had ceased being a hobby and became a serious, scientific avocation. Along with this heightened sense of the importance of charitable donations came a change in the motives and purposes of charitable associations. No longer confident that alms would "cover their sins" or that their donations would make England a more prosperous and powerful nation, the philanthropists of this era seemed determined to use charity instead as an instrument of national regeneration. Charity was to aid in the development of character, in the maintenance of a firm determination to remain free from the humiliation of accepting alms. The new charity was to be an important element in the foundation of a new Christian England. Rather than merely relieving the poor, as donors in premodern England had been content to do, or rehabilitating them through a sheltered period of vocational training, as mid-eighteenth-century philanthropists had attempted, the new charity hoped to reform the minds and morals of the laboring poor. Unlike earlier givers who had hoped to win heaven through individual beneficence, or those optimists who had attempted to conquer poverty through associated philanthropy, the charitably inclined of the later period argued that the only real assistance that the rich could confer upon the poor that was of real and permanent value was aid grounded in

> a personal inspection of their conduct and management; a calm and constant attention to their wants, and to the most eligible methods of relieving them; to encourage and stimulate their habits of industry, sobriety and economy; to fur-

---

[3] This change, and its long-lasting effects, is nowhere better seen than in the obituary of C. S. Loch, secretary and historian of the Charity Organization Society: the *Times*, January 25, 1923, noted that "self respect [was] . . . the greatest charity of all."

nish them with such knowledge as may be useful in their pursuits and in their station of life as well as to confirm in their minds the importance of fulfilling their religious and moral duties; to connect them with the higher orders by the ties of kindness and gratitude, without inducing that sense of dependence which diminishes a just confidence in their own exertions, is to confer intrinsic and lasting benefits which do not terminate with our lives but form a useful example to be transmitted to our posterity.[4]

What the nation now stood most in need of, many philanthropists contended, was some system that would provide a common purpose, that would impose on all classes obligations and duties, that would subsume individual interests into some larger interest. The peculiar amalgamation of political economy, science,[5] and evangelical religion that occurred in this period provided such a coherent system of beliefs and values. Sweeping across class lines, it criticized the aristocrat as well as the pauper, and attempted to provide similar moral imperatives for both. In this way, the attempt to save the souls of the nation, by using charity as an important weapon in its battle with sin, was also an attempt to reunite the classes and the nation under the banner of a new and revitalized Christianity.

Thus, though the charity of the early nineteenth century appears so different from its eighteenth-century predecessors, an important element of continuity connects the two. Believing both in the possibility and necessity of improving the world, London's citizens used charity as an important agent in that social change. From the late seventeenth century onward, charity became a central element in domestic police, a central area for social experimentation, and central avenue for individual and social action.

[4] *The Philanthropist*, 1:215.

[5] For example, John Duncan, in *Collections Relative to Systematic Relief of the Poor* (1815) noted that "as justice, reduced to rules, becomes the subject of legal science, so charity, reduced to rules, may be considered as the subject of a science of beneficence": quoted in Sir Leon Radzinowicz, *A History of English Criminal Law and its Administration from 1750*, 4 vols. (London: Stevens, 1948), 4:33.

Major Donors

I HAVE GONE through the subscription lists for two periods, 1740–1769 and 1790–1819, and listed those donors who gave to a majority of the charities considered in this book. For the first period, to qualify as a major donor an individual had to contribute to at least three of the following charities in the twenty year period: the Foundling Hospital, the Marine Society, the Lambeth Asylum, the Lying-in Charity, the Magdalen Hospital, or the British Lying-in Hospital. To qualify for inclusion in the latter period, one had to contribute to four major charities, including the above six charities with the addition of the Philanthropic Society or the Lock Hospital.

The total number of charities that any individual donated to will include not only the ones we have examined, but any other charities I have been able to find to which they subscribed. These "other" charities are described as "nonlisted." A donor is described as the director of a charity when he has sat on a governing board of that charity. The phrase "traditional bequests" includes such things as money for bread or coal for the poor at Christmas, contributions to almshouses, schools, and so forth.

1740–1769

Sir Richard Adams died 1774, will read, no charitable bequests. Baron of Court of Exchequer. Brother-in-law, Sir George Amyand, contributor. Gave to four charities.

Michael Adolphus died 1785, will read, traditional bequests and £10 each to the British Lying-in Hospital and the Marine Society. Merchant and contributor to government loans. Jew. Gave to six charities and director of the Marine and the Lambeth Asylum.

Isaac Akerman died 1792, will read, no charitable bequests. China merchant. Brother and wife givers. Son-in-law William Noble and his executor Robert Dent major donors in later period. Other executor giver. Gave to seven charities and was director of the Magdalen and the Lambeth Asylum.

Lady Anson died 1760. Daughter of the first earl of Hardwicke. Husband naval hero. Husband, son, and daughter-in-law givers. She gave to three charities.

Sir Charles Asgill died 1788, will read, no charitable bequests. Banker and alderman of London. Partner Nightingale and wife gave. Donated to five charities, director of the Magdalen.

Sir John Barnard died 1764, will read, traditional bequests, bequests to nonlisted charities, and £50 to the Foundling Hospital. Underwriter and marine insurance. M.P. and alderman. Strict Anglican. Daughter married Thomas Hankey, major donor. Executor John Small major donor. Wife gave. Donated to seven charities, director of the Foundling and the Marine Society.

John Barnes died 1782. Stockbroker. Gave to five charities, director of the Magdalen and the Foundling.

Anne, Viscountess Bateman died 1769. Husband gave. Gave to three charities.

John, seventh duke of Bedford, died 1771. Gave to six charities.

George Bond supported the Society for Promoting Religious Knowledge among the Poor. Wife gave. Gave to four charities.

Jacob Bosanquet died 1767, will read, traditional bequests. East India and Levant Company director. Brother and sons givers, as was brother-in-law, John Hanbury. Son-in-law, S. R. Gaussen, major donor. Gave to four charities.

Samuel Bosanquet died 1765, will read, traditional bequests. Director of Royal Exchange Assurance and Turkey Company. Brothers and sons givers, as was son-in-law, Peter Gaussen. Gave to five charities.

John Browne died 1785, linen draper. Gave to five charities.

Robert Butcher died 1788. Steward to duke of Bedford, who was major giver. Gave to seven charities.

George, fourth earl of Cardigan, died 1790. Wife gave. Gave to four charities.

Nathaniel Castleton died 1782, will read, no charitable bequests. Knightley and Poyntz, his executors, charitable subscribers. Gave to three charities, director of the Magdalen.

Charles Child, will dated 1766, left £100 to Foundling. Insurance broker. Gave to four charities, director of the Foundling.

Richard Chiswell died 1772, will read, traditional bequests and bequests to nonlisted charities. Turkey merchant, M.P., and Bank of England director. Father gave. John Wowen, his executor, major giver, and other executor, Muilman, gave. Gave to four charities.

Samuel Clarke gave to eight charities. Wife giver. Director of the Foundling.

George Colebrooke died 1809. M.P. East India Company and government contractor, stockbroker, and banker. Partners Franks, Joseph Martin, and Barlow Trecothick major donors. Other partners, Nesbitt and Hanbury, charitable givers, as was his wife and his brother James. Gave to six charities and director of the Marine Society.

John Cornwall died 1803. Rope maker, banker, Bank of England and Russia Company director. Son and wife donated. Gave to ten charities, director of the Magdalen and the Marine Society.

Sir James Creed died 1793, East India merchant. M.P. Wife and partner, Peter Burrell, contributors. Gave to five charities and was director of the Marine Society.

James Crockatt died 1769, will read, no charitable bequests. South India trader and Carolina merchant. Gave to four charities, on directing committee of Magdalen.

Benjamin Mendes DaCosta died 1764, will read, traditional bequests. Merchant. Wife, brothers, and son donors. Gave to five charities.

Richard Dalton died 1791, will read, no charitable bequests. Keeper of king's drawings. Wife donor. Gave to ten charities.

William, second earl of Dartmouth, died 1801. Brother, wife, and son givers. Well known for his religious piety. Gave to nine charities, director of the Lambeth Asylum and the Foundling.

John Delme died 1789, will read, traditional bequests and £50 to each charity of which he was governor. Banker. Brother major donor. Gave to nine charities, director of the Magdalen.

Peter Delme died 1770, will read, traditional bequests. Banker and M.P. Wife and son donors, brother major donor. Gave to ten charities, director of the Foundling.

Mary Countess Denbigh died 1782. Father and husband gave. Gave to three charities.

Robert Dingley died 1781. London silk merchant, Bank of England and Russia Company director. Wife and brother givers. Gave to three charities and director of the Foundling.

Peter Dobree Guernsey merchant and common councillor. Supporter of the SPCK. Son gave, and son-in-law, Paul LeMesurier, major donor. Gave to four charities.

Richard Duhorty, merchant. Gave to four charities, director of the Marine.

John Fielding died 1780, will read, no charitable bequests. Magistrate. Brother gave, and associate, Saunders Welch, major giver. Gave to five charities, director of the Marine and the Lambeth Asylum.

Samuel Fluyder died 1768, will read, no charitable bequests. Alderman and M.P. Packer, cloth merchant, blackwellhall factor, government contractor. Brother and brother-in-law, earl of Cardigan, major donors. Gave to six charities.

Thomas Fluyder, died 1769. Alderman and M.P. Government contractor. Brother major donor. Wife and father-in-law, Sir George Champion, gave. Gave to six charities.

Jacob, first earl of Folkestone, died 1761. M.P. Grandson, earl of Radnor, and son-in-law, Robert Lord Romney, major givers. Gave to seven charities, director of the Marine.

Alexander Fordyce died 1789. Banker. Brother gave. Gave to five charities.

Aaron Franks died 1777. East India merchant. Jew. Brother and wife donors. Gave to seven charities.

Naphtali Franks, East India merchant. Jew. Brother and wife givers. Gave to five charities.

Richard Fuller died 1782. Banker and M.P. Dissenter. Son[?] major giver, as was partner, Frazer Honeywood. Gave to three charities.

Peter Gaussen died 1788, will read, traditional bequests, bequests to nonlisted charities, and £100 each to the Foundling and the Magdalen. Bristol silk merchant, Bank of England director. Son gave, and father-in-law, Sam Bosanquet, major donor. Gave to five charities.

Lady Betty Germain died 1769, will read, traditional bequests. Gave to nine charities.

Sampson Gideon died 1762. Financier. Jew. Son major donor. Gave to four charities.

Peter Godfrey, East India Company director and supporter of the SPCK. Gave to three charities.

Stephen P. Godin died 1787, will read, traditional bequests and £50 each to the Foundling and the Magdalen. Insurance broker. Brother and three sons-in-law, John Cornwall, Godfrey Thornton, and John Shiffner, givers. Gave to five charities and directed the Magdalen and the Marine.

George Grenville died 1770. M.P. Wife major donor. Gave to three charities.

Mrs. George Grenville died 1769. Husband major donor. Gave to three charities.

John Grubb gave to three charities.

J. C. Hankey died 1802. Banker. Father, cousins, and uncle donors. Gave to five charities, director of the Lambeth Asylum.

Sir Joseph Hankey died 1769, will read, no charitable bequests. Banker and alderman. Son, brothers, and nephews givers. Gave to eight charities, director of the Marine and the Lambeth Asylum.

Thomas Hanson died 1770, will read, traditional bequests, bequests to nonlisted charities, and £500 each to the Foundling and the Magdalen. Merchant. He was executor of Benjamin Longuet, major donor, as was one of his executors, James Matthias; the other, Richard Goodall, gave. He gave to three charities.

Jonas Hanway died 1786, will read, no charitable bequests. Russia merchant and supporter of the SPCK. Brother giver. Gave to seven charities, on directing committees of the Magdalen, the Foundling, and the Marine.

Sir Thomas Harrison died 1765, will read, traditional bequests and bequests to nonlisted charities. Son donor. Gave to five charities.

William N. Hart died 1765. Banker. Son and wife donors. Gave to four charities.

William Heberden died 1801. Doctor. Son major donor. Gave to six charities.

Abraham Henckell died 1761. Merchant. Nephew major donor. Gave to six charities.

Isaac Henckell, Hamburg merchant. Uncle major donor and brothers gave. Gave to eight charities.

Francis, fourth marquis of Hertford, died 1794. Wife gave and son major donor. Gave to five charities.

Thomas Hill died 1790, will read, no charitable bequests. Director of the Royal Exchange Assurance. Gave to six charities.

Henry Hoare died 1785, will read, no charitable bequests. Banker, M.P., and supporter of the SPCK. Sons, brother, and nephews major donors. Gave to three charities.

Richard Hoare died 1777. Banker. Brother and nephews major donors. Gave to three charities.

Mrs. Jane Holden, wife of Samuel Holden, Russia Company and Bank of England director. Friend, Joseph Fawthorp, a charitable donor, as was husband and daughters or sisters-in law. Gave to five charities.

Thomas Hollis died 1774, will read, traditional bequests and money to establish libraries. Heir, Thomas Brand Hollis, donor. Gave to three charities.

Frazer Honywood died 1764, will read, no charitable bequests. Banker, M.P., and monied man. Brother, wife, and father-in-law, Abraham Atkins, donors. Partner, Richard Fuller, major donor. Gave to six charities, director of the Magdalen and the Marine.

Edward Hooper died 1793, commissioner of the customs house. Gave to four charities, director of the Marine.

John Horne, Italian merchant. Brother major donor. Gave to six charities.

Samuel Horne died 1777, will read, no charitable bequests. Italian merchant. Brother major donor. Gave to five charities, director of the Magdalen.

Vansittart Hudson died 1768, will read, traditional bequests, bequests to nonlisted charities and £100 to the Foundling. Gave to four charities, director of the Foundling.

John Hyde died 1771. London Assurance director and wholesale hardwareman. Wife, son, and daughter donors. Gave to six charities.

John Jackson, merchant. Gave to three charities, director of the Marine.

Stephen T. Janssen died 1777, will read, traditional bequests. M.P. and alderman. Owner of French enamel works. Father giver. Gave to eight charities.

Anthony Keck died 1767, will read, no charitable bequests. M.P. and supporter of the SPCK. Son and wife donors. Gave to five charities.

Dr. George Kelley gave to three charities.

Edward Knipe died 1786. Brother and wife donors. Gave to three charities.

Ralph Knox died 1783, will read, traditional bequests. Director of Royal Exchange Assurance. Wife subscriber. Gave to three charities.

Edwin Lascelles died 1795, will read, no charitable bequests. M.P., West Indies merchant, and sugar factor. Brother and nephew donors. Gave to six charities, director of the Foundling.

John Lefevre died 1790, will read, no charitable bequests. Malt distiller, brewer, and banker. Supporter of the Society for Promoting Religious Knowledge among the Poor. Brothers givers, and banking partners, the Raikes family, major donors. Gave to four charities.

Benjamin Longuet died 1761. Bank of England, South Sea Company, and Russia Company director. Nephew donor, and executor, Thomas Hanson, major donor. Gave to five charities. Left Foundling £100.

Rev. Martin Madan died 1790, will read, no charitable bequests. Methodist and supporter of the SPCK and the Society for Promoting Religious Knowlege among the Poor. Gave to four charities, director of the Foundling and the Lock Hospital.

Horatio Mann died 1786. Diplomat. Nephew donor. Gave to five charities.

Joseph Martin died 1776, will read, traditional bequests. Banker and speculator in government funds, M.P., and Alderman. Supporter of the SPCK. Brothers donors; parliamentary patron, George Colebrooke, major donor. Gave to five charities.

James Matthias died 1782, will read, traditional bequests, bequests to nonlisted charities and £50 to the Marine Society. Hamburg merchant, director of London Assurance, Russia Company, and dealer in government loans. He was executor of Francis Craiestyn, charitable subscriber. Gave to six charities, director of the Marine.

Charles, Baron Maynard died 1775. M.P. Gave to four charities.

Welbore, Baron Mendip died 1802. M.P. Wife and son donors. Gave to six charities.

J. H. Mertins died 1776, will read, no charitable bequests. Merchant. Wife donated. Gave to six charities.

Richard Morhall died 1773[?] Supporter of the SPCK. Wife and uncle donors. Gave to six charities, director of the Magdalen.

Letitia Munday, hat warehouse. Gave to three charities.

Robert Nettleton died 1774, will read, traditional bequests and bequests to nonlisted charities. Bank of England and Russia Company director. Wife gave. Partner of Raikes and Hanway, major donors. Gave to nine charities, director of the Foundling and the Magdalen.

James Norman died 1787, will read, no charitable bequests. Merchant. Brother, brother-in-law, and wife gave. Gave to eight charities.

Hugh, third duke of Northumberland, died 1786. M.P. Wife and heir gave. Donated to five charities.

Miss Anne Pigott gave to four charities.

Frederick Pigou died 1792, will read, no charitable bequests. Gunpowder merchant, East India Company and Sun Fire Office director. Two of his sons, as well as his business partner, Miles P. Andrews, donors. Gave to three charities.

Francis Plumer died 1779. Common councillor. Gave to seven charities.

William Pococke died 1786, leather seller and merchant. Supporter of the SPCK. Wife donor. Gave to eight charities.

William, second duke of Portland, died 1762. M.P. Wife, brother, and son gave. Donated to three charities, director of the Foundling.

George Prescott died 1790, will read, no charitable bequests. Italian trader, banker, and M.P. Partner Andrew Grote giver. Gave to five charities.

Sir William B. Proctor died 1773, will read, no charitable bequests. M.P. Uncle donor. Gave to six charities.

Lady Ravensworth died 1794. Husband donor and brothers, John and Peter Delme, major donors. Gave to five charities.

Samuel Richardson died 1772, printer and novelist. Gave to three charities.

Mary, Marchioness Rockingham died 1804. Husband donor. Religious woman. Gave to four charities.

Robert, second Baron Romney died 1782. Son major donor and wife and daughters subscribers. Evangelic. Gave to four charities, president of the Marine and director of the Magdalen.

Hugh Ross died 1775, will read, no charitable bequests. Merchant. Gave to four charities, director of the Magdalen.

George Ruck gave to three charities.

J. A. Rucker, merchant and Russia Company director. Brother and son or nephew donated. Gave to six charities, director of the Magdalen and the Lambeth Asylum.

Joseph Salvador died 1787. Merchant and financier, East India Company director. Brother donated. Gave to five charities, on directing committee of the Marine.

Sir George Savile died 1784. M.P. Gave to four charities.

Charles G. Say, printer of *Daily Gazeteer*. Gave to four charities.

Col. John Schutz died 1773. Supporter of the SPCK. Brother or son giver. Gave to three charities.

Anthony, fourth earl of Shaftesbury, died 1771. M.P. Wife, sister of Jacob, Lord Folkestone, major donor, gave. Gave to four charities.

William, second earl of Shelburne, died 1805. M.P. Gave to three charities.

Henry Shiffner died 1795, will read, no charitable bequests. Russia merchant, London Assurance Company director, and M.P. Related to the Grenvilles, major donors. Father's business partner Samuel Holden, husband of Jane, major donor. After bankruptcy, one of his trustees was John Thornton, major donor, and other trustees, George Amyand and Nicholas Linwood, subscribers. Brother and wife (whose family, the Dorriens, were major givers) subscribed. Gave to five charities, director of the Marine.

Hon. Mrs. Shirley died 1778, will read, traditional bequests. Gave to four charities.

John Small died 1786, will read, traditional bequests. Turkey and Russia merchant. Executor of Sir John Barnard, major donor. Gave to three charities.

John Smith died 1783, will read, traditional bequests and bequests to nonlisted charities. Lisbon merchant and director of South Sea Company. Gave to three charities, director of the Foundling.

Mary, Duchess Somerset died 1768. Gave to five charities.

Grace, Lady Sondes died 1777. Husband and father donors. Gave to four charities.

Hon. Edward Southwell died 1777. M.P. Gave to seven charities.

Hon. Mrs. Southwell died 1765. Gave to four charities.

John, Earl Spencer died 1783. M.P. Son and wife donated. Gave to four charities.

Thomas Spencer gave to three charities, director of the Magdalen and the Marine.

Hon. Charles Stanhope gave to three charities.

Hon. Philip Stanhope gave to three charities.

William, fourth earl of Strafford, died 1791. M.P. Wife and sister donors. Gave to four charities.

Dr. Robert Taylor died 1762, will read, no charitable bequests. Gave to six charities.

Andrew Thom[p]son died 1795, will read, traditional bequests. Brother donor and son[?] major donor. Gave to eight charities.

John Thornton died 1790, Russia Company director and high sheriff of Surrey. Supporter of the SPCK. Sons, brothers, nephews givers. Gave to 12 charities, director of the Magdalen and the Foundling.

Sir John Thorold died 1775. Sheriff of Lincolnshire. Supporter of the SPCK. Son gave. Donated to five charities.

Hon. Charles Townshend died 1767. M.P. Brother and son donated. Gave to five charities.

Barlow Trecothick died 1775, will read, traditional bequests, bequests to nonlisted charities and £500 to the City of London Lying-in Hospital. M.P., alderman, and North America merchant. Supporter of the SPCK. Business partner, George Colebrook, and executor, Thomas Plumer, major donors. Gave to seven charities, director of the Marine and the Foundling.

Horatio Walpole died 1797. M.P. Gave to three charities.

John Walsh died 1766, will read, traditional bequests. Music printer. Gave to four charities.

John Waple died 1763, will read, no charitable bequests. Treasurer of Grey's Inn. Executor, Timothy Waldo, gave to charity. Gave to four charities, on the directing committee of the Foundling.

Saunders Welch died 1784, will read, no charitable bequests. J.P. for Middlesex. Colleague, John Fielding, major donor. Gave to six charities, director of the Magdalen.

John Whiston died 1780, will read, traditional bequests, bequests to nonlisted charities and £50 each to the Lambeth Asylum. and the Magdalen and a posthumous continuation of his subscription to the Lying-in Charity. Bookseller and printer. Gave to seven charities.

James Whitchurch supported the SPCK and gave to seven charities.

Louisa, Lady Willoughby de Broke died 1798. Husband major donor. Gave to three charities.

George Wombwell, died 1780, will read, no charitable bequest. East India Company director, M.P., government contractor, and victualling in America. Brother and wife subscribers. Gave to six charities, director of the Magdalen.

John Wowen died 1786, will read, no charitable bequests. Executor, Richard Chiswell, major donor. Gave to six charities.

1790–1819

John Proctor Anderdon, merchant and London Dock Company director. Evangelic supporter of the SPCK. Son and wife gave. Donated to eight charities.

Sir Joseph Andrews died 1801, will read, traditional bequests. Brother and wife gave, as did one of the executors of his will, John Kingston. Gave to eight charities, director of the Marine and the Philanthropic.

John J. Angerstein died 1823, will read, no charitable bequests. Insurance broker and M.P. Son and daughter or sister gave. Wife's first husband, James Crockatt, major donor. Angerstein was executor of the estate of Thomson Bonar, major donor, and one of his executors, A. H. Thompson was a giver. Evangelic. Gave to nine charities, director of the Magdalen, the Philanthropic, the Marine, and the Society for Bettering the Condition and Improving the Comforts of the Poor (SBCP).

Edmund Antrobus died 1827, will read, no charitable bequests. Stockbroker and Sun Fire Company director. Brothers and nephews gave, and Thomas Coutts, for whom Edmund was executor, was major donor. Gave to ten charities.

Jasper Atkinson, merchant. Supported the SPCK. Gave to six charities.

Heneage, fourth earl of Aylesford, died 1812, will read, no charitable bequests. M.P. Wife and brother gave. Gave to eight charities.

John Bagwill, stockbroker. Gave to eight charities.

Richard Baldwyn died 1812, will read, bequest to nonlisted hospital. Treasurer of St. Bartholemew's Hospital. Executor of Benjamin Kenton, major donor. Gave to five charities, director of the Marine.

Joseph Ballard gave to five charities. Wife gave. Director of the Foundling.

Charles Barclay died 1856, will read, no charitable bequests. Banker and M.P. Many members of extended family givers. Donated to six charities.

Robert Barclay died 1830, will read, no charitable bequests. M.P. and banker. Many members of extended family givers. Donated to ten charities.

Alex Bennett, attorney and sworn clerk of the Court of Exchequer, died 1819[?] Wife subscriber. Member of the SPCK. Gave to nine charities.

John Blades, glass manufacturer. Sheriff and evangelic. Sister or daughter and son gave. Gave to eleven charities, director of the Philanthropic.

Thomas Boddington died 1821, will read, no charitable bequests. Common councillor, West Indies merchant and director of Royal Exchange Assurance, London Dock Company and the Bank of England. Supporter of the Society for Promoting Religious Knowledge among the Poor. Brother and nephew or son also gave. Gave to sixteen charities, director of the Marine.

Charles Boldero, banker. Business partners, Adey and Lushington, gave, as did several family members. Gave to five charities.

Edward Gale Boldero, banker and director of Pelican Life, died 1848. Business partners, Adey and Lushington, donated, as did several family members, including his wife. Gave to six charities, director of the Philanthropic.

Thomson Bonar died 1813, will read, no charitable bequests. Russia merchant, director of Eastlands and London Flour Company. Wife and son gave. J. J. Angerstein, major donor, was his executor. Gave to eleven charities, director of the SBCP, the Philanthropic, and the Magdalen.

Samuel Bosanquet died 1806, will read, traditional bequests, bequests to nonlisted charities and £50 to the Philanthropic. Bank of England, Levant Company director. J.P. and high sheriff for Essex. Devotely Anglican and supporter of the SPCK. Father and son major donors, various members of family subscribers. Gave to six charities.

Samuel Bosanquet died 1848, will read, no charitable bequests. Evangelic supporter of the SPCK. Grandfather and father major donors, many family members subscribers. Gave to seven charities, director of the Marine, the Philanthropic, and the SBCP.

Hon. Bartholomew Bouverie died 1835, will read, no charitable bequests. M.P. Related to Earl Radnor, Lord Folkestone, and Hon. Philip Pusey, major donors; wife also gave. Subscriber to the SPCK. Gave to nine charities, director of the Magdalen.

Mrs. Ann Bowyer, Worcester. Gave to six charities.

Nathaniel Brassey, banker. Father and brother gave. Gave to four charities.

Mrs. Brewer, Worcester. Gave to six charities.

John Brickwood, North America merchant. Son gave. Supporter of the SPCK. Gave to five charities.

Isaac Hawkins Browne died 1818, will read, traditional bequests and bequests to nonlisted charities. M.P. and sheriff of Shropshire. Wrote works on religion and morals. Member of the SPCK. Wife gave. Subscribed to fifteen charities, director of the Lock Asylum and the SBCP.

Thomas C. Bunbury died 1821, will read, no charitable bequests. M.P. Father gave, as did his brother-in-law, Sir Patrick Blake. Donated to four charities.

Thomas Burne, broker. Member of the Society for Promoting Religious Knowledge among the Poor. Son gave. Gave to four charities.

John, fourth earl of Bute, died 1814. M.P. Father, mother, and wife subscribed; father-in-law, Thomas Coutts, major donor. Gave to five charities, on directing committee of the SBCP.

Thomas Cadell died 1803, will read, no charitable bequests. Printer and alderman. Gave to seven charities, director of the Foundling.

John Capel died 1846, will read, no charitable bequests. Stockbroker and M.P. Wife donated. Gave to ten charities.

Philip, fifth earl of Chesterfield, died 1815, will read, no charitable bequests. M.P. Father and wife gave. Donated to four charities.

Thomas T. Clarke. Wife and son donors. Gave to nine charities.

Sir Robert Clayton died 1799, will read, traditional bequests. M.P. Wife, father, grandfather, and daughter or sister donated. Gave to five charities.

John Clutton, attorney. Wife donated. Gave to eight charities, director of the Philanthropic.

Benjamin Cole, stockbroker. Gave to five charities.

John Conyers, M.P. Father and wife donors. Gave to eight charities.

Thomas Cope, merchant and grocer. Wife and daughter or sister donated. Gave to six charities.

Thomas Coutts died 1822, will read, no charitable bequests. Banker. Brother and wife gave, son-in-law major donor. Gave to eleven charities.

John Deane gave to four charities.

John H. Deffell, merchant. Wife subscribed. Gave to eight charities.

Cornelius Denne, banker and director of Union Fire Office. Member of the Society for Propagating the Gospel. Gave to six charities, director of the Foundling and the Philanthropic.

Robert Dent died 1805, will read, no charitable bequests. Banker and M.P. Executor, George Smith, and brother, William, major donors; son subscribed. Gave to eight charities.

William Dent died 1823, will read, no charitable bequests. Merchant and director of the South Sea Company. Brother, Robert, major donor, sister or daughter gave. Supporter of the SPCK. Gave to ten charities, director of the Marine and the Lambeth Asylum.

William Magens Dorrien died 1849. Banker and M.P. Father, mother, brothers, and wife donated. Gave to eight charities, directed the Magdalen.

Thomas Edwards Freeman died 1808, will read, traditional bequests, bequests to nonlisted charities and £100 to the Lock Hospital. South Sea merchant and M.P. Son gave. Member of the Society for Propagating the Gospel and the SPCK. Gave to ten charities, director of the SBCP and the Magdalen.

John Frederick, third duke of Dorset, died 1799, will read, no charitable bequests. Wife donated. Gave to five charities.

George, third earl of Dynevor, died 1852, will read, no charitable bequests. M.P. Gave to six charities, director of the SBCP.

Nathaniel Fenn, wholesale grocer. Son donated. Gave to the Society for Promoting Religious Knowledge amongst the Poor. Gave to eleven charities, director of the Foundling.

William Field, Russia merchant. Gave to four charities.

William Fry, wholesale tea dealer and Imperial Insurance Company director. Brother and wife gave. Quaker. Gave to twelve charities.

William Fuller died 1800, will read, traditional bequests. Father or uncle, Richard Fuller, major donor, brother and executors gave. Supporter of the Society for Promoting Religious Knowledge among the Poor. Donated to eight charities.

James Gambier died 1833, will read, left money to religious societies. Admiral. Evangelic. Wife gave. Donated to eleven charities.

Sir William Garrow died 1840, will read, no charitable bequests. Lawyer, attorney general, and M.P. Member of the SPCK. Gave to nine charities, director of the Foundling and the SBCP.

Stephen Gasalee gave to eight charities, director of the Philanthropic.

Sampson Gideon died 1824. M.P. Father and wife gave. Gave to fifteen charities.

Rev. Thomas Gisborne died 1846, will read, traditional bequests. Evangelic and friend of Wilberforce and Thorntons, major donors. Member of the Society for Propagating the Gospel and the SPCK. Gave to eight charities, on directing committee of the SBCP.

Rev. Samuel Glasse died 1812, will read, traditional bequests and annual subscription to the British Lying-in Hospital. Evangelic. Son subscribed. Gave to eight charities, director of the Marine and the Magdalen.

George Godwin, stockbroker and director of Pelican Life Assurance Company. Wife, son, and daughter gave. Gave to seven charities.

Thomas Griffith, auctioneer and appraiser. Wife and brother[?] donated. Supported the Society for Promoting Religious Knowledge among the Poor. Gave to nine charities.

James Hardie, merchant and insurance broker. Gave to four charities.

Jeremiah Harman, merchant and Bank of England director. Partners, the Hoares, major donors. Father, mother, wife, and sons donated. Although High Church, an evangelical sympathizer. Gave to twelve charities, director of the Philanthropic.

Quarles Harris, insurance broker. Son donated. Member of the SPCK. Gave to ten charities.

Benjamin Harrison died 1856, will read, no charitable bequests. Wine merchant, director of Hudson's Bay Company, Hand in Hand, and London Life Assurance. Grandfather, father, uncle, and brother givers. Member of the SPCK and evangelic. Gave to ten charities, director of the Philanthropic.

John Hatsell, woolen draper and mercer. Wife and brother[?] gave. Member of the SPCK. Gave to eleven charities.

Michael Heathcote, Manchester warehouseman. Gave to eight charities, on directing committees of the Philanthropic and the Foundling.

William Heberden died 1845, will read, no charitable bequest. Physician to George III. Grandfather, father, brother, and wife givers. Gave to eight charities.

Richard Heron died 1805. Lawyer, commissioner of bankruptcy and re-memberancer in Exchequer, M.P. Gave to four charities.

Francis, fifth marquis of Hertford, died 1822, will read, bequests to non-listed charities. Father major donor and mother subscribed. Gave to ten charities, director of the SBCP.

George Hibbert died 1837, will read, no charitable bequests. West Indies merchant, M.P., and alderman. Wife and sons[?] gave. Donated to eight charities.

John Hillman gave to five charities.

Charles Hoare, banker. Entire family givers. Member of the SPCK. Gave to eight charities, director of the SBCP.

Henry Hoare died 1817. Banker. Entire family donors. Member of the SPCK and the Society for Promoting Religious Knowledge among the Poor. Gave to fifteen charities, director of SBCP and the Philanthropic.

Samuel Hoare, banker. Entire family donors. Gave to eight charities.

Eusebius Horton, sheriff of Derbyshire. Member of the SPCK. Gave to seven charities.

Henry Hughes, printer. Wife gave. Member of the SPCK. Gave to nine charities, director of the Foundling.

William Hussey died 1813, will read, traditional bequests. Clothier and M.P. Gave to five charities.

John Jane gave to six charities.

George Jeffrey, Russia merchant and director of Union Fire Office. Supporter of the Society for Promoting Religious Knowledge among the Poor. Gave to eleven charities, director of the SBCP.

Rev. Richard Kaye died 1810, will read, traditional bequests. Prebendary of York and dean of Lincoln. Supporter of the SPCK and the Society for Propagating the Gospel. Gave to six charities, director of the Marine.

Benjamin Kenton died 1800, will read, traditional bequests, bequests to nonlisted charities and £200 for the Lying-in Charity, £1,500 to the Magdalen, £300 to the Society for Sunday Schools, £3,000 to the Philanthropic Society, £2,000 to the Marine and City of London Lying-in Hospital, £1,500 to the Foundling, and £2,000 to the Lambeth Asylum. Wine merchant. Son-in-law, D. P. Watts, major donor. Supporter of the SPCK. Gave to eight charities.

John Kingston, director of Albion Fire and Life Assurance. Supporter of SPCK. Gave to five charities, director of the Foundling and the Marine.

Paul Le Mesurier died 1805, will read, no charitable bequests. M.P., alderman, and director of East India Company. Wife and son gave, father-in-law major donor. Member of the Society for Propagating the Gospel. Gave to ten charities.

Sir William Leighton died 1826, will read, bequests to nonlisted charities. Alderman and coal merchant. Wife gave. Donated to ten charities.

Beeston Long died 1820, will read, no charitable bequests. Banker and director of Bank of England, London Dock Company, and Royal Exchange Assurance. Mother, father, and father-in-law gave. Gave to six charities, on directing committee of the Marine.

Mrs. W. Long, supporter of the SPCK. Gave to five charities.

William Manning died 1835, will read, no charitable bequests. M.P. and West Indies merchant, director of Bank of England and Royal Exchange Assurance. Evangelic and member of the SPCK. Gave to fourteen charities, director of the Magdalen, the SBCP, and the Marine.

John Marriott, member of SPCK. Gave to five charities and director of the Foundling.

James Martin died 1810, will read, no charitable bequests. Banker and M.P. Unitarian and supporter of the SPCK. Brothers and wife givers. Gave to eleven charities.

William Mellish died 1838, will read, no charitable bequests. M.P. and merchant. Evangelic. Father and grandfather gave. Gave to eight charities, director of the Marine.

Sir Charles Middleton died 1813. Comptroller of the navy and M.P. Wife subscribed, and father-in-law, James Gambier, major donor. Connected with William Wilberforce, major donor, and uncle by marriage of W. M. Pitt, major donor. Evangelic and member of the Society for Promoting Religious Knowledge among the Poor and the SPCK. Gave to nine charities, director of the Lock Asylum.

George, fourth viscount of Midleton, died 1836. Wife and daughter or sister also gave. Gave to five charities.

Langford Millington died 1807, will read, no charitable bequests. Member of the Society for Propagating the Gospel. Gave to six charities, director of the SBCP.

William Noble, banker. Father-in-law, I. Akermann, major donor. Partners, Devaynes and Dawes, subscribers. Gave to five charities.

George Norman, merchant and director of the Eastland Company. Father or uncle major donor. Gave to seven charities.

James Allen Park died 1838, will read, no charitable bequests. Judge. Devoutly religious, member of the SPCK and the Society for Propagating the Gospel. Gave to eleven charities, director of the Magdalen and the Philanthropic.

Thomas S. Penoyre, wholesale druggist and chemist. Gave to five charities.

Peter Perchard died 1806, will read, traditional bequests, bequests to nonlisted charities and £70 to the City of London Lying-in Hospital and £20 to the Lying-in Charity. Common councillor and merchant goldsmith. Father gave. Supporter of the SPCK and the Society for Propagating the Gospel. Gave to seven charities.

Charles Pieschell died 1824. Russia merchant and Imperial Insurance director. Member of the Society for Promoting Religious Knowledge among the Poor. Gave to eight charities.

William Morton Pitt died 1836, will read, no charitable bequests. M.P. Wife and various relations givers. Son-in-law, Lord Marsham, major donor. Evangelic and supporter of the SPCK. Gave to twelve charities, director of the Magdalen, the Society for Sunday Schools, the Philanthropic, and the SBCP.

Thomas Plumer died 1824, will read, no charitable bequests. Lawyer, M.P., and director of West India Dock Company, Imperial Insurance Company, and London Assurance. Supporter of the SPCK. Wife gave. Donated to ten charities, director of the Foundling and the Society for Sunday Schools.

Josiah DuPre Porcher died 1820, will read, no charitable bequests. East Indies merchant and M.P. Wife donated. Gave to nine charities, director of the SBCP.

William Henry, third duke of Portland, died 1809, will read, no charitable bequests. Prime minister. Father, mother, and sister donated. Gave to four charities.

Robert Pott, vinegar maker. Brother and wife gave. Donated to eight charities, director of the Magdalen.

John C. Powell died 1847, will read, no charitable bequests. Merchant and director of London Assurance. Sister and brother gave. Supporter of the SPCK. Gave to eight charities, director of the Magdalen.

Sir Charles Price died 1818. Alderman and M.P. Evangelic. Wife donated. Gave to four charities.

Hon. Philip B. Pusey died 1828, will read, traditional bequests and £100 to the Magdalen. Father and brothers major donors. Supporter of the SPCK. Gave to fourteen charities, director of the Magdalen and the Philanthropic.

Jacob, sixth earl of Radnor, died 1828, will read, traditional bequests, bequests to nonlisted charities and religious societies and £200 to the Magdalen. M.P. Grandfather and brother major donors, many other relatives givers. Gave to eight charities, director of SBCP.

J. M. Raikes died 1833. Russia Company, London Dock, and Eastlands Company director. Uncle major giver, many members of family also donated. Supporter of the SPCK. Gave to five charities, director of the Magdalen.

Thomas Raikes died 1814, will read, no charitable bequests. Bank of England and Russia Company director. Nephew major donor, many members of family also gave. Partners Thornton and Wilberforce major donors. Supporter of the SPCK and the Society for Promoting Religious Knowledge among the Poor. Gave to nine charities, director of the Marine.

Thomas Roberts, tea broker. Evangelic supporter of the SPCK and the Society for Promoting Religious Knowledge among the Poor. Wife gave. Gave to eight charities.

Charles, third baron of Romney, died 1811, will read, no charitable bequests. M.P. Father major donor, son and wife donated. Gave to four charities, director of the Marine and the SBCP.

D. H. Rucker, Russia Company and Sun Fire Company director. Relatives and wife donated. Gave to twelve charities.

J. A. Rucker, Russia Company and London Assurance director. Relatives donated. Gave to eight charities.

Jesse Russell, soapboiler. Supporter of the SPCK and the Society for Propagating the Gospel. Son and wife gave. Donated to eight charities, director of the Lambeth Asylum.

William Salte, wholesale linen draper and director of Hand in Hand Fire

Company. Male relatives gave. Donated to six charities, director of the Foundling and the Lambeth Asylum.

Sir James Sanderson died 1798, will read, traditional bequests, bequests to nonlisted charities and £100 each to the Philanthropic, the Magdalen, and the Foundling. Banker, M.P., and alderman. Wife and son gave. Donated to ten charities, director of the Magdalen.

George Scholey died 1839, will read, traditional bequests, and bequests to nonlisted charities. M.P., alderman, and hop and brandy merchant. Supporter of the Society for Promoting Religious Knowledge among the Poor. Gave to four charities.

Thomas Scott, auctioneer. Gave to seven charities, director of the Lambeth Asylum.

Charles Selwin died 1795, will read, bequests to nonlisted charities, £500 each to the Marine, the Magdalen, and the Foundling, and £100 each to the Lambeth Asylum and the Philanthropic. Gave to five charities, director of the Foundling.

George Sharp, Russia and Spanish broker and common councillor. Brother and son gave. Donated to six charities.

Samuel Shore died 1828, will read, no charitable bequests. Banker and member of the Society of Protestant Dissenters. Wife and son gave, as did father-in-law, Freeman Flower. Donated to four charities.

William Skirrow, hop merchant. Supporter of SPCK. Wife and son gave. Donated to five charities, director of the Lambeth Asylum.

George Smith died 1836, will read, no charitable bequests. Banker and M.P. Wife subscribed, brother John major donor. Gave to nine charities, director of the Marine.

John Smith died 1827, insurance broker, director of the Imperial Insurance Company. M.P. Brother George major donor. Gave to five charities.

William Smith died 1836. M.P. Wife gave. Supporter of the Society for Promoting Religious Knowledge among the Poor and the Academic Institute for Protestant Dissenters. Donated to seven charities.

Westgarth Snaith died 1816, will read, no charitable bequests. Banker. Wife gave. Supporter of the SPCK. Gave to six charities.

George John, second earl of Spencer, died 1834, no charitable bequests. M.P. Father major donor, mother gave. Gave to seven charities, on directing committee of the Philanthropic and the SBCP.

Samuel Stratton, Russia merchant. Supporter of the Society for Promoting Religious Knowledge among the Poor. Gave to ten charities.

Michael Angelo Taylor died 1834. M.P. and supporter of the SPCK. Gave to five charities, director of the Magdalen.

John Thom[p]son, insurance broker. Father or uncle Andrew major donor, wife gave. Gave to seven charities, director of the Magdalen.

Claude G. Thornton died 1866. Bank of England, South Sea Company, Sun Fire Office, Russia Company director and sheriff of Hertfordshire. Brother, uncles, father, father-in-law, wife, and grandfather, S. T. Godin, gave. Gave to eight charities, director of the Magdalen.

Henry Thornton died 1815, will read, bequest of £50 to the Society for Sunday Schools. Russia Company director, contributor to government loans, M.P., and supporter of the SPCK and the Society for Promoting Religious Knowledge among the Poor. Father, brother, and wife donors. Gave to ten charities, director of the Lock Asylum, Marine, and Foundling.

Robert Thornton died 1826, will read, no charitable bequests. Director of the South Sea Company, the Russia Company, and the East India Company. M.P. Brothers, wife, father gave. Supporter of the SPCK and the Society for Promoting Religious Knowledge among the Poor. Gave to twelve charities, director of the Lock Asylum and the Marine.

Mrs. Robert Thornton, husband and in-laws gave, including several major donors. Gave to seven charities.

Samuel Thornton died 1838, will read, no charitable bequests. Bank of England and Russia Company director, spokesman for the Greenland merchants and M.P. Father, brothers, and cousins gave. Supporter of the SPCK and the Society for Promoting Religious Knowledge among the Poor. Gave to ten charities, director of the Magdalen, the Lock Asylum, the Marine, and the Society for Sunday Schools.

Stephen Thornton died 1850, will read, no charitable bequests. Royal Exchange Assurance director. Father, brothers, and cousins major donors. Gave to five charities, director of the Marine.

Richard Till died 1824, will read, no charitable bequests. Clerk to City Commission of Land Tax, secretary to London Bridge water works, and director of the Amicable Society. Son gave. Donated to nine charities.

Peter Vere, banker. Gave to six charities.

John Walker died 1830, will read, no charitable bequests. Physician and author. Gave to six charities.

John Warburton died 1808, will read, left bequest of £100 to the Asylum for Orphaned Girls. Timber merchant. Gave to five charities, director of the Lambeth Asylum and the SBCP.

General George Warde died 1803, will read, traditional bequests and £50 each to the Magdalen, the Lambeth Asylum, and the Philanthropic. Brother[?] gave. Donated to four charities.

James Ware died 1815, will read, traditional bequests. Surgeon and oculist. Supporter of the Society for Promoting Religious Knowledge among the Poor. Wife, sons, and daughters gave. Donated to eight charities, director and founder of the School for the Indigent Blind.

David Pike Watts died 1816, will read, no charitable bequests. Wine merchant. Father-in-law major donor, daughter married the son of Jesse Russell, major donor. Supported the SPCK. Gave to fifteen charities, director of the SBCP, the London Hospital, and the Magdalen.

Rev. Dr. Stephen White died 1824. Father gave. Donated to four charities, treasurer of the Foundling.

John Whitmore died 1826. M.P. and Bank of England director and merchant. Son gave. Supported the SPCK. Gave to six charities, director of the SBCP.

William Wilberforce died 1833, will read, no charitable bequests. M.P. and Russia Company director. Supporter of the SPCK and the Society for Promoting Religious Knowledge among the Poor. Leader of the evangelics. Gave to ten charities, director of the SBCP.

William Willis died 1831. Banker. Wife gave. Donated to six charities, director of the Lying-in Charity and the Marine.

John, Lord Willoughby de Broke, died 1816, will read, traditional bequests. Wife major donor. Gave to nine charities.

George Wolffe died 1828. Danish consul, merchant, and shipper. Brother and wife givers. Member of the Society for Promoting Religious Knowledge among the Poor and evangelic. Gave to eleven charities.

Rev. Francis Wollaston. Father and daughter or sister gave. Donated to six charities, director of the Magdalen and the Lambeth Asylum.

Index

Adolphus, Michael, 77n, 84, 90n, 203
Aiken, John, 106, 163, 166
Akerman, Isaac, 90, 203
Anson, Lady, 91, 203
Asgill, Sir Charles, 88, 204
Asylum for Orphaned Girls at Lambeth,
74n, 75n, 81n, 155, 185; beginnings of,
115–19, 116n, 117–18n; and other char-
ities, 120, 120n, 127, 130, 130n, 131; in
crisis, 158–60, 158n, 159n
Atterbury, Francis, 13, 16, 16n, 20, 47n

Bank of England directors/philanthropists,
64, 76, 91, 167
Barbon, Nicholas, 31, 32n
Barnard, Sir John, 90, 90n, 204
Barrow, Isaac, 13, 15, 15n
Bedford, Duke of, 89n, 204
Bell, William, 92n, 95
Bellers, John, 23, 26, 27–28, 29n
Benson, Martin, 12n, 13, 20n
Bernard, Thomas, 9, 137, 157, 179, 181,
184n, 200; and SBCP, 174–77, 174n,
177n
Bicheno, James, 172n, 184n
Blewitt, George, 35, 37n, 41
Boddington, Benjamin, 113
Boddington, Thomas, 214
Bosanquet, Jacob, 75, 90, 91n, 113, 204
Bosanquet, Samuel, 90, 91n, 214
Braddon, Lawrence, 23–24, 27, 36
British Lying-in Hospital, 72, 75n, 132,
133n; donation to, 86, 87, 88, 88n, 113;
at midcentury, 102–4, 105, 108, 109n;
origins of, 65–68; under attack, 179,
180, 180n, 181, 181n
Brown, John, 92n, 93, 95
Burnet, Gilbert, 17–18, 18n
Butler, John, 82n
Butler, Joseph, 8, 12n, 20n, 35, 38, 39, 40,
41

Cardigan, Earl of, 89n, 204
Cary, John, 26n, 27, 28, 30
Charity: associated, 49, 49n, 54, 197, 198;
benefits of, 3, 20, 59, 197; by bequest,
19, 40, 40n, 42, 46–48, 46n, 47n, 48n,
49, 64, 64n, 77–80, 89–90, 113; and
charity school movement, 29, 34n, 46,
49–51, 51n, 54, 59, 170, 170n, 171,
171n; and childcare, 109–10, 184, 195;
and Christianity, 10, 10n, 12–22, 41,
59–60, 102, 109, 113, 125, 165, 165n,
168, 171, 197; dangers of, 48, 49; and
dependency, 140, 145, 153, 155–62; and
domestic economy, 175, 175n, 200; and
hospitality, 143n; and management,
174; and money raising, 9–10, 61, 79–
82, 85, 133; and national policy, 4, 53,
54, 56, 58–60, 67–69, 97, 102n, 126,
195–97; and philanthropy, 5, 5n; and
poverty, 34; purposes of, 165, 194–96;
as reward for virtue, 154, 176; science
of, 169, 174n, 176, 177n, 184, 202n;
and self-help, 134, 195, 200, 201n; and
soup kitchens, 175, 175n, 177n; and
Sunday schools, 171n. See also Commerce; Discrimination; Employment;
Justice; Moral reformation; Poor Law;
Property; Sunday schools; Sympathy;
War; Workhouse
Chetwood, Knightly, 13, 14, 14n, 21
Child, Josiah, 23, 27, 29n, 30
City of London Lying-in Hospital: donors
and donation, 74, 75n, 87, 87n; at midcentury, 102, 103, 105, 128, 132; origins of, 65–69, 66n, 72, 72n
Clagget, Nicholas, 18, 21
Colebrooke, Sir George, 89n, 90, 91, 205
Colebrooke, James, 90, 91n
Colquhoun, Patrick, 137, 183n; and moral
reform, 171n, 173, 175n, 176n; and
prostitution, 188, 190, 190n
Commerce: and charity, 15, 21, 22, 35–36,
41–43, 68–69, 102, 102n, 111, 115,
123, 126, 183, 186, 197; and Christianity, 30, 95, 137, 137n; criticisms of, 93,
95, 149–51, 156; and population, 24,
146, 147, 148, 178; and science, 137;
and slavery, 142, 143; value of, 25, 25n,
31–32, 96, 111, 136, 138, 142, 152–53,
156; and virtue, 34n, 152, 153. See also